Nicholas Lander views menus from a highly unusual perspective as the only restaurant critic to have owned and run one of London's most successful restaurants. He established L'Escargot in Soho in the 1980s when he was among the first British restaurateurs to write his menus in English and to change them according to the seasons.

For the past 27 years he has reviewed restaurants and menus from around the world in his role as restaurant critic for the *Financial Times*.

His first book, *The Art of the Restaurateur* (Phaidon, 2012), profiled 20 of the world's best restaurateurs and was named a Book of the Year by *The Economist*.

NICHOLAS LANDER

ON THE MENU

The world's favourite piece of paper

unbound

This edition first published in 2016

Unbound

6th Floor Mutual House, 70 Conduit Street, London W1S 2GF

www.unbound.com

Text Design by Carrdesignstudio.com

Art Direction by Mark Ecob

A CIP record for this book is available from the British Library

ISBN 978-1-78352-242-2 (trade hbk)
ISBN 978-1-78352-243-9 (ebook)
ISBN 978-1-78352-304-7 (limited edition)

Printed and bound in Italy by L.E.G.O. S.p.A.

1 3 5 7 9 8 6 4 2

For Jancis

Dear Reader,

The book you are holding came about in a rather different way to most others. It was funded directly by readers through a new website: Unbound. Unbound is the creation of three writers. We started the company because we believed there had to be a better deal for both writers and readers. On the Unbound website, authors share the ideas for the books they want to write directly with readers. If enough of you support the book by pledging for it in advance, we produce a beautifully bound special subscribers' edition and distribute a regular edition and e-book wherever books are sold, in shops and online.

This new way of publishing is actually a very old idea (Samuel Johnson funded his dictionary this way). We're just using the internet to build each writer a network of patrons. Here, at the back of this book, you'll find the names of all the people who made it happen.

Publishing in this way means readers are no longer just passive consumers of the books they buy, and authors are free to write the books they really want. They get a much fairer return too – half the profits their books generate, rather than a tiny percentage of the cover price.

If you're not yet a subscriber, we hope that you'll want to join our publishing revolution and have your name listed in one of our books in the future. To get you started, here is a £5 discount on your first pledge. Just visit unbound.com, make your pledge and type ONTHEMENU in the promo code box when you check out.

Dan, Justin and John
Founders, Unbound

ACKNOWLEDGEMENTS

This book, long lurking at the back of my memory, would never have seen the light of day without the intervention of my friend Bill Emmott. It was he who, in the summer of 2014, kindly pointed me in the direction of Unbound.

Therefore, it is to this one individual and my eventual publishers that I owe the biggest thanks. My eternal gratitude is owed to all the team at Unbound but particularly to John Mitchinson, a man whose appetite for food and menus seems to be as unlimited as his interest in books.

And, of course, via everyone at Unbound, to the over 130 friends and those interested in the whole subject of menus who have so generously funded the publication of *On the Menu*.

To my old friend, Danny Meyer, I owe great thanks for suggesting the title of this book, so much better than its original title. To the late Bill Baker, and his wife Kate, whose house near Bristol provided the scene for the chapter 'The Menu as Travel', and to Michel Roux Jr for the time spent at Le Gavroche and for writing such an inspiring foreword.

To all the following chefs, restaurateurs, bar gurus, sommeliers and designers whom I interviewed, my grateful thanks:

Michael Anthony	Daniel Boulud	Mary Lewis
Jonathan Arana-Morton	Ferran Centelles	Bruce Poole
Paul Baldwin	Claire Clark	René Redzepi
Robbie Bargh	Sally Clarke	Ruth Rogers
Joe Bastianich	Terry Coughlin	Xavier Rousset
Mario Batali	Arnaud Donckele	Shaun Searley
Shannon Bennett	Peter Gilmore	Charlotte Sager-Wilde
Enrico Bernardo	Bill Granger	Marie-Pierre Troisgros
Heston Blumenthal	Shaun Hill	Michel Troisgros
April Bloomfield	Miles Kirby	Charlie Young
Massimo Bottura	Frank Langello	

I would also like to thank two lawyers from Olswang, Marcus Barclay and Joel Vertes, without whom the chapter 'Protecting the Menu' could not have been written. And I would like to thank Eugen Beer of *Love Menu Art* in New York and Henry Voigt of *The American Men*u, based in Wilmington, Delaware, for providing many of the menus reproduced in this book.

I would also like to thank all of their PAs for making their time available.

Finally, my heartfelt thanks go out to two very different groups of individuals. Firstly, to all my friends and family who have shown such faith in me and in this book. And, secondly, to chefs, past, present and future for writing their menus, their interpretation of the piece of paper that undoubtedly gives the world the greatest pleasure.

CONTENTS

Foreword 1
Introduction 3

Chapter 1   The Menu as Travel.................................. 7
Chapter 2   The Origins of the Menu........................... 27
Chapter 3   Planning the Menu................................... 41
             Michael Anthony – *Untitled & Gramercy Tavern*.......... 43
             Shannon Bennett – *Vue de monde*................. 53
             April Bloomfield – *The Spotted Pig & The Breslin*...58
             Heston Blumenthal – *The Fat Duck*.............. 64
             Massimo Bottura – *Osteria Francescana*......... 73
             Daniel Boulud – *Bar Boulud*..................... 82
             Arnaud Donckele – *La Résidence de la Pinède*.....89
             Peter Gilmore – *Quay*........................... 98
             Shaun Hill – *The Walnut Tree Inn*.............. 103
             Bruce Poole – *Chez Bruce*...................... 107
             René Redzepi – *Noma*........................... 112
             Ruth Rogers – *The River Cafe*.................. 119

Chapter 4   The Ever-Expanding Menu........................ 125
             The Breakfast & Brunch Menu.................... 127
             The Afternoon Tea Menu......................... 136
             The Dessert Menu............................... 145
             The Cocktail Menu.............................. 151

Chapter 5   Designing the Menu............................... 157
Chapter 6   The Menu as Fundraiser.......................... 173
Chapter 7   Protecting the Menu.............................. 183
Chapter 8   The Wine List................................... 197
Chapter 9   The Menu Briefing at Babbo, New York......... 225
Chapter 10   The Menus as Memento........................... 235
Chapter 11   The Menu as Edible Art......................... 251
Supporters 283

FOREWORD

———

As a chef and restaurateur, I know and fully appreciate the importance of a menu.

Growing up with a father who was a chef, I was privileged enough to be exposed to the culinary world from a young age. I remember my mother and father sitting down at the kitchen table discussing food and wine to compose a menu, toing and froing from our heaving bookshelf of old cookbooks to finally agree on what should be served at the next family reunion. Given so much importance and attention were placed on creating a meal at home, you can imagine how much thought had to go into a restaurant menu.

Those childhood memories are one of the reasons why I became a chef; curating a menu is as creative as the cooking itself.

A menu is a reflection of one's self; so much can be seen and revealed by a menu. It should have a personality, akin to looking at an artist's canvas – a story is set before you to excite the senses, to entice, to question and to enjoy.

I have a vast collection of menus and, much to my wife's chagrin, it keeps on growing. Some are framed and well over a hundred years old, others are from royal banquets, delicately woven in silk and featuring particularly unusual dishes that you would not find on a menu today.

They are a constant source of inspiration and I never tire of reading them. I try to imagine the kind of person who wrote them and what challenges the chef had to surmount to achieve perfection of those elaborate concoctions. I hope that one day, one of my menus will be looked at in the same way.

Michel Roux Jr, 2016

BIBENDUM

NUNC EST BIBENDUM

MENU

Bibendum, London

The classic Simon Hopkinson menu after he, Sir Terence Conran and the late Paul Hamlyn had completed their tasteful renovation of the original Michelin building in London, whose motto is *Nunc est Bibendum*: now is the time to drink.

<table>
<tr><td>

Consommé
Soupe de poisson
Cream of celery soup

•

Endives au gratin
Saucisson aux lentilles
Piedmontese peppers
Escargots de Bourgogne
Jambon de Bayonne
Baltic herrings à la crème
Calves brains and capers
Smoked salmon
Terrine de foie gras
Risotto alla Milanese
Grilled aubergine with pesto
Champignons à la Grecque
Salade composée
Filets de rouget en escabèche
Oeufs en meurette
Salade de museau
Six native oysters
Gratin de moules aux épinards
Crab mayonnaise
Pork rillettes

•

Fillets of sole meunière
Fillet of sea bass, sauce vierge
Grilled lobster, garlic butter
Fried fillet of plaice, tartare sauce
Grilled fillets of trout Bordelaise
Grilled turbot, beurre blanc

Prices include VAT

</td><td>

for two
Poulet de Bresse rôti
Côte de boeuf grillée, sauce Béarnaise
Canette rôtie aux pommes
Carré d'agneau persillé

•

Roast quails
Tête de veau, sauce ravigôte
Steak au poivre
fillet   rump
Entrecôte marchand de vin
Roast lamb, sauce soubise
Sauté de veau aux morilles
Onglet sauté aux échalottes
Poulet poché à la crème et crêpes Parmentier
Tripes Lyonnaise
Ris de veau, beurre noisette
Boiled bacon with split peas and carrots
Grilled rabbit, mustard sauce

</td></tr>
</table>

Carottes Vichy		Haricots verts		Roast onions
	Cabbage		Spinach	
Pommes frites	Boiled potatoes		Mashed potatoes
	Green salad	Chicory salad	

INTRODUCTION

—◆—

On the Menu began its life as a companion volume to my first book, *The Art of the Restaurateur*. Both books attempt to cast greater light, understanding and credit on two aspects of the restaurant business that have long been overlooked. I have felt for many years that the requisite talents of restaurateurs have been cast into the shadows by those of chefs. In the same way, I believe that we – by which I mean every single person who enjoys restaurants – have overlooked and taken for granted the immense pleasure the menu generates every time we sit down and pick one up.

Whenever I have been in conversation with someone who has asked me what I am working on, I have mentioned the title of this book and then responded to their often quizzical look by adding that, in my opinion, 'The menu is the single piece of paper that gives the world the most pleasure.' To date, nobody has successfully challenged me.

I have inevitably challenged myself. As potential rivals as pleasure-giving documents, I have thought of bank statements, but they are only cheering if you are in credit. I have thought of pieces of paper containing more worldly and important news, such as a peace treaty. But this piece of paper implies that one side has lost, so by necessity it conveys pleasure only, at the very most, for the victors. I have thought of documents that have brought me personal pleasure – school certificates, my marriage certificate, the birth certificates of my children and grandchildren – but they affect far fewer people and are only pored over very infrequently. And, of course, there is the real possibility that in a few years' time none of these sorts of documents will exist in a physical form at all, as they all inevitably will be digitised.

Menus do appear on the internet – although I try never to look at them before going to any restaurant so as not to spoil the surprise – but they will have to continue in a physical form as they are a vital ingredient in the make-up of every restaurant, one of the very few businesses that can never move entirely into cyberspace. We need to take our bodies along with us to enjoy restaurants and for as long as this situation does not change, we will inevitably be handed a menu as soon as we are seated – unless the restaurant still relies on an old-fashioned blackboard menu or a more modern iPad or tablet.

There has also been a second, very common reaction from those I have spoken to about this book. Almost everyone has said, 'I wish you had told me about your book a few weeks or months ago. I had an enormous pile of old menus which I've only just thrown out.' This response provided further proof that menus fulfil a role no other single piece of paper can match as a relatively long-lasting memento of a special event, a celebration or just an exceptional lunch or dinner.

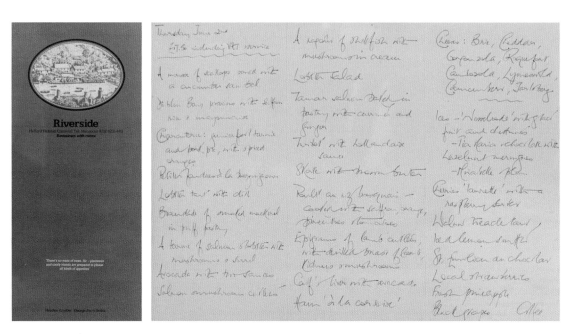

Riverside, Cornwall

From an era when George Perry-Smith, a disciple of the food writer Elizabeth David, was running his restaurant with rooms overlooking the bay at Helford, Cornwall.

The principal goals of this book will become obvious, I hope. How menus represent the least expensive form of travel. The slow evolution of the menu since it first appeared in the Parisian restaurants of the early 19th century. The highly divergent aims and ambitions of several of the world's top chefs as they sit down to create what are today remarkable and very personal menus. How menus have managed to raise so much money for innumerable worthy causes. And how certain menus, printed to commemorate historic events, remain the closest we can get to what it must have been like to live through the Siege of Paris in 1870 as a customer, or to face the havoc about to be inflicted on your profession as a restaurateur in the US on the eve of Prohibition in 1920.

But in particular, I hope that this book will also be a wake-up call to many in the restaurant business. I believe that far too many menus are still lazily, thoughtlessly and hastily put together; that they suffer from a lack of creative imagination and colour; and that they singularly fail to take advantage of the considerable improvements in printing and technology that have taken place recently. Many of today's menus could be far more interesting and appetising.

This belief was corroborated by a particularly entertaining 'Lunch with the *FT*' column that appeared in the *Financial Times* on June 13th 2015. My colleague, then a media correspondent and currently a political correspondent, Henry Mance, interviewed the British newspaper proprietor Richard Desmond at the Coq d'Argent restaurant in the City of London and wrote, 'The menu features a few dozen French dishes, typed in the kind of dull font that is better suited to reading mortgage terms and conditions.' Far too many menus are written in such an uninspiring style, particularly in the larger restaurants and hotels. They can easily, and should, do much better.

The final aim of this book, therefore, is to act as a spur to many restaurateurs and chefs to write more attractive, colourful and eye-catching menus. These improvements will in turn, I believe, serve only to give the world's restaurant-goers even greater pleasure than the menus that first emerged in revolutionary Paris over 200 years ago.

THE MENU AS TRAVEL

———

Every year, just before New Year's Eve celebrations, I would set off on a tour of the most acclaimed restaurants across Europe.

I would start in London, head across the Channel to Bruges in Belgium, then down eastern France to two of its most fascinating wine regions, Alsace and Burgundy.

Then I would head south to Beaujolais and the Rhône Valley before travelling to south-west France for the very different cooking styles of the two Michels: Michel Bras at Laguiole and Michel Guérard at Les Prés d'Eugénie close to the Spanish border. Finally, I would turn east once more, traverse the Riviera into Italy and travel down the coast for my ultimate meal in the centre of Florence.

This trip took about 30 minutes and regrettably involved neither food nor drink. But it was great fun and it could not have been easier. All I had to do was walk along the corridor in the former mill house that belonged to an old friend and his wife in the depths of the Somerset countryside.

The walls of this corridor, and in fact numerous staircases and lavatory walls, were covered in menus that had been collected at the end of each meal these friends had enjoyed, before being carefully framed and treated with great respect. They provided the most mouth-watering aperitif to the good food and wine we were about to enjoy as we welcomed in the New Year.

This collection of menus appealed on many levels. The most poignant, of course, were those that gave an intimation of a restaurant where, regretfully, I would never have the good fortune to eat.

There on one wall was a menu from the late Alain Chapel's restaurant in Mionnay just outside Lyon. Chapel had been the world's most respected chef when he passed away, far too young at the age of 53 in 1990, shortly after I had sold my restaurant in London. As the *Financial Times*'s restaurant correspondent by then, I was free to travel but sadly fate had intervened and I would never eat Chapel's cooking.

Then there was a menu from Paul Bocuse's three-star Michelin restaurant, L'Auberge du Pont de Collonges in Lyons, which immediately conjured up for me the alluring combination of what was then the most highly regarded restaurant in France alongside France's most revered chef. To add extra piquancy, this menu had been signed in the corner 'To Bill from Paul', uniting two men whom, once I had met them both, I came to appreciate shared the same gargantuan appetite for food and wine.

This brief, inexpensive, virtual tour of Europe's top restaurants via this expansive display of menus had an enormous effect on me.

Above all, it put me in a very good mood. I was immediately excited by the sound of all the dishes that swam before my greedy eyes and I was delighted to be part of a profession in which one piece of paper could universally convey such instant pleasure. These simple documents, some in colour, several illustrated with line drawings but never anything too fancy, made me feel remarkably happy.

And while they naturally made me even hungrier than the aromas emanating from our friends' kitchen, they also induced a particular sense of professional curiosity. Over the years I used to read these menus from three different perspectives: initially as a restaurateur; then as a restaurant reviewer; and always as a prospective customer.

Reading them as a restaurateur inevitably took me behind the swing door of the kitchen. I would start to imagine the layout of the kitchen, the colours

and aromas of the raw ingredients as they were being assembled and the banter between the chefs before the rhythm of the service. And then the silence that fell, the hallmark of a top kitchen, as the service got under way.

Then I would imagine the interaction that would occur in these restaurants, inevitably the creation of one very strong, determined and talented chef, as the waiting staff began to flood into the kitchen with the orders. The whole kitchen would spring to attention: all the various sections would be busy; chaos and confusion would be narrowly averted; and, after the hubbub, the savoury aromas would give way to the more delicate charms of the pastry section as desserts and plates of petits fours brought the curtain down for at least a few hours.

Most appetisingly, I would wander along this row of menus and try to decide which dishes I was going to eat and just when we could in reality slip across the Channel to return not just with the memories but also with our own copy of the restaurant's menu. That was unquestionably the most exciting part of this tour – the notion of long-distance eating, a notion that led to one incontrovertible fact: one day, I was going to sit down to choose and to eat from all these menus.

That, above all, was the biggest and most long-lasting effect of walking up and down this one corridor and ogling all these menus: they made me want to travel. And not just to Belgium, France and Italy or back to Bibendum in London, where my friend's wife had once worked, but to any, and every, restaurant in the world that serves good food.

And not just to those places that 20 years ago were then on my culinary radar – Paris, San Francisco, Hong Kong, New York, Sydney, Tokyo and Rome – but to all those places that, in the intervening years, have become such unlikely centres of great food and wine around the world: Barcelona and Roses, Copenhagen, Shanghai, Lima, Fäviken in northern Sweden, Singapore and on to Melbourne.

Menus are for me – and I suspect for many like me who are keen on travel, and are greedy and enthralled by restaurants – the swiftest and most exciting form of travel. They take you to a table in a place where others are going to have to work extremely hard and carefully over long hours to make you happy.

And I know, from the past 35 years in and around the restaurant business, quite how hard these chefs, restaurateurs, waiters and sommeliers (not to mention the members of their washing-up teams) will be working. And I also know, from having helped to write numerous menus as a restaurateur and surveyed far more as a writer on this exciting profession, quite how much thought, effort, skill and knowledge goes into writing a menu.

The final selection in this book is mine and, therefore, obviously highly subjective. All these menus appeal to me for various reasons, not least of course because they make me want to travel straight to the restaurant. But menus can also tell a story, of why a trip was planned, what happened as a consequence – reasons for which the menu is less a record of what was eaten and drunk but rather a conduit for the overall experience. I want to begin this tour, therefore, with three different menus that have hung in my kitchen for several years, although one now hangs on the wall of our son's restaurant, The Quality Chop House, in London.

L'ESCARGOT BIENVENU

From some time in the 1960s

This is the French restaurant in London I took over in 1980, when I shortened the name from L'Escargot Bienvenu to L'Escargot, and I remember finding this menu (*pages 12–13*) in a drawer before the builders moved in. For me it represents not just a past I inherited and passed on to successive restaurateurs, but also a piece of London's social history.

Although it is now impossible to decipher the precise date under Menu du Jour, I believe it dates from some time in the early 1960s. The telephone numbers, GERRARD 8460 and 4460, date from the system known as 3L-4N, when the first three letters of the exchange, GER, were followed by four numbers – and this was abolished in 1968.

By then L'Escargot Bienvenu had been in business since 1926 when it opened as London's first French bourgeois restaurant under restaurateur Georges Gaudin. It is he who bestrides the snail on the menu cover, proudly holding aloft the slogan 'Slow and Sure'.

It is pride that oozes from this menu despite the passage of time. Restaurants can no longer sell cigars and cigarettes, once a considerable source of profit, and these prices look ridiculous by today's standards. First courses at 20–40p and main courses under 50p bear testament to a bygone era, but the layout of this menu is a model of clarity.

The never-changing ingredients on this menu are clearly and concisely printed in red. These range from the 6 old pence cover charge (2.5 pence in today's money) in the top left-hand corner to the unmistakable notice that the restaurant is firmly closed on a Sunday. The sections of the menu, again very clearly delineated in a red, capitals-only typeface, easily take your eye and your stomach to the various parts of what was definitely an extensive daily menu.

A clear turtle soup may not be to everyone's taste today, but I do wish I had tried the consommé of snails, a dish that must have been created specifically for

MENU.

L'Escargot Bienvenu

Restaurant

MAISON FRANÇAISE

———

GEO. GAUDIN, *Proprietaire*.

48, GREEK STREET,

SHAFTESBURY AVENUE,

W.1

'Phone: GERRARD **8460**

COUVERTS 6D

Menu du Jour.

Date .... 19........

HORS D'OEUVRES

Hors d'Oeuvres Variés 3/- Saucisson à l'ail 2/6 — Salami 2/6
Oeuf Mayonnaise 2/- Salade Russe 1/- Pâté Campagne 2/-
Pâté Geo. 4/-

POTAGES

Potage Cultivateurs 1/6 — Consommé d'Escargots 2/-
Consommé Vermicelli 1/6 — Tortue Claire 3/6

POISSONS

Sardines Grillées 4/6 — Moules Marinière 4/6
Quenelles de Brochet Nantua 7/6 — Sole Grillée St Tartare 7/6 —
Turbot Mornay 6/6 — Truite Bordelaise 7/6
St Jacques Beurre d'Escargots 7/6 — Grenouilles Provençales 8/6

Grenouilles Provençales 8/6

OEUFS

[illegible]

PLAT du Jour **Crêpes de Volaille Gratinées 6/6**

ENTREES

Carré de Porc Rôti Choux de Bruxelles 7/6
Rognons Grillés Vert Pré 6/6
Tête de Veau Vinaigrette 7/-
Chop de Chevreuil Provençale 8/6
Jambon Braisé aux Épinards 7/6
Tripes à la Mode de Caen 5/6
Grain Grillé p. 2 pers 16/- ou en Cocotte Bonne Femme p. 2 pers 20/-
Râble de Lièvre au Porto p. 2 pers 16/-
Saucisse Toulouse Haricots Blancs 5/-
Boudin Pommes Purée 5/-

ROTIS

Poulet Rôti: Cuisse 7/6 Aile 8/6
Caneton Rôti S.G.

LEGUMES ET SALADE

Haricots Vert 3/- Haricots Blancs 1/3 — Choufleurs 2/- Choux de Bruxelles 2/6
Pois Étuvées 2/6 — Carottes 1/6 — Épinards 2/6 — Céleris 2/- Endives Braisées 2/-
Pommes Rissolées. Lyonnaises. Sautées. Frites. Allumettes. Nature 1/3
Salade de Saison 2/6

ENTREMETS

[illegible]
[illegible]
... Pêche Fraîche 3/-

FROMAGE

Port Salut 2/- Camembert 2/- Gorgonzola 2/- etc...

CAFE 1/6

CIGARES ET CIGARETTES

FERMÉ LE DIMANCHE

CLOSED ON SUNDAY
.....
PHONE: GERRARD 4460

this restaurant and would have used the snails that were bred in the former coal cellars that run under Greek Street. The fish section ranges from inexpensive grilled sardines to turbot Mornay (a béchamel sauce with grated cheese that may well have overpowered this delicate fish) to frog legs Provençale, a dish they obviously had plenty of to sell that day as they listed it twice. And I like the manner in which the main meat section ranges from inexpensive crêpes stuffed with chicken – a great way to use leftovers – to the classic saddle of hare for two with a port sauce. There are two prices for the roast chicken, depending on whether white or dark meat is chosen, and there is a separate section for egg dishes, something that is only now reappearing on menus.

But what this menu exudes for me is a sense of confidence in all that its kitchen prepares. It is resolutely and unquestionably French, and in that era French cooking ruled the world. Chefs had not begun to travel the world as they started to do in the following decade, a trend that led to an exchange of information, ideas, recipes and ingredients that would have been inconceivable to the chefs in L'Escargot Bienvenu's basement kitchen at that time.

EL BULLI
April 30th 2011

The menu on the next page is, obviously, more than just a single menu. It is a compilation of the list of dishes we ate shortly before El Bulli closed in the summer of 2011, and the montage of photos and images (*pages 18–19*) are from the building's unlikely inception in 1963 to 2014 when its world-famous chef Ferran Adrià planned to reopen it as a culinary foundation; it conveys so much – and not just about somewhere that was, for over a decade, unquestionably the world's most exciting, influential and inspirational restaurant.

First of all, the date of April 30th 2011. While so many around the world were celebrating the marriage of HRH Prince William to Kate Middleton in Westminster Abbey, we were visiting the family-run Hotel Almadraba Park in Roses for the first time, before saying goodbye to our friends at El Bulli whom we had first met in the 1990s.

This particular menu was very different from what we ate on those first occasions. In those days, although everything was given more than a twist, there was an à la carte menu, and most dishes bore some resemblance to dishes we had enjoyed elsewhere.

Not so by 2011 when Adrià, and the late Juli Soler, his restaurateur and partner, had travelled the world, particularly to China, Japan and Peru, and become acquainted with so many novel ingredients. And, in turn, their collective renown, fuelled by the internet, had begun to act as a magnet for young, hard-working cooks who wanted to work 12-hour shifts for six months of the year in El Bulli's extremely cramped kitchens, often unpaid – and then go out to party afterwards.

These influences are obvious in the dishes: two versions of the Cuban mojito; two dishes with Parmesan; Thai prawn brain; almost a dozen small plates with a very strong Japanese theme; a Mexican Oaxaca taco; a classic game cappuccino (Adrià became so fascinated with cooking game that he extended the restaurant's

elBulli

mojito - caipirinha sugar cane
mojito and apple flute
pillow like a cocktail
hibiscus
pistachio ravioli
pistacho with her shell
cod fish crust
shrimps "tortilla"
parmesan cheese "macaron"
parmesan cheese "porra"
olive oil chip
bloody-mary
drunk oil caviar with olive soup
boiled shrimp
Thai prawn brain
roses with ham won-ton and melon water
ham and ginger canapée
quails with carrot "escabeche"
soy matches and yuzu with miso
soy cristal
sea urchin niguiri
nori seaweed with lemon
marrow and belly of tune-sushi
miso soup
Umeboshi
tiramisu
caviar cream with hazelnut caviar
liquid hazelnut "porra"
germinated pinenuts
sea cucumbers in sashimi with kalix
octopus shabu-shabu
cold sea anemone with bernacles
lulo "ceviche" and mollusk
clams "ceviche"
Oaxaca "taco"
prawn two firings
oysters Gillardeau with black sand and bone marrow
peas 2011
"gazpacho" and "ajo blanco"
tomatoe tartar
hare "buñuelo"
game meat capuccino
blackberries risotto with game meat sauce
hare ravioli with "boloñesa" and blood
mimetic chestnuts
pond
sugar cube with tea and lime
yogurt blini
Saint-Félicien dollar
gruyère with kirsch
"coca de vidre" - crystal cake
mini-donuts
apple rose

0,5 l. **Fino Piedra Luenga**
Bodegas Robles @ Montilla-Moriles (D.O.)

0,75 l. **Fino La Panesa**
Emilio Hidalgo @ Jerez (D.O.)

0,5 l. **Fino Antique**
Bodegas Rey Fernando de Castilla @ Jerez (D.O.)

0,75 l. **Châteauneuf-du-Pape 2000**
Henri Bonneau @ Châteauneuf-du-Pape (A.O.C.)

0,5 l. **Estela Solera**
Mas Estela @ Empordà (D.O.)

0,75 l. **Oloroso Dulce Matusalem**
González Byass @ Jerez (D.O.)

opening dates to accommodate this enthusiasm); then a series of small desserts that incorporated a wide range of textures and flavours.

But while this menu appears as a matter of record only, what this display reveals are aspects of restaurant life in the late 20th century that changed the world of restaurants forever.

The first, made possible by the flexibility and simplicity of this style of menu design, is quite how easy it is to incorporate ingredients and dishes from around the world on a single piece of paper. At this level, it is not the customer who chooses the menu but the chef, with the only point of discussion being any particular food allergies the customer may have.

On the tour of the kitchen that every guest at El Bulli was taken on, I vividly remember seeing numerous copies of this long list of dishes lying on the pass, close to where Adrià stood, with numbers cross referencing them to the tables and horizontal lines through each dish as they were sent out. This is an example of a menu where the chef, not the customer, is in charge.

The second example of how menus have changed is the short list of wines by the glass that were served during our dinner – listed in the bottom left-hand corner. This combination, often given too much credence by many, was an important change in the restaurant-going experience from the late 1990s onwards. As multi-course meals became increasingly common, everyone benefited: the customer, most obviously, in terms of pleasure; the restaurant in terms of average spend; the winemakers, whose profile was augmented; and the sommeliers, who now took a far more active role in the restaurant and played a far more significant role in the restaurant's overall profitability. How best to unify a menu and wine list will be dealt with in a subsequent chapter.

The montage graphically demonstrates the evolution of this white-painted building by the sea, from a combination of grill room, apartments and minigolf in 1963, via its ownership by a German couple with a penchant for bulldogs, to a restaurant specialising in French cuisine, to its most esoteric culinary evolution, until its final incarnation as the elBulli Foundation.

GRILL-ROOM BAR 1963 EL BULLI CALA MONTJOY PETIT-GOLF APARTAMENTOS

"El Bulli"

Diner Gastronomique
DE LA SAINT SYLVESTRE 1977 /78

HAZIENDA "El Bulli"
GRILL-ROOM - BAR - APA

1 9 8 3
Felices Fiestas
1 9 8 4
El Bulli

EL BULLI
restaurant

Restaurante "El Bulli"

restaurante "El Bulli" ROSAS

restaurante "El Bulli"
CALA MONTJOY ROSAS

MENTOS

El Bulli

El Bulli
RESTAURANT

El Bulli

El Bulli

El Bulli

4156

El Bulli
RESTAURANT

elBulliFoundation

elBullirestaurante

2014

And although this development may seem most unlikely, it is only one of many unlikely aspects of the development of restaurants over the past two decades. Is a minigolf course any less likely a setting for the world's most exciting menu than a 16th-century English pub or a warehouse originally built around the same period to store the furs and other bounty Denmark's traders brought back from the northern Arctic?

The buildings that came to house El Bulli, The Fat Duck in Bray, Berkshire, and Noma in Copenhagen respectively have these unlikely origins. But while they are all different in aspect, they also have one commercial common denominator that was crucial to each of their menu's success: they were all, at the outset, available at a ridiculously inexpensive rent. Their chefs, Adrià, Blumenthal and Redzepi, could dream and create menus in very different styles and completely different settings because a fundamental foundation to their restaurants' future success was inadvertently in place: they were all based within distinctive, undervalued and underappreciated buildings. Regrettably, because of rising property prices worldwide, I am not sure whether we may ever see similar examples of this phenomenon ever again.

RESTAURANT JULIEN

October 15th 1900

This piece of paper (*pages 22–25*) from Paris at the height of La Belle Époque serves as another distinctive example of just what pleasures a menu can generate: pleasures that in this instance, however, have nothing to do with the taste of food and wine. This document highlights just how a menu can be a lasting historical document, a purpose that so many menus can serve by recording every kind of anniversary or special event.

I can still recall where and why I bought this menu. It is from T. McKirdy, a small company based in Brighton that every quarter used to publish a small catalogue of antiquarian cookbooks, posters, menus and food and wine memorabilia. Their catalogue was a food lover's treasure trove and I remember seeing this menu as a separate item, headed simply 'Dîner de Faveur' and the date. I bought it sight unseen and think I paid no more than £5 for it.

I bought it for a special purpose. At the time I was working as a restaurant consultant on the renaissance of St Pancras station as the new home for Eurostar in London. The basis upon which we were working was to reinject the elegance that once existed in continental train travel into the reality of the early 21st century. I thought that this could act as a totem for what we were aiming to do.

I still don't believe that I have ever seen such an elegant menu, everything about it seems so understated, so simple yet so refined. This *dîner de faveur*, or special dinner, took place on Monday, October 15th 1900 at the Restaurant Julien, hosted by Mademoiselle Louise Willy, an actress with the Theatre of the Palais Royal, and Monsieur Auguste Germain, the theatre correspondent of *The Paris Echo*. It is the latter's portrait in the centre, complete with bow tie, cigarette and a moustache he obviously took great pride in.

The menu, for what I assume was a late post-theatre supper, is written with such brevity and style. *Potage de Santé*, a healthy consommé to rejuvenate body and spirit; a special *Bouchée* (mouth-sized), named after, and obviously a favourite

Menu

Potage de Santé

Bouchées à la Willy

Turbot sauce Mousseline

Gigot Catalane

Faisan rôti

Salade de Chicorée

Glace Rossi

Fromages - Fruits

Desserts

VINS

Médoc supérieur

Chablis 1re — Clos-Ponchon

G. H. Mumm Cordon rouge

Café & Liqueurs

Pippermint Get glacé

M. AUGUSTE

Imp. Paul Lemaire, 7 & 9, rue Abel-Hovelacque.

GERMAIN

"Dîner de Faveur"

du

Lundi 15 Octobre 1900

PRÉSIDÉ PAR

Mlle LOUISE WILLY

DU THÉATRE DU PALAIS-ROYAL

ET

M. AUGUSTE GERMAIN

COURRIÉRISTE THÉATRAL DE « L'ÉCHO DE PARIS »

Faveur

of, the leading lady; turbot, the king of fish, with a rich Mousseline sauce (a hollandaise with whipped cream); and then two meat main courses: a leg of lamb with a spicy Catalan sauce of anchovies and garlic, alongside some plainly roasted pheasants, right at the beginning of the game season, with a simple chicory salad. Ice cream, cheese, fruit and petits fours brought the dinner to a gentle conclusion, in the early hours of October 16th 1900, I suspect.

One final, small but significant feature of this menu is how well it has survived the past 115 years, a tribute to the printing skills of M. Paul Lemaire in the rue Abel-Hovelacque, whose name and address appear bottom left. This menu survives as a window into another world.

A menu read online, or posted outside a restaurant, can set the senses racing. Looking it over while at the table, discussing it with a well-informed waiter or, as I often do, keeping the menu by my side during the meal, increases the pleasure while I am eating. And taking menus as souvenirs, storing them as I have done for years in a large box, is a wonderful way in which to recall past pleasures.

Holding and reading a well-written menu brings great satisfaction, inordinate pleasure and, in many cases, a sense of travelling through time and space to those restaurants. Before analysing why certain of the world's most inspiring menus can create such sensations, I would like to start at the beginning: what are the origins of today's menus?

THE ORIGINS OF
THE MENU

Three of the world's original restaurant menus – from the Beauvilliers, Lavenne and Veron et Baron restaurants that once flourished in Paris – now hang proudly on the walls of Le Gavroche, the two-star Michelin restaurant run by its chef/proprietor Michel Roux Jr in London's West End.

These menus (*pages 28–30*) date from the early 19th century when restaurants were mushrooming across Paris – in the 20 years from the early 1790s, more than 500 restaurants opened – but it is impossible to say precisely when they were compiled as they are not dated. It is possible to say with some certainty, however, that the Lavenne menu was on offer around 1805 – the same year as the Battle of Trafalgar – because the vintage of the Chateau Lafitte (sic) listed is 1802 and in those days even the best wines were drunk young.

This era of change and tumult in France was to witness the birth of the menu, following on from the emergence of both the concept of a restaurant and the profession of the restaurateur, both of which had emerged in Paris several decades earlier.

Then there was only one dish on offer, a court-bouillon, or soup, that had the aim of 'restoring' whoever enjoyed it to good health. The soup was called 'un restaurant' and those who sold it 'un restaurateur' – hence the mistake that persists today of putting an 'n' into the word restaurateur.

BILL OF FARE IN FRENCH AND ENGLISH.

VÉRON ET BARON,

Restaurateurs,

AU CAFÉ DE FRANCE, PALAIS-ROYAL, GALERIE VITRÉE, N° 216.

POTAGES.	SOUPS.
Au riz	Rice soup.
Au vermicelli	Vermicelli.
Aux croûtons	Best soup, with some fried bread cut into dice.
Aux choux	Cabbage soup.
A la Julienne	Vegetable soup.
Au parmesan	Macaroni soup, with some grated parmesan cheese served a part.
Consommé	Jelly broth.
Lait au riz	Rice with milk and sugar.

HORS-D'ŒUVRES.	HORS-D'ŒUVRES.
Deux œufs frais	A couple of new-laid eggs.
Beurre frais, la douzaine	Fresh oysters, the dozen.
Citron	Lemon.
Beurre	Fresh butter.
Radis	Radishes.
Melon, la tranche	Melon, the slice.
Olives de Lucques	Olives of Lucca.
Salade d'anchois	Anchovy sallad.
Canapé à l'anchois	Anchovy toast.
Cornichons	Gherkins.

ENTRÉES DE BŒUF.	ENTRIES OF BEEF.
Bœuf au naturel	Boiled beef.
Bœuf aux choux	Ditto with cabbage.

ENTRÉES DE MOUTON.	ENTRIES OF MUTTON.
Filet en chevreuil piqué	Larded fillet dressed as roe-buck's.
Deux côtelettes au naturel	Two broiled chops.

ENTRÉES DE VOLAILLE.	ENTRIES OF POULTRY.
Chapon au gros sel, le quart	Capon boiled, the quarter.
Poulet au riz, le quart	Ditto with rice, the quarter.
Poulet au gros sel, le quart	Fowl boiled, the quarter.

ENTRÉES DE VEAU.	ENTRIES OF VEAL.
Tête de veau, sauce tomate	Calf's head, with love apple sauce.
Tête de veau à la vinaigrette	Ditto with parsley, oil and vinegar.
Oreille à la vinaigrette	Calf's ear, served at the head.

ENTRÉES DE PÂTISSERIE.	ENTRIES OF PASTRY.
Deux petits pâtés au naturel	Two petty patties.
Idem au jus	Ditto with gravy and a stuffing.

ENTRÉES DE POISSON.	ENTRIES OF FISH.
Saumon, sauce aux câpres	Salmon, caper sauce.
Saumon à l'huile	Ditto with oil and vinegar.
Turbot à l'huile	Turbot, the same way.
Turbot, sauce aux câpres	Turbot, caper sauce.

ROTS ET GIBIER.	ROAST AND GAME.
Idem, la moitié	Ditto, the half.
Idem, le quart	Ditto, the quarter.
Veau rôti, chaud	Roast veal, hot, with gravy.
Pigeon	Pigeon.
Grive	Thrush.
Caille	Quail.
Bécasse	Woodcock.
Perdreau	Young partridge.
Trois mauviettes	Three larks.

SALADE. — SALLAD.

ENTREMETS. — ENTREMETS.

Coquille aux huîtres	Scalloped oysters.
Coquille aux champignons	Scalloped mushrooms.
Huîtres au gratin	Oysters stewed in their shells.
Croûte aux champignons	Crust and mushrooms.
Truffes au vin de Champagne	Truffles boiled in Champagne.
Asperges à la sauce	Asparagus with butter sauce.
Artichaut à la sauce	Artichoke with butter sauce.

FROMAGES.	CHEESE.
Fromage de Gruyère	Swiss cheese.
Idem de Hollande	Dutch ditto.
Idem de Brie	Brie ditto.
Idem de Neufchâtel à ., moitié	Neufchatel ditto à ., the half.
Idem de Chester	Cheshire ditto.
Idem de Roquefort	Roquefort ditto.

ENTREMETS AU SUCRE.	SWEET DISHES.

DESSERT.	DESSERT.

There are ____ up-stairs, public and private rooms for company.

(*Soups and luncheons at all hours.*)

VINS ROUGES (RED WINES.)	VINS BLANCS. (WHITE WINES.)	VINS DE LIQUEUR (LIQUOR WINES.)	LIQUEURS FINES (FINE LIQUORS.)
Bourgogne (Burgundy)	Chablis	Madère sec (Dry Madeira)	Extrait d'absinthe. (Wormwood brandy)
	Bordeaux blanc	Malaga	Crème d'absinthe. (Cream of wormwood)
	Meursault	Alicante	Eau-de-vie de Cognac. (Cognac brandy)
	Pouilly fumé	Rota	
	Graves	Muscat	

LAVENNE, RESTAURATEUR.

Table particulière de Société, et par tête.

DÉJEUNERS CHAUDS ET FROIDS.

L'on prie les Sociétés de prévenir la veille, pour être mieux servies.

PRIX FIXE DES METS POUR UNE PERSONNE.

Les articles portés en ville augmentent de deux sous par portion.

Les articles dont les prix ne sont pas indiqués, manquent. *Et si l'on ne donne pas de vin au Garçon*

Pain . . . 4

POTAGES.

Riz au naturel ou à la purée .	
Idem à la turque .	6
Vermicelle au naturel ou à la purée .	6
À la Julienne .	6
Aux choux ou aux herbes .	6
Consommé .	8

HORS-D'OEUVRE.

Huîtres .	14
Beurre frais .	4
Radis .	
Deux œufs frais .	8
Trois rognons à la brochette .	15
Rognons au vin .	15
Cornichons .	5
Olives .	8
Artichauts à la poivrade .	8
Melon , la tranche .	12
Figues .	
Salé aux choux ou à la purée .	12
Un citron .	6
Salade d'anchois .	15
Thon mariné .	12
Deux saucisses à la purée .	8
Idem au naturel .	
Pieds de cochon à la Ste.-Menehould .	10
Saucisse aux choux ou choux-croûte .	12
Boudin noir .	10
Idem blanc .	6
Côtelette de porc frais , sauce Robert .	15
Pied de cochon aux truffes .	
Andouillette de Troyes .	12
Jambon frais .	8

BOEUF.

Bœuf au naturel .	8
Idem aux racines .	8
Idem , sauce aux cornichons .	8
Idem aux choux ou à la choux-croûte .	8
Idem , sauce tomate .	8
Idem à la mode .	12
Palais de bœufs au gratin, à l'Italienne ou à la poulette .	
Hatelet de palais de bœuf .	15
Entre-côte , sauce italienne .	12
Filet de bœuf sauté dans sa glace .	
Idem aux truffes .	
Idem rôti à la sauce piquante .	15
Idem , sauté au vin de Madère .	1
Rotsbiff à l'anglaise .	
Bifteck aux cornichons ou au cresson .	15
Idem au beurre d'anchois .	15
Idem aux pommes de terre .	15
Langue à la sauce piquante .	
Choux-croûte de Strasbourg garnie .	

ENTRÉES DE VEAU.

Ris de veau à la financière .	1 5
Idem aux pois .	1 5
Idem piqué au jus ou à l'oseille .	1 5
Idem à la chicorée ou sauce tomate .	1 5
Idem en papillote .	
Blanquette de veau .	12
Foie à la bourgeoise .	
Idem sauté au vin .	15
Fraise de veau .	15
Tête de veau en tortue .	1 10
Idem à la vinaigrette .	12
Pied au naturel au frit .	12
Poitrine de veau farcie .	15
Fricandeau à l'oseille ou à la sauce tomate .	
Idem à la chicorée .	12
Idem aux pois .	12
Idem aux pointes d'asperges .	
Tendons de veau aux pois .	
Idem à l'oseille ou à la poulette .	12
Pois au jambon .	
Oreilles frites ou à l'Italienne .	15
Idem aux champignons .	18
Idem farcies , frites .	
Côtelette en papillote .	
Idem panée , grillée .	12
Idem aux fines herbes .	
Cervelle frite ou à la poulette .	15
Idem en matelotte ou au beurre noir .	15
Langue en papillote .	
Veau à la gelée .	12

ENTRÉES DE MOUTON.

Deux côtelettes au naturel .	12
Idem à la minute .	15
Idem à la maître d'hôtel .	15
Une côtelette aux racines .	10
Gigot braisé , à l'oseille ou aux haricots .	
Idem à la chicorée .	12
Idem aux navets ou aux carottes .	12
Pieds à la poulette .	12
Filet de chevreuil .	15
Poitrine panée et grillée .	12
Idem sauce tomate ou aux navets .	12
Idem aux pointes d'asperges .	
Idem à la chicorée ou à l'oseille .	
Queue de mouton à la purée .	8
Épigramme d'agneau .	

ENTRÉES DE VOLAILLE.

Carick à l'Indienne .	1 10
Quart de chapon ou gros sel .	1 5
Idem au riz .	
Poulet au riz , le quart .	1 4
Idem à l'estragon ou tomate .	18
Idem aux truffes , le quart .	1
Idem aux champignons , le quart .	1 4
Idem à la Maringo , le quart .	
Quart de poulet , sauce Robert .	1
Quart de poulet à la tartare .	1
Fricassée de poulet garnie .	1
Fritaux de poulet , le quart .	1
Cuisse de poulet en papillote .	1
Marinade de poulet .	
Suprême de volaille .	1
Idem aux truffes .	
Croquettes de volailles .	1 4
Blanquette de volaille .	1 4
Salade de volaille .	15
Coquille de volaille aux truffes .	1 6
Financière de crêtes de coqs .	
Galantine de dinde aux truffes .	15
Pigeon à la crapaudine .	5
Idem aux petits pois .	8
Un demi-pigeon en compote .	
Quart de canard aux pointes d'asperges .	
Idem aux pois .	
Quart de canard aux navets ou à la purée .	15
Ailerons aux navets .	

VOL-AU-VENT.

Vol-au-vent à la financière .	1
Idem de cervelle à l'allemande .	
Vol-au-vent de filets de volaille .	18
Vol-au-vent de ris de veau .	18
Vol-au-vent d'anguilles .	18
Vol-au-vent de morue .	18
Deux pâtés au jus .	12

ENTRÉE DE POISSON.

Matelotte d'anguille ou à la poulette .	1
Anguille à la tartare .	1
Merlan grillé , sauce aux câpres .	
Idem au gratin ou au sel .	15
Esturgeon à l'Italienne .	
Carlet sur le plat .	15
Alose aux câpres ou à l'oseille .	
Deux harengs, sauté à la moutarde .	
Filets de soles au gratin .	15
Sole au gratin .	15
Turbot à la Hollandaise .	15
Idem à l'huile ou sauce aux câpres .	15
Idem à la maître-d'hôtel .	
Idem à la provençale .	12
Idem à la hollandaise .	
Idem au gratin .	
Raie sauce aux câpres ou au beurre noir .	
Saumon sauce aux câpres ou à l'huile .	15
Maquereau à la maître-d'hôtel , entier .	15
demi-maquereau .	18
Moules à la poulette .	
Barbue aux câpres ou à l'huile .	15
Béchamelle de poisson .	12
Cabillot aux câpres ou à la flamande .	15
Truite , sauce aux câpres ou à l'huile .	15
Brochet, sauce aux câpres .	15
Écrevisses de Seine .	
Boudin blanc de merlan .	12

ENTRÉES DE GIBIER.

Salmi de bécasse aux truffes .	12
Salmi de perdreau , la moitié .	15
Idem aux truffes .	
Civet de lièvre .	15
Gibelotte de lapreaux .	15
Mauviettes au gratin .	
Caille au Gratin .	12
Demi perdrix aux choux .	1 10
Idem à la purée ou sauce tomate .	5
Salmis de canard sauvage .	

ROTS.

Poularde aux truffes .	
Poularde fine rôtie , le quart .	1
Quart de poularde au cresson .	1
Dindonneau , le quart .	1
Poulet gras au cresson , le quart .	1
Idem aux truffes , entier .	
Canard sauvage , la moitié .	
Sarcelle .	
Bécassine .	
Perdreau rouge .	5
Caille rôtie .	
Bécasse .	
Pluvier doré .	
Perdreau gris .	
Mauviettes .	
Grive .	
Filet de bœuf .	15
Gigot de Présalé .	
Pigeon de volière .	5
Veau de Pontoise .	12
Sole frite .	15
Carpe frite , la moitié .	
Goujons frits .	
Éperlans frits .	
Merlan frit .	
Limande ou carlet frits .	10
Agneau rôti .	
Salade .	5

ENTREMETS.

Asperges à la sauce ou à l'huile .	
Croquettes de pommes de terre .	12
Idem de ris .	12
Petits pois au sucre .	12
Idem à l'anglaise .	
Salsifis à la sauce blanche ou frits .	15
Épinards au jus ou au sucre .	
OEufs à la tripe .	12
Haricots blancs à la maître d'hôtel .	12
Haricots verts .	12
Idem à l'anglaise .	12
Choux-fleurs au beurre ou à l'huile .	
Chicorée au jus .	12
Pommes de terre frites ou à la maître d'hôtel .	
Cardons au jus .	
Céleri au jus .	
Artichaut à la sauce .	12
Artichauts frits .	12
Artichaut à la barigoulle .	
Croûte aux champignons .	
OEufs pochés au jus .	12
OEufs brouillés .	12
Idem à la béchamelle .	
Idem brouillés aux truffes .	
Idem brouillés , aux pointes d'asperges .	
Idem à l'oseille ou au beurre noir .	
Omelette aux pommes .	
Omelette au jambon .	15
Omelette aux rognons .	
Idem aux fines herbes .	12
Idem au sucre .	15
Idem aux confitures .	
Idem soufflée .	
Soufflé de ris ou de pommes de terre .	5
Charlotte de pommes .	5
Beignets de pommes .	
Idem de pêches .	
Idem d'abricots .	15
Macaroni .	15
Petites fèves de marais .	
Navets au jus .	12
Coquille aux champignons .	15
Macédoine de légumes .	12
Asperges aux petits pois .	
Petit pot de crème .	
Truffes au vin de Champagne .	
Croûtes aux truffes .	
Truffes à l'Italienne .	12
Laitue au jus .	

DESSERT.

Compote de poires ou de pommes .	
Idem de cerises .	10
Fraises au sucre ou framboises .	12
Cerises .	
Poires .	
Pommes .	
Pêche .	10
Abricots .	8
Prunes .	8
Raisin de Fontainebleau .	
Biscuit .	4
Noix vertes .	
Cerneaux .	8
Pruneaux en compote .	
Confitures de groseilles .	12
Idem de cerises .	12
Idem d'abricots .	12
Marmelades de pommes .	12
Idem d'abricots ou prunes .	12
Meringue à la crème .	
Idem aux confitures .	
Fromage de Gruyère .	4
Idem de Roquefort .	10
Idem de Chester .	10
Idem de Brie . ou Neuchatel .	4
Idem à la crème .	
Orange au sucre .	
Salade d'orange .	
Mendians .	10
Marons .	
Figues .	
4 Macarons .	8
Cerises à l'eau-de-vie .	8
Prune à l'eau-de-vie .	8
Abricot à l'eau-de-vie .	8
Pêche à l'eau-de-vie .	12

VINS ROUGES.

Vin ordinaire .	1 5
Vin de Macon .	1 10
Vin de Bourgogne .	2 5
Vin de Beaune .	2 5
Vin de Pomard .	3
Vin de Volney .	3 10
Vin de Bordeaux .	2
Vin de Bordeaux Médoc .	4
Vin de Bordeaux Lafitte .	5 6
Vin de Chambertin .	6
Vin de côte rôtie .	6
Vin de l'Hermitage .	5
Vin de Porto .	6

Bierre .	10
Porter .	15

VINS BLANCS.

Vin de Tonnerre .	10
Vin de Chably .	1 10
Vin de Mulsault .	3 15
Vin de Soterne .	3
Vin de Champagne .	5
— la demi-bouteille .	3 15
Vin de Champagne rosat .	5
Vin de Champagne , tisanne .	5
Vin de Grave .	3
Vin de l'Hermitage .	4
Vin de Côte-Rôtie .	4
Vin de Saint-Perret .	4
Vin de Condrieux .	4

VINS DE LIQUEURS, le verre.

Malaga .	15
Madère .	15
Malvoisie .	18
Chypra .	1 5
Rota .	12
Alicante .	12
Lunel .	12
Muscat Frontignan .	12

CAFÉ ET LIQUEURS.

Café , la demi-tasse .	8
Eau-de-vie de Cognac .	8
Eau-de-vie d'Andaye .	12
Eau-de-vie de Dantsick .	12
Marasquin .	12
Anisette de Bordeaux .	12
Idem de Hollande .	12
Senhac ou huile de rose .	12
Kirschwater .	12
Fleur d'orange .	10
Crème de vanille .	10
Crème de Rhum .	10
Crème de Menthe .	10
Crème de Moka .	8
Noyau de Phalsbourg .	8
Extrait d'Absinthe .	
Curaçao .	
Rhum .	
Huile de vanille .	

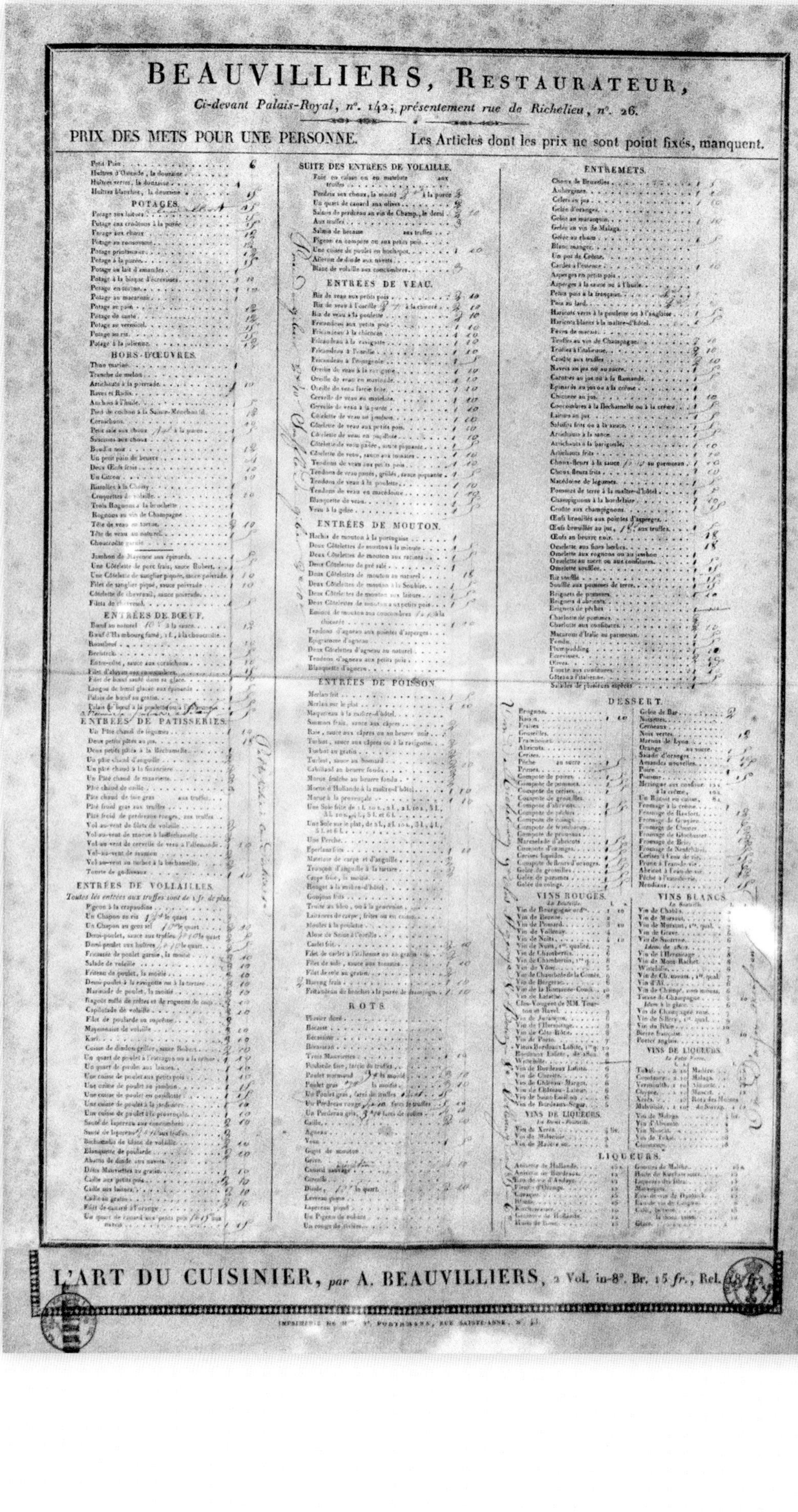

BEAUVILLIERS, RESTAURATEUR,

Ci-devant Palais-Royal, n°. 142; présentement rue de Richelieu, n°. 26.

PRIX DES METS POUR UNE PERSONNE. Les Articles dont les prix ne sont point fixés, manquent.

Petit Pain 6
Huîtres d'Ostende, la douzaine ....
Huîtres vertes, la douzaine ....
Huîtres blanches, la douzaine ....

POTAGES.

Potage aux laitues ....
Potage aux croûtons à la purée ....
Potage aux choux ....
Potage au consommé ....
Potage printanier ....
Potage à la purée ....
Potage au lait d'amandes ....
Potage à la bisque d'écrevisses ....
Potage au tapioca ....
Potage au macaroni ....
Potage au pain ....
Potage au carte ....
Potage au vermicelli ....
Potage au riz ....
Potage à la julienne ....

HORS-D'OEUVRES.

Thon mariné ....
Tranche de melon ....
Artichauts à la poivrade ....
Raves et Radis ....
Anchois à l'huile ....
Pied de cochon à la Sainte-Menehould .....
Cervelas ....
Petit oie aux choux ....
Saucisses aux choux ....
Boudin noir ....
Un petit pain de beurre ....
Deux œufs frais ....
Un Cervat ....
Rissoles à la Chancy ....
Croquettes de volaille ....
Trois Ragoûts à la brochette ....
Rognons au vin de Champagne ....
Tête de veau au tortue ....
Tête de veau au naturel ....
Choucroûte garnie ....

Jambon de Bayonne aux épinards ....
Une Côtelette de porc frais, sauce Robert .
Une Côtelette de sanglier piquée, sauce poivrade
Filet de sanglier piqué, sauce poivrade ...
Côtelette de chevreuil, sauce poivrade ....
Filets de chevreuil ....

ENTRÉES DE BŒUF.

Bœuf au naturel ....
Bœuf d'Hambourg farci, à la choucroûte ....
Rosbif ....
Bifteck ....
Entre-côte, sauce aux cornichons ....
Filet d'aloyau aux cornichons ....
Filet de bœuf sauté dans sa glace ....
Langue de bœuf glacée aux épinards ....
Palais de bœuf au gratin ....
Palais de bœuf à la poulette ....

ENTRÉES DE PATISSERIES.

Un Pâté chaud de légumes ....
Deux petits pâtés au jus ....
Deux petits pâtés à la Béchamelle ....
Un pâté chaud d'anguille ....
Un pâté chaud à la financière ....
Un Pâté chaud de mauviettes ....
Pâté chaud de caille ....
Pâté chaud de foie gras ... aux truffes ...
Pâté froid gras aux truffes ....
Pâté froid de perdreaux rouges, aux truffes
Vol-au-vent de filets de volaille ....
Vol-au-vent de morue à la Béchamelle ......
Vol-au-vent de cervelle de veau à l'allemande
Vol-au-vent de saumon ....
Vol-au-vent en turbot à la béchamelle .....
Tourte de godiveaux ....

ENTRÉES DE VOLAILLES.

Toutes les entrées aux truffes sont de 3 fr. de plat.

Pigeon à la crapaudine ....
Un Chapon au riz ....
Un Chapon au gros sel ....
Demi-poulet, sauce aux truffes ....
Demi-poulet aux huîtres ....
Fricassée de poulet garnie, la moitié .....
Salade de volaille ....
Poulet à la reine, la moitié ....
Demi-poulet à la vinaigrette, la moitié ...
Mayonnaise de poulet, la moitié ....
Ragoût mêlé de crêtes et de rognons de coq
Capilotade de volaille ....
Mayonnaise de volaille ....
Filet de poularde en mayonnaise ....
Kari ....
Cuisse de dindon grillée, sauce Robert ....
Un quart de poulet à l'estragon ou à la tartare
Un quart de perdreau aux laitues ....
Une cuisse de poulet aux petits pois ......
Une cuisse de poulet au jambon ....
Une cuisse de poulet en provisions ....
Une cuisse de poulet à la jardinière ......
Une cuisse de poulet à la provençale ......
Sauté de laperaux aux concombres ....
Sauté de laperaux aux truffes ....
Béchamelle de blanc de volaille ....
Blanquette de poularde ....
Abatis de dinde aux navets ....
Dites Mauviettes au gratin ....
Caille aux petits pois ....
Caille aux laitues ....
Caille au gratin ....
Filet de caneton d'Orange ....
Un quart de caneton aux petits pois ....

SUITE DES ENTRÉES DE VOLAILLE.

Filet en cuisse en aspic matelote, aux truffes
Perdrix aux choux, la moitié ... à la purée
Un quart de canard aux olives ....
Salmis de perdreaux au vin de Champagne, le demi
Aux truffes ....
Salmis de bécasse ... aux truffes ....
Pigeon en compote ou aux petits pois ......
Une cuisse de poulet en hochepot ....
Aileron de dindon aux navets ....
Blanc de volaille aux concombres ....

ENTRÉES DE VEAU.

Ris de veau aux petits pois ....
Ris de veau à l'oseille ... à la tartare ..
Ris de veau à la poulette ....
Fricandeau aux petits pois ....
Fricandeau à la chicorée ....
Fricandeau à la ravigote ....
Fricandeau à l'oseille ....
Escalopes à l'écarlate ....
Oreille de veau à la ravigote ....
Oreille de veau en marinade ....
Oreille de veau farcie frite ....
Cervelle de veau au matelote ....
Cervelle de veau à la purée ....
Côtelette de veau au jambon ....
Côtelette de veau aux petits pois ....
Côtelette de veau au papillote ....
Côtelette de veau grillée, sauce piquante .
Côtelette de veau, sauce au tomate ....
Tendons de veau aux petits pois ....
Tendons de veau panés, grillés, sauce piquante
Tendons de veau à la poulette ....
Tendons de veau en macédoine ....
Blanquette de veau ....
Veau à la gelée ....

ENTRÉES DE MOUTON.

Haches de mouton à la portugaise ....
Deux Côtelettes de mouton à la minute .....
Deux Côtelettes de mouton aux racines .....
Deux Côtelettes de pré salé ....
Deux Côtelettes de mouton au naturel ......
Deux Côtelettes de mouton à la Soubise ....
Deux Côtelettes de mouton aux laitues .....
Deux Côtelettes de mouton e et petits pois
Émincé de mouton aux concombres ou à la chicorée
Tendons d'agneau aux pointes d'asperges ...
Épigramme d'agneau ....
Deux Côtelettes d'agneau au naturel ....
Tendons d'agneau aux petits pois ....
Blanquette d'agneau ....

ENTRÉES DE POISSON

Merlan frit ....
Merlan sur le plat ....
Maquereau à la maître-d'hôtel ....
Saumon frais, sauce aux câpres ....
Raie, sauce aux câpres ou au beurre noir ..
Turbot, sauce aux câpres ou à la ravigote .
Turbot au gratin ....
Turbot, sauce au homard ....
Cabillaud au beurre fondu ....
Morue fraîche au beurre fondu ....
Morue à Hollande à la maître-d'hôtel ......
Marne à la provençale ....
Une Sole frite de 1 fr., 1 fr. 50 c., 2 fr.
Une Sole sur le plat de 1 fr. 50 c., 2 fr., 3 fr. 4 fr.
Une Perche ....
Éperlans frits ....
Matelote de carpe et d'anguille ....
Tronçon d'anguille à la tartare ....
Carpe frite, le moitié ....
Rouget à la maître-d'hôtel ....
Goujons frits ....
Truite au bleu, ou à la genevoise ....
Laitances de carpe, frites ou en caisse ...
Moules à la poulette ....
Aloze au Soleil à l'oseille ....
Cadet frit ....
Filet de carlet à l'allemande ou au gratin
Filet de sole, sauce aux tomates ....
Riz à vette de goujon ....
Hareng frais ....
Fritandeau de brochets à la purée de Bruxelles

RÔTS.

Plouver doré ....
Bécasse ....
Bécassine ....
Bécasseau ....
Trois Mauviettes ....
Poularde fine, farcie de truffes ....
Poulet ordinaire, le moitié ....
Poulet gras ... le moitié ....
Un Poulet gras, farci de truffes ....
Un Perdreau rouge, sans être farci de truffes
Un Perdreau gris ... farci de truffes .....
Caille ....
Agneau ....
Veau ....
Gigot de mouton ....
Genet ....
Canard sauvage ....
Sarcelle ....
Dinde ... le quart ....
Levreau piqué ....
Laperau piqué ....
Un Pigeon de volière ....
Un rouget de rivière ....

ENTREMETS.

Choux de Bruxelles ....
Aubergines ....
Céleris en jus ....
Gelée d'oranges ....
Gelée au marasquin ....
Gelée au vin de Malaga ....
Gelée au citron ....
Blanc manger ....
Un pot de Crème ....
Cardon à l'essence ....
Asperges en petits pois ....
Asperge à la sauce ou à l'huile ....
Petits pois à la française ....
Pois au lard ....
Haricots verts à la poulette ou à l'anglaise
Haricots blancs à la maître-d'hôtel ....
Fèves de marais ....
Truffes au vin de Champagne ....
Truffes à l'italienne ....
Croûte aux truffes ....
Navets au jus au sucre ....
Carottes au jus ou à la flamande ....
Épinards au jus ou à la crème ....
Chicorée au jus ....
Salsifis frits ou à la sauce ....
Artichauts à la sauce ....
Artichauts à la barigoule ....
Artichauts frits ....
Choux-fleurs à la sauce ... au parmesan ...
Choux-fleurs frits ....
Macédoine de légumes ....
Pommes de terre à la maître-d'hôtel ....
Champignons à la bordelaise ....
Croûte aux champignons ....
Œufs brouillés aux pointes d'asperges .....
Œufs brouillés au jus ... aux truffes .....
Œufs au beurre noir ....
Omelette aux fines herbes ....
Omelette aux rognons ou au jambon ....
Omelette au sucre ou aux confitures ....
Omelette soufflée ....
Riz soufflé ....
Soufflé aux pommes de terre ....
Beignets de pommes ....
Beignets d'abricots ....
Beignets de pêches ....
Charlotte de pommes ....
Charlott aux confitures ....
Macaroni d'Italie au parmesan ....
Fondu ....
Plum-pudding ....
Pruneaux ....
Olives ....
Toutes nos confitures ....
Gâteaux à l'italienne ....
Salades de plusieurs espèces ....

DESSERT.

Brugnons ....
Raisin ....
Poires ....
Groseilles ....
Framboises ....
Abricots ....
Cerises ....
Pêche .... au sucre ....
Prunes ....
Compote de poires ....
Compote de pommes ....
Compote de cerises ....
Compote de groseilles ....
Compote d'abricots ....
Compote de prunes ....
Compote de coings ....
Compote de mirabelles ....
Compote de pruneaux ....
Compote de Bourdelais oranges ....
Marmelade d'abricots ....
Compote d'oranges ....
Gelée de groseilles ....
Gelée de pommes ....
Gelée de coings ....

Grain de Bar ....
Noisettes ....
Cerneaux ....
Noix vertes ....
Marrons de Lyon ....
Orange ....
Salade d'oranges ....
Amandes nouvelles ....
Pain ....
Pommes ....
Meringue sur commande ....
À la crème ....
Un Biscuit en caisse ....
Fromage à la crème ....
Fromage de Roquefort ....
Fromage de Gruyère ....
Fromage de Chester ....
Fromage de Gloucester ....
Fromage de Brie ....
Fromage de Neufchâtel ....
Cerises à l'eau-de-vie ....
Prunes à l'eau-de-vie ....
Abricot à l'eau-de-vie ....
Pêche à l'eau-de-vie ....
Meridaux ....

VINS ROUGES.

La bouteille.

Vin de Bourgogne ord. ....
Vin de Beaune ....
Vin de Pomard ....
Vin de Volnay ....
Vin de Nuits ....
Vin de Nuits, 1re. qualité ....
Vin de Chambertin ....
Vin de Chambertin, 1re. qualité ....
Vin de Vône ....
Vin de Chambolle de la Cômée ....
Vin de Bregnac ....
Vin de la Romanée-Conti ....
Vin de Juliénas ....
Clos-Vougeot de MM. Tournon et Bareil .....
Vin de Juliénas ....
Vin d'Hermitage ....
Vin de Côte-Rôtie ....
Vin de Paris ....
Vins Bordeaux-Lafitte, 1re. ....
Bordeaux Estève, de 1800 ....
Wancollie ....
Vin de Bordeaux Latite ....
Vin de Cherubin ....
Vin de Château-Margau ....
Vin de Château-Laine ....
Vin de Saint-Émilion ....
Vin de Bordeaux-Ségur ....

VINS DE LIQUEURS.

Le demi-bouteille.

Vin de Xérès ....
Vin de Malvoisie ....
Vin de Madère vieux ....

VINS BLANCS.

La bouteille.

Vin de Chablis ....
Vin de Beaune ....
Vin de Meursau, 1re. qual. ....
Vin de Grave ....
Vin de Sauterne ....
Idem. de 1800 ....
Vin de l'Hermitage ....
Vin de Mont-Rachet ....
Wancollie ....
Vin de St. Péray ....
Vin d'Aï ....
Vin de Champ. sans mousse ....
Tisane de Champagne ....
Idem à la glace ....
Vin de Cluny ....
Vin de Sillery, 1re. qual. ....
Vin du Rhin ....
Bierre Française ....
Porter anglais ....

VINS DE LIQUEURS.

Le demi-bouteille.

Tokai .... Muscat ....
Constance ..... Malaga ....
Vermouth ...... Alicante ....
Chypre .... Muscat ....
Xérès .... Rota des Moines ....
Malvoisie ..... du Bourg ....
Vin de Malaga ....
Vin d'Absinthe ....
Vin de Tokai ....
Cassanaya ....

LIQUEURS.

Anisette de Hollande ....
Anisette de Bordeaux ....
Marasquin de Zara ....
Marasquin d'Andaye ....
Fleur d'Orange ....
Curaçao ....
Bitters ....
Kirchwasser ....
Parfait-amour ....
Crème de Hollande ....
Crème de Rose ....
Grenades de Malthe ....
Huile de Vénus ....
Huile de Mocka ....
Liqueurs des îles ....
Maraquin ....
Eau-de-vie de Dantzick ....
Eau-de-vie de Cognac ....
Rhum ....
Eau de Cognac vieux ....
Genièvre ....

As the profession developed, the menu (a word derived from minute, meaning small or made shorter) came into being – a process that coincided with the emergence of revolutionary France. The most informative, detailed account of this transformation is Rebecca L. Spang's excellent book *The Invention of the Restaurant*, but even this book cannot explain how menus suddenly emerged and how their contents immediately numbered several hundred dishes, as these three menus do.

There are, I believe, several different reasons. France, at the time, was a predominantly agricultural country and labour was inexpensive. No ground rules had yet been laid down as to how people were to eat, to enjoy or even to behave in their restaurants – the influence of writers such as Grimod de La Reynière and Brillat-Savarin lay several years in the future. And, most crucially, in this power vacuum everyone was free to experiment – as in cooking so in the emergence of the menu, necessity appears to have been the mother of invention.

But of course the design of the menu has always been highly dependent on the printing technology available at the time. These original Parisian menus look like sheets of a newspaper because that is all that could be printed inexpensively in the early 19th century.

They are large, single-folio sheets packed with columns of closely printed type, all of which follow a similar layout. There are *potages* (soups) top left and then a string of different headings with minor variations on their final preparation: approximately 20 beef dishes, then the same number incorporating veal, chicken or lamb. This is followed by a smaller number of offerings involving *vols-au-vent* then an even larger number headed *entremets*, smaller dishes served between courses, and finally about 30 desserts. The bottom right-hand corner is given over to a list of wines, coffee and liqueurs. These pages may read like a menu but they look very much like pages from the shipping news of that era.

Evolving printing technology during the 19th century changed menu design. From the large folio it became a small leather booklet covered and bound with silken cord. Then it again became a single sheet, decorated with images of

languid goddesses and stylised flowers, and finally during the Belle Époque era the menu took on the overtones of poster art. By this stage, as Spang writes, 'the menu had become a sort of literary product, the restaurant's most marked generic innovation.'

And as Spang also makes clear, these early menus presented the then-known culinary world on a single sheet of paper, beyond which dwelt the monstrous unknown because – although taverns and auberges existed in the provinces – restaurants were a strictly Parisian phenomenon. Menus had begun the process that continues to this day of taking hold of our imaginations.

That these menus belong to Michel Roux Jr (one was offered to him by a customer, the other two he bought from the *bouquinistes* by the side of the river Seine) is extremely fitting, as the Roux family has been responsible for maintaining the French culinary standards that emerged in the early 19th century since they moved to London in the late 1960s. Michel Jr took over from his father Albert at Le Gavroche in 1991; his uncle, Michel, owns the three-star Michelin restaurant The Waterside Inn at Bray near Maidenhead; and Michel Jr's daughter Emily is, not surprisingly, an emerging culinary talent.

At 9.30am, as his waiting staff were busy preparing the dining room, I sat down opposite Roux and his morning cup of tea, drunk from a Manchester United mug, in the Chef's Library – a book-lined private dining room that seats six – to discuss, firstly, how any chef could have run a kitchen that offered as many dishes as these three restaurants once did, and then how he has adapted his restaurant's menu for the 21st century.

He began by explaining how kitchens in those days must have been radically different from those of today. There would have been very limited refrigeration, so fresh produce would have had to be delivered several times a day. The stoves, burning either coal or wood, would have made the kitchen extremely hot, with temperatures similar to those of a steam locomotive, and the stoves would have been kept burning constantly. There would have been staff everywhere, and the cooking process would have been very different. 'There would have been three

or four sauces that differentiated the dishes but otherwise there would have been a significant overlap in the style in which the lamb or the chicken or the beef would have been served. It would have been more like an old-fashioned Indian restaurant, with the main dishes distinguished by their sauces rather than their style of cooking. That's the only way they could have offered this vast array of choice,' Roux explained.

The menus were printed in bulk and then added to by hand to incorporate all the ingredients that became available at some time or another during the year. These were, in effect, menus for all seasons. And yet as Roux, the celebrated TV chef, stood in front of the Lavenne menu, written 210 years earlier, he confessed that every time he looks at these menus he finds something fascinating, as though looking through a window into his profession's past.

'I wonder what Lavenne's *huile de vanilla* tasted like as a dessert, or this liqueur from Lunel, a little medieval village south-west of Nîmes. Here they're offering an English cheese that has come all the way from Chester. And the fact that there are eight different soups on the menu reminds me that when we first opened Le Gavroche there were at least three soups on our menu, including a soup of the day.'

Then Roux spotted a dish called *oeufs à la tripe*, eggs cooked like tripe, and roared with laughter. 'This is a dish I used to prepare when I was doing my military service as a cook in the Elysée Palace in Paris. It's a great dish. You prepare hard-boiled eggs then chop them up. Then you make a sauce by blanching onions in lots of milk seasoned with salt and nutmeg, and then you pour this béchamel over the eggs and you *gratiné* it in the oven. We used to make it for the staff lunch, but if there was a meeting that day and the ministers and their secretaries discovered that we were preparing it, we had to make extra portions for them too, because they all knew what a satisfying dish it is. They wanted mini portions, of course.'

But while these menus provide a link to the dishes we used to eat, they do not reflect the significant changes in how and what we want to eat today. The French cooking of the early 19th century is very different from that of today and that is

a particular challenge Roux has had to confront. He used various aspects of his menu to overcome it.

When he took over Le Gavroche from his father the first thing he did was to introduce a new menu cover to announce this significant change (*pages 37–39*). He commissioned the Irish painter Pauline Bewick to draw in watercolour Michel's face centre stage on the menu cover with several of his favourite ingredients around him: a wild salmon, a round of cheese, cherries, half a lemon and a glass of wine. Significantly, the faces of his father and uncle appear within the frame of a mirror in the background. It is a painting that leaves no doubt which chef is now in charge.

The menu Michel inherited was heavy on cream and butter. Heavily reduced sauces and those based on roux (however appropriate linguistically) were not really the kind of food a man who has completed over 20 marathons would like to eat or even to cook today. But when he tried to take one of the restaurant's signature dishes, the Soufflé Suissesse – a double-baked cheese soufflé cooked in double cream – off the menu, he received so many complaints that after four months he admitted defeat and restored it.

But the recipe for his Soufflé Suissesse is radically different from his father's. He has increased significantly the quantity of egg white in the blend to lighten the whole dish up and, in a classic example of 'menu engineering', he has moved the dish from the à la carte menu to the tasting menu so that it is served in half the size of its former incarnation. The dish's popularity remains undimmed: on Friday and Saturday nights, Roux confessed somewhat wearily, it can be ordered by at least half the tables in the restaurant.

Roux cited changes to two other classic dishes – the lobster mousse with caviar and champagne sauce and the luscious Omelette Rothschild dessert – as further examples of how his menu has to satisfy the 21st-century palate but not diverge too far from its traditional French roots. In the former there is now more lobster meat, three medallions not two as before, and less mousse, less cream and more caviar: 'If you're going to serve caviar, you have to be generous,' Roux

explained. In the latter dish, there is still plenty of butter but the ingredients have been simplified so that the overall taste is lighter and fresher.

Another dish that Roux is proud of is a crab salad served alongside a soft shell crab, an ingredient that has excited him since he cooked in Hong Kong. 'There is a lot of white meat from the crab, olive oil, balsamic vinegar and coriander. It sounds very non-French until you look at that book over there, *Memoires des Chefs*, and realise that Alain Chapel was serving a dish called *Crêpe Japonaise* with lots of fresh ginger 60 years ago at his three-star Michelin restaurant in Mionnay.'

Roux speaks passionately about the traditions the restaurant industry must maintain – his kitchen's knives are still sharpened by a company run by the London-based descendants of those who initiated this profession in Carisolo, northern Italy, and whenever possible he likes to buy onions, garlic and shallots from the itinerant 'Onion Johnnies' from Brittany – and in two respects, both connected to the wine list, he has maintained his menu's popularity.

Roux has always been more aware and appreciative of his wine list than many of his peers. He knows what it can do for any restaurant's profitability, and he has always written his menu so that the customer can enjoy it and the wine list together for maximum pleasure. 'Whenever we are serving a fillet of a classic fish, for example, I will make sure that there is a classic buttery sauce to go with it. The dish shines and so will the wine. The same is true for a good red wine. If a customer wants to enjoy a good red burgundy, he will want a good piece of beef with a great red wine sauce. I would want that myself, so we have to make this possible.'

While this option is open to any chef to follow, the secret behind the success of Le Gavroche's lunchtime menu is probably not. During the recession of the early 1990s it was noticed that, for the first time, customers were not ordering wine at lunch, but if and when they did, it was reported back to the restaurant that their expenses were not being readily accepted (this was particularly true of the American companies then moving into Mayfair).

The solution was breathtakingly simple and has proved highly successful for the past two decades. The price of the lunchtime menu would henceforth include half a bottle of wine and half a bottle of mineral water per person but neither would be itemised on the bill. It would simply be described as lunch.

The consequence of this set price menu has been a restaurant packed with relatively high-spending clientele during the week – something every restaurateur dreams of. And Le Gavroche's clientele is remarkably diverse, as Roux appreciates every time he makes a tour of the dining room towards the end of service. 'There are tables of those in the financial world, tables celebrating a special occasion and those whom we refer to as "Gavroche virgins" – those who are drawn here for their very first time by the price of lunch but then invariably return when they have a particular occasion to mark. This menu, created by my father and Silvano Giraldin, our former general manager, has been fundamental to the ongoing success of Le Gavroche.'

But what is most striking about this menu, so in tune with the style of food customers want to eat today and so representative of the cooking style of a chef who has made such a success on television, is that it is on offer in a room whose walls are lined with the world's first restaurant menus.

Over 200 years ago, in a single city, menus were merely lists, albeit very long ones, of all the dishes a restaurant kitchen could deliver. Today, all over the world, menus are much more concise, highly effective marketing tools created by highly talented, strongly opinionated chefs who use the menu to express their personal creativity. Over this period, chefs have incorporated technology, travel and hugely diverse culinary inspiration to express themselves while the menu, the piece of paper that expresses these ambitions and ideas, has just got smaller and smaller.

LE MENU

LE 'BLOODY MARY' AU CRABE

OU

LES OEUFS DE MOUETTE BROUILLES ET POINTES D'ASPERGES

OU

*FILET DE MAQUEREAU POELE A LA MOUTARDE
ET COURGETTE*

******

PAVE DE CABILLAUD ROTI, PETITS POIS A LA FRANCAISE

OU

FRICASSEE DE VOLAILLE ET TRESORS DES BOIS

OU

ROGNONS DE VEAU, TAGLIATELLES FRAICHES ET ESTRAGON

******

PLATEAU DE FROMAGES

OU

LES GLACES ET SORBETS MAISON

OU

*PANNA COTTA A LA VANILLE ET AU RHUM
FRUITS ROUGES ET TUILE CROUSTILLANTE*

******

CAFE ET PETITS FOURS

LES VINS

HUGEL "GENTIL" – DOMAINE HUGEL & FILS 2013
Alsace

CHATEAU DE SOURS BLANC 2013
Bordeaux

-------0-------

B DE BIAC 2010
Cadillac – Côtes de Bordeaux

DOMAINE LA TOUR DE GATIGNE 2012
Duché d'Uzès - Languedoc

~~~~~~~~~~~

Lunch menu @ £55.00 per person inclusive of vat
1/2 bottle of Wine &
1/2 Bottle of Speyside Glenlivet Still
or Sparkling Mineral Water per person
there will be a 12.5% discretionary service charge

CHAPTER

3

PLANNING THE MENU

A nyone who knows even a little about how restaurant menus are written will appreciate that they are the epitome of a team effort.

No chef ever creates a dish on his or her own. Dishes, and the subsequent menus that evolve from them, are the culmination of one individual's creativity supplemented by the input of his team in the kitchen; by his sommeliers; by his restaurateur partner; and, often, in response to demand from his customers.

And yet, I hope that the following interviews with 12 of the world's leading chefs will yield more than just the fact that each of them relies to an extraordinary degree on others, and, as they each acknowledge, on the quality of the chefs, and often their spouses, who surround them.

The insecurity inherent in the personality of anyone who tries to reach the top of this precarious profession determines what will appear on the menu, as does knowing what you can cook well – qualities cited by Bruce Poole of Chez Bruce in London. Then there is the importance of the correct spelling, particularly of foreign words, in the physical presentation of any menu, characteristics instilled in Shaun Hill by his journalist father.

Although in my interviews with Heston Blumenthal, Massimo Bottura, Arnaud Donckele and René Redzepi each chef acknowledges the importance of their colleagues, friends and families, these interviews also underline quite how

talented and determined each of them has been to reach their current standing. They also show how each of them has faced particular challenges because of the state of cooking in the countries where they began.

In certain respects, life was somewhat easier for Blumenthal and Redzepi because the respective standards of cooking in the UK and Denmark were so much lower than those in France and Italy at the time they began to create the menus that were to make The Fat Duck and Noma so respected. In my interview with Bottura, he went on at length about how every Italian still believes that their way of preparing a dish is the best, and therefore, by definition, the only way of cooking it. And Donckele, born in the north of France, had to travel to the south of his native country to find the region that would fire his culinary imagination.

Travel has played an increasingly important role in the creation of these menus, not just the travel that brings these chefs closer together and leads to greater inspiration, but also the travel that allows for the easier cross-fertilisation of so many different ingredients. Those who now have restaurant empires benefit from travel that allows the chefs themselves to move so effortlessly: Daniel Boulud from his native Lyon to New York and then to outposts in London, Singapore and Montreal; April Bloomfield, born in Birmingham, trained in London, who has now made New York her culinary home – the same city that has allowed Michael Anthony, born in Cincinnati, to write his menus at Gramercy Tavern and Untitled, after having travelled widely in France and Japan.

Finally, to two Australian chefs, Peter Gilmore and Shannon Bennett, who continue to operate in the cities in which they were born, Sydney and Melbourne respectively, and yet who over the past 10 years have had such a profound impact on how the raw ingredients from that bountiful continent are enjoyed by those who live there and the increasing numbers of those who visit.

The interviews that follow provide a snapshot of how these chefs create and write their menus today. They would be the first to acknowledge that they stand on the shoulders of the chefs who taught them. They are also well aware that those whom they teach will, in turn, write very different menus again.

MICHAEL ANTHONY

UNTITLED & GRAMERCY TAVERN

Michael Anthony, the Executive Chef of Gramercy Tavern and Untitled at the Whitney Museum in New York, looks every inch the part, whether in his chef's whites or not.

Softly spoken and broad-shouldered, with a smile never far from his lips, he embodies the confidence of many of America's top chefs today and has the can-do attitude that is so typical of many who, like him, hail from the Midwest. This combination is perhaps the key to understanding why Anthony is so widely admired and liked across the city he has adopted and that has adopted him as he, seemingly effortlessly, manages the kitchens of two such physically diverse restaurants.

Gramercy Tavern, whose stoves Anthony took over from Tom Colicchio in 2006, is the very successful and vibrant embodiment of the American hospitality of yesteryear, displayed through the produce and colours of today's Union Square Greenmarket only a few blocks away. This cosy restaurant in a historic landmark building serves 500 customers a day via six or seven different menus on offer in its more relaxed Tavern and its more formal Dining Room – with its chefs introducing on to the menu two to three new dishes a week to many who consider this restaurant a home from home.

By contrast, Untitled occupies the ultra-modern glass corner of Renzo Piano's architectural creation by the redeveloped High Line that opened only in the summer of 2015 but already serves 500 a day in its restaurant, 600 a day in the café on its eighth floor, and attracts predominantly those who are there for the art or are visiting the city as tourists.

Anthony manages to write menus for both that have been influenced by his time spent working in France, Japan and the US, but in autumn 2015 he was taking on board what he had learnt on a recent trip to South Korea. There, for much longer than in the US, they have considered food as a medicine and

are far more relaxed about the remedial effects of barks, roots and herbs. This approach, he believes, is extremely relevant to the menus he writes, however unlikely it may seem in super-urban New York of all places.

Anthony's approach is underpinned by two other strong beliefs. The first is that what can generate the longest, happiest memories for any visitor to any city is the time they spend in restaurants. 'These two restaurants may be very different physically but the food that is served, as well as the approach and enthusiasm of our predominantly young waiting staff, can connect the customer immediately with the beating heart of the city, with what New Yorkers can and should be really proud of,' he explained.

Although it is a team effort to deliver this, Anthony feels particularly strongly about one aspect of menu design that is entirely the responsibility of the executive chef: the question of portion size.

The chef and the restaurateur enter into an unwritten two-part contract with every customer: to feed and to nourish is the obvious first part but equally important is that the customer does not leave disappointed. This is the professional tightrope every chef must walk to ensure that customers go on their way feeling energetic and vibrant rather than lethargic and guilty. This challenge represents for Anthony an aspirational goal not just for his restaurants but also for the whole industry. 'I want the calling card of dining in America in the future to be that we serve not just dishes that are of the appropriate size but that are also suitably balanced.' Sensibility and common sense have to play roles as important in the writing of menus as technique and the inclusion of seasonal ingredients.

Over lunch – a bowl of Vermont Cabot cheddar fondue topped with shiitake mushrooms and diced pickled pear, followed by fettuccine with bok choy and littleneck clams – Anthony explained how Gramercy Tavern and Untitled had presented him with very different challenges.

The popularity he inherited at the former was very welcome but also stood firmly in the path of the changes he wanted to make. His decision to take the beef tenderloin dish off the menu, hitherto its most popular, but one that he felt

lacked integrity, brought letters of protest and complaint from many. But he stood his ground and eventually won over his many critics. In the process, he learned an important lesson in the world of customer relations.

'I learned how to be a better leader and in any organisation the leader needs to clearly explain the path the group is headed on and why. To choose a path, the leader must have a sense of whether the group can embrace that decision, understand it and then believe in it. Hence, my decision to replace the grilled fillet of beef with a rotating set of dishes all developed from utilising every last piece of the whole side of beef.'

These included: grilled flat iron steak, celery root, kale and green garlic sauce; Gramercy Tavern pastrami with home-made pickles; beef tartare, quail egg and pine nuts; open ravioli of braised beef; ragu of beef bolognaise and house-made pappardelle; smoked kielbasa with red cabbage sauerkraut; Fontina stuffed meatballs and Tavern burger (which is ground daily and limited to 30 per day). This list is not exhaustive but ongoing in its drive for creativity and thrift.

Writing the menu for Untitled involved no backtracking, 'no handcuffs' as Anthony phrased it, and the restaurant came with the extra attraction of an open kitchen and one in which all the cooks can see all their customers. Although the design gurus of the museum were involved, which led to a notable absence of colour from the menu, Anthony was clear about how the menu would be composed.

First of all, there were to be no category headings: the menu contains five vegetarian dishes but these were not to be highlighted or treated differently from the other dishes despite his own affinity for cooking vegetables. Secondly, the dishes were to be listed as more than a series of ingredients but with quite brief descriptions. 'They are to be a conversation starter, an invitation to pleasure and not to be so long or so cumbersome that they get in the way of a discussion between the customer and the waiting staff,' Anthony explained. This sentiment is picked up also by the wine list, where there is an Untitled wine poured by the glass and described as 'a glass of something different'. This changes every week and prompts the same kind of dialogue.

Untitled

Uplifter: sparkling wine, grapefruit liqueur, bitters	14
Henry's Tipple: gin, apple fennel syrup, tonic	14
Gansevoort Shandy: pilsner, cappelleti, lemon	14
Cider House Rules: bourbon, hot apple cider	14

Untitled pastries	20
Sunchoke and spinach quiche, feta, dill	9
Cabot cheddar fondue, soft scrambled eggs, maitake, kale	11

Chicory caesar salad, broccoli, aji amarillo	16
Apple and pear salad, arugula, brussels sprouts	15
Smoked arctic char, soft boiled egg, capers, potato pancake	17
Parsnip soup, kabocha squash, ruby red shrimp	16

Carrots, yogurt, honey, savory granola	15
Beets, candied walnuts, tatsoi	14
Delicata squash, chorizo, collard greens	16
Cauliflower, cardamom custard, lemon	15
Sweet potatoes, chili, black garlic	14

Fritatta, caramelized onions, bacon bits	25
Fettuccine, shiitake, broccoli rabe	29
Black bass, spaghetti squash, daikon, shiso	33
Roasted and fried chicken salad, cashews	28
Pork hash, kohlrabi, fried egg	27

Banana hazelnut praline cake, concord grapes	12
Sticky toffee cake, pears, chai	12
Triple chocolate chunk cookie with milk	9

11:00am - 2:30pm
5pm - 10pm (Sundays until 9pm)

Michael Anthony, Executive Chef
Suzanne Cupps, Chef de Cuisine

Untitled

Marinated winter vegetables	11
Spinach and sunchoke dip, feta, dill	12
Cabot cheddar fondue, maitake, asian pear	14
Carolina rice fritters, chicken liver, pickled carrots	14
Lamb meatballs, peanuts, guajillo	14
Chicory caesar salad, broccoli, aji amarillo	16
Cured fluke, carrot, preserved lime	17
Smoked arctic char, wild rice, celery root, apples	16
Beef tartare, chestnut, delicata squash	18
Ruby red shrimp, parsnip soup, kabocha squash	16
Potatoes, buttermilk, capers, trout roe	14
Salsify and carrots, bacon, honey mustard	15
Delicata squash, chorizo, collard greens	16
Cauliflower, cardamom custard, lemon	15
Sweet potatoes, chili, black garlic	14
Fettuccine, shiitake, broccoli rabe	29
Black bass, spaghetti squash, daikon, shiso	33
Monkfish, bok choy, barbecue, kohlrabi	30
Roasted and fried chicken, kale, radicchio	32
Country rib, cabbage, brussels sprouts	30

Michael Anthony, Executive Chef
Suzanne Cupps, Chef de Cuisine

Untitled

Cheese Plate   12
Goat, Goat Lady Dairy, 'Sandy Creek'
Cow, Uplands Cheese Company, 'Pleasant Ridge Reserve'
Sheep, Hidden Springs Creamery, 'Bohemian Blue'

Dessert
Pumpkin cheesecake, cranberry, spiced brittle   10
Quince chiffon pie, pistachio, basil   10
Banana hazelnut praline cake, concord grapes   10
Sticky toffee cake, pears, chai   10
Chocolate hot fudge cake, raspberries   10
Triple chocolate chunk cookie with milk   8

Coffee/Tea
Coffee   5
Espresso   5
Cappuccino, Latte   6
Tea—Black, Green, Oolong, White, Mint, Chamomile   6

Wine
Sauternes, Petit Guiraud '11   10
Banyuls Grand Cru, Jacques Laverrière 'Clos Chatart' '93   10
Oloroso Sherry, Valdespino '1842 Solera'   10

Untitled

Sparkling

Mata i Coloma, 'Cupada No. 15 Reserva' Cava	13
Diebolt-Vallois 'Tradition Brut' Champagne	20
Billecart-Salmon Brut Rosé Champagne	25

White

Sauvignon Blanc, Villalin 'Grandes Vignes' Quincy, Loire '14	15
Riesling, Weiser-Künstler, Mosel '14	13
Chenin Blanc, Laffourcade, Savennières, Loire '11	16
Pinot Blanc, Silas 'Enna Hay' Willamette '14	14
Chardonnay, Tyler Winery, Santa Barbara '13	20
Roussanne & Marsanne, Bernard Ange, Crozes-Hermitage, Rhone '14	15

Red

Pinot Noir, Gachot-Monot, Côte de Nuits-Villages, Burgundy '12	18
Cabernet Franc, Château du Hureau, Saumur-Champigny, Loire '12	14
Merlot, Maison Blanche 'Piliers' Montagne-St.Émilion, Bordeaux '09	16
Touriga Nacional & Tempranillo, Ramilo, Lisbon '12	12
Old Vines Blend, Sean Thackrey 'Pleiades XXIV' California	16
Grenache, Monpertuis, Châteauneuf-du-Pape, Rhone '09 (Magnum)	20

Untitled

A glass of something different	14

Cocktails

Little 12th Fizz: Gin, Campari, Chartreuse, Sweet Vermouth, Soda	15
Highliner: Bourbon, Maraschino, Sour, Mint	15
Westside Cowboys: Rye, Carpano Antica, Bitters, Orange	15
The Gertrude: Gin, Dry Vermouth, Citrus Essences	15
Tempest: Rum, Chartreuse, Lemon, Cocchi, Violette	15

Beer

Pilsner: Stoudt's 'Pils' Pennsylvania	9
Hefeweizen: Erdinger 'Weiss' Germany	9
IPA: Singlecut 'Half-Stack' New York	9

Soft Drinks

Spiced Pear	6
Apple-Fennel	6
Concord Grape	6

GRAMERCY TAVERN

FIRST COURSES

Butternut Squash Soup
Almonds, Brussels Sprouts and Pickled Shallots
12.

Cauliflower Cappelletti
Grapes, Capers and Brown Butter
16.

Beet Salad
Almonds, Fregola and Stone Fruit
14.

Lobster Salad
Corn Custard, Honshimeji Mushrooms and Yellow Squash
17.

Beef Tartare
Tomatoes and Peppers
16.

Corn & Grain Salad
Cherry Tomatoes, Almonds and Pecorino
12.

GRAMERCY TAVERN

SECOND COURSES

Smoked Arctic Char
Corn, Shishito Peppers and Stone Fruit

Sea Bass
Cucumber, Shiitake Mushrooms and Black Garlic Vinaigrette

Flounder
Yellow Squash, Pine Nuts and Sherry Sauce

Pork Loin & Deckle
Sweet Peppers, Polenta and Plums

Pasture Raised Chicken Breast & Thigh
Apples, Barley and Pumpkin

Lamb Loin & Shoulder
Eggplant, Yogurt and Peppers

THREE COURSE MENU 92.

EXECUTIVE CHEF MICHAEL ANTHONY
CHEF DE CUISINE HOWARD KALACHNIKOFF

GRAMERCY
TAVERN

SEASONAL TASTING MENU

Marinated Scallops
Fluke, Almonds and Plums
Rkatsiteli, Dr. Konstantin Frank, 2014, Finger Lakes, New York

Black Rice
Sea Urchin, Shiitake Mushrooms and Ruby Red Shrimp
Riesling, Egon Müller, Scharzhof, 2014, Mosel Valley, Germany

Poached Halibut
Tomatoes, Shell Beans and Olives
Pouilly-Loché, Clos des Rocs, Monopole, 2012, Burgundy, France

Farfalle
Calamari, Chorizo and Mussels
Ciliegiolo, Bussoletti, Rosso Narni, 2014, Umbria, Italy

Vermont Wagyu Beef
Caraflex Cabbage, Blueberries and Juniper
Zinfandel, Sky, 2011, Mt. Veeder, Napa Valley, California

Quince
Vanilla Rice Pudding, Pomegranate, Pistachio and Basil
Vin Santo del Chianti, Santa Vittoria, 2009, Tuscany, Italy

TASTING MENU 120.
WINE PAIRING 75.

TASTING MENUS REQUIRE THE PARTICIPATION OF THE ENTIRE TABLE.

GRAMERCY
TAVERN

VEGETABLE TASTING MENU

Tomato Gazpacho
Cucumber, Peppers and Sourdough Croutons
Cabernet Franc/Gamay Rosé, Bellwether, 2014, Finger Lakes, New York

Blue Cheese Custard
Watermelon, Hazelnuts and Beets
Riesling, Egon Müller, Scharzhof, 2014, Mosel Valley, Germany

Roasted Squash
Wheat Berries, Scallion and Mint
Grüner Veltliner Federspiel, Hirtzberger, Rotes Tor, 2013, Wachau, Austria

Braised Onion
Sweet Corn, Cheddar and Pickled Chiles
Tokaji Sec, Királyudvar, 2012, Tokaji, Hungary

Fried & Smoked Eggplant
Heirloom Tomatoes, Olives and Basil
Pinot Noir, Enderle & Moll, Liaison, 2013, Baden, Germany

Apple
Caramel Flan, Walnuts, Maple Syrup and Sorrel
Moscatel, César Florido, Dorado, Chipiona, Spain

TASTING MENU 105.
WINE PAIRING 75.

TASTING MENUS REQUIRE THE PARTICIPATION OF THE ENTIRE TABLE.

These decisions about the layout and composition of the menu came about as Untitled was in the final stages of construction and planning, when a trip to London changed Anthony's perception of what the restaurant should be. Initially, his mind was set on establishing a restaurant with a much stronger identity than has actually emerged, with a style of cooking that he described 'would have shown off more'.

What changed his mind was a lunch at London's River Cafe and an appreciation of what had allowed that restaurant to prosper for 30 years. 'I realised that there is only so much time and manipulation ingredients can take, and that restraint is often a vital and overlooked component if you want to establish somewhere with longevity, where your customers will look forward to coming back over and over again.'

This visit also led to a significant change in how the Untitled menu was to be presented. The initial plan had been to attach it to a clipboard or a weighted object that would hold it firm, but this notion was rejected in favour of a single piece of paper that fulfilled several different objectives: it was immediately accessible; it would evoke spontaneity because it is so easy to handle; and it would prove inexpensive to reprint.

Although the particular styles of Gramercy Tavern and Untitled as restaurants may differ, at each of them the dishes on offer aim to be expressions of colour and respect for the ingredients, while acting as vehicles for their chefs' improvisation so that they may evolve and change.

SHANNON BENNETT

VUE DE MONDE

I spent an hour sitting directly opposite Shannon Bennett, the chef from Melbourne, Australia, who has made the city's Vue de monde restaurant on top of the Rialto Tower so well known.

During that time, I had his undivided attention. We were sitting, quite comfortably, in a friend's private plane that was flying us from Essendon Airport, just outside Melbourne, to Hobart, Tasmania, where the following day Bennett was taking several people fishing for bluefin tuna with Mark Eather, one of Bennett's heroes.

For the first ten minutes, Bennett spoke somewhat wistfully of his initial years as a chef. He had begun as a kitchen hand when he was 15 before several years in the UK – initially at John Burton-Race's L'Ortolan Restaurant in Berkshire and then at the Hyde Park Hotel under Marco Pierre White. This brought home to him one of the fundamental requirements for success: 'Never take yourself too seriously,' he explained with his trademark smile.

He returned to his home town, borrowed AUS$70,000 from a friend of his father whom he repaid with interest within a few years, and opened the first Vue de monde in a suburban street. Having moved the restaurant twice in the ensuing years, Bennett now employs over 85 chefs in his main restaurant, in four Cafés du monde, in an events business and at Jardin Tin, a Vietnamese restaurant that Bennett encouraged his Vietnamese kitchen hands to open.

Our discussion then turned to Vue de monde's menu, my recollection of eating there and my memory of the edible penny pieces, filled with honey and ginger, which were some of the petits fours served. These harked back to the game of two-up played by Australian gold miners in the 19th century. Bennett smiled and said that it was important for him to use his menu to recall what the city and its history had meant to his grandparents.

But then he became more serious. 'My menu is, I hope, more important than that. A menu, above all, has to be delicious. A chef is charged with striving to create dishes that meet this mark and if you don't you're in trouble. And the customer has to be in a position at the end of the meal to say, I would come back and I would eat that again.'

His restaurant's menu currently achieves these goals via an extensive tasting menu only, served at lunch and dinner. But Bennett emphasised the word currently. His menu has reached this stage via his personal evolution and that of his customers, both of which he is more than aware are changing. 'I've matured and my young chefs, who are more talented cooks than I ever was, will not have the same philosophy as I once had. And dining out is evolving too and I can see our menu changing back to three or four courses that customers choose from a more structured à la carte menu in a couple of years' time.'

But whereas Bennett's menu may change, his philosophy and approach will not; in fact, these will only strengthen. Both involve the opportunity to promote and work with producers who, he explained, earn his highest respect for the selflessness with which they breed their animals. He mentioned David Blackmore for his Wagyu beef raised in Alexandra, Victoria; Steve Felletti of the Moonlight Flat Oyster Company in Bateman's Bay, New South Wales; and Mark Eather, whom we were about to meet. 'What unites them all is their commitment to a stress-free environment for their produce when they are alive and a stress-free method of killing them at the end.'

Bennett had first made contact with Eather four years earlier when fellow Australian chef Neil Perry had been most impressed by the quality of the red snapper available at the Tsukiji Fish Market in Japan. He had been even more impressed when he heard that the fish had originated in Australia, and his own acquaintance with Eather began.

Perry passed on Eather's details to Bennett, who contacted him straight away but had had to wait 18 months for a positive response. But Bennett was soon convinced of Eather's quality, integrity and professionalism. He may be

TUESDAY 29ᵀᴴ MARCH, 2016

Chiko roll
Moonlight flat, Angasi oysters, green grapes
~

King George whiting, parsley, cucumber
2014 Muros Antigos 'Loureiro', Vinho Verde, Portugal
~

Bowen Mud crab, seaweed, corn sauce, macadamia
2014 François Chidaine 'Les Argiles' Vouvray, Loire Valley, France
~

Marron snag
&
Marron tail, pork and mussel emulsion, cherry crumble
NV Charles Heidsieck 'Brut Reserve', Reims, France
~

Crushed Yukon Gold Potatoes, Yarra Valley Trout Roe and Black Shellfish Sauce
2001 Bannockburn 'Museum Release.' Chardonnay, Geelong, Victoria

Lemon myrtle, wood sorrel

Lamb sweetbreads, Asian greens, macadamia
2006 Capçanes 1/VB Montsant, Spain

David Blackmore Wagyu tenderloin, plums, mustard
2009 Quinta da Gaivosa, Douro, Portugal

Aged Milla's Farm duck breast, wild berries, beetroot
2012 Paradigm Hill 'L'Ami Sage' Pinot Noir, Mornington Peninsula, Victoria

Peach Lolly

Kensington Pride mango, lime, coconut
2013 Punt Road Botrytis Semillon, Riverina, New South Wales
~

Chocolate soufflé
2012 Mas Amiel Rouge, Maury AOC, France

Assortment of cheeses, bread, jams
2014 Eric Bordelet Poiré Granit, Normandy, France

A selection of petit-fours

paying the highest price for his fish, but he and his customers are guaranteed the highest quality.

Eather is, at first, a rather gruff Australian, broad-shouldered and absolutely passionate about the quality of the fish he, and the 25 other fishermen who sell via him to Japan, physically deliver. All the fish are killed according to the standards of *ikejime* by the insertion of a spike behind the eye, a process that immediately causes brain death, after which the fish relaxes. Eather has become, in turn, an educator – tirelessly pointing out to anyone who will listen that aquaculture is the future if we want to feed the world's growing population, and that the concept of cheap fish does not stand up. Sustainable and ethical fishing are, in his opinion, the only way forward.

Eather has spent a great deal of time educating Bennett and his kitchen team about the fish he supplies them with, most notably their flavour and texture, and which fish actually improve with age. Bar cod is better after at least five days, Bennett explained, while all the tuna that reaches Tsukiji has been frozen as soon as it has been caught. It is best eaten a day or two after it has been defrosted when all the moisture has had time to evaporate.

Bennett cited as many as 12 different suppliers like Eather who support Vue du monde throughout the year before pulling out his iPhone excitedly. 'And these are some photos of my last trip to Flinders Island, now famous for its export of wallaby – the country's only real game, in my opinion – lamb and wasabi. The meat I buy from James Madden, who is a pilot and the son of David, who founded the Flinders Island Meat Company, is fantastic. I admire all these guys so much. Their financial returns are so small, the dedication that they have to display has to be so extreme.'

It is this dedication on the part of his suppliers that Bennett now instils into his menus and via a masterclass that he holds for all the apprentices who have just joined his growing company, on the second Wednesday of every month in the kitchen of Vue du monde, on the 55th floor of the city's iconic Rialto building with its sweeping views over Melbourne and the surrounding countryside.

He preaches: 'Ingredients are everything. What makes a great restaurant is where and how the pigeon that is on the menu has been reared, whether it has been reared locally or not, and its relevance to the city.'

APRIL BLOOMFIELD

THE SPOTTED PIG & THE BRESLIN

April Bloomfield was easy to spot across the dark, bustling dining room that is The Breslin in the Ace Hotel, New York. She was standing to the left of the pass over which was a sequence of hot lamps and behind which was a brigade of male chefs. But even from a considerable distance it was quite obvious that Bloomfield was making her views clear and doing so firmly but politely.

She then disappeared into one of the booths that line one side of the restaurant and I was ushered into her presence. We embraced – I had first interviewed her 13 years before as she was leaving London's River Cafe to open The Spotted Pig in New York – then she looked at her iPhone and explained that she had about 20 minutes instead of the hour I had been promised. Such, however, is her passion for food that in the end she spoke for even longer.

New York has brought Bloomfield justified renown as a chef. After The Spotted Pig and The Breslin, she opened The John Dory, an oyster and fish bar, as well as Salvation Taco and Salvation Burger, all in New York. She was just back from San Francisco where she and her business partner Ken Friedman who, following a midlife crisis, switched from the fire of the music business to the frying pan of opening restaurants, have also opened Tosca.

Female intuition led her to give her opinion on the respective challenges of writing menus for customers on the East and West Coasts. 'Because the pace here is fast, furious and fun, New Yorkers may go to three or four different places in an evening whereas in San Francisco going to a restaurant is still more of a "big night out". I have to write my menus accordingly.'

The common theme of Bloomfield's New York menus – strong flavours that can be executed swiftly – has justified Friedman's initial hunch over a decade ago that the city was more than ready for the food of a British gastropub. Since then the appetite for this style of cooking has only grown and it forces Bloomfield to think carefully, not just about the combination of ingredients but the efficiency

THE SPOTTED PIG

Lunch

Wednesday, October 14, 2015

Bar Snacks
* Deviled Egg $4
* Roasted Almonds $4
* Marinated Olives $4
* Pot of Pickles $6
* Chicken Liver Toast $9
* Roll Mops $9

Plates
* Oysters with Mignonette 6 for $18 / 12 for $36
* Market Salad with Aged Pecorino & Pomegranate $16
* Smoked Haddock Chowder with Pancetta & House Made Crackers $17
Apple Salad with Mrs. Quicke's Cheddar & Toasted Walnuts $16
Stracciatella with Wild Mushrooms $17
* Pork Rillette with Mustard, Pickles & Toast $17
Grilled Cheese Sandwich with Onion Marmalade & Mustard $18
* Chargrilled Burger with Roquefort Cheese & Shoestring Fries $22
Spanish Mackerel with Sweet Potato Mash $22
Cubano Sandwich with Arugula Salad $19

Sides
* Shoestring Fries $9
* Broccoli Rabe $9

Desserts
* Flourless Chocolate Cake $9
* Banoffee Pie with Whipped Cream $9
* Crème Caramel $9
* Cheese Plate 2 for $10 / 3 for $15

* These Items Are Also Available for Late Lunch from 3:00 - 5:00 P.M.
Eating Undercooked Meat & Raw Shellfish Could Increase Your Risk of Food Borne Illness

The BRESLIN
BAR & DINING ROOM

DINNER

SNACKS

BOMBAY MIX
6

SALT & PEPPER CRISPS
5

SPICED ALMONDS
5

CARAMEL POPCORN
5

SCRUMPETS
MINT VINEGAR
9

SCOTCH EGG
9

BOILED PEANUTS
FRIED IN PORK FAT
7

CHICKEN LIVER PARFAIT
9

BEEF & STILTON PIE
10

TERRINE BOARD
34

SERVED WITH PICKLES,
PICCALILLI AND MUSTARD

GUINEA HEN
WITH MORELS

RUSTIC PORK
WITH PISTACHIO

RABBIT & PRUNE

HEAD CHEESE

LIVERWURST

SMALL

WELLFLEET OYSTERS DILL PICKLE JUICE	6 for 20
CHANTERELLES A LA PLANCHA HOUSE CURED COPPA & MANZANILLA SHERRY	16
PORK RILLETTE BRUSSEL SPROUTS, RADISH & MUSTARD VINAIGRETTE	16
HERBED CAESAR SALAD ANCHOVY CROUTONS	15
TUSCAN KALE & CHICORY SALAD CHARRED BROCCOLINI, CRISPY PARSNIP, PURPLE CABBAGE, FLAX SEED & MIREPOIX VINAIGRETTE	16
SUCRINE SALAD SCALLIONS, RADISH, MUSTARD GREENS & BUTTERMILK DRESSING	15
SEAFOOD SAUSAGE BEURRE BLANC & CHIVES	19
BLOOD SAUSAGE FRIED EGG & CREAMY TARRAGON DRESSING	16
TEMPURA FRIED OCTOPUS RED PEPPER JAM, WATERMELON, CILANTRO & PICKLED RIND	18
HALLOUMI & SPINACH LAMB SAUSAGE HARICOTS VERTS, CRISPY QUINOA & PICKLED GREEN TOMATO	17

LARGE

CHARGRILLED LAMB BURGER FETA, CUMIN MAYO & THRICE COOKED CHIPS	23
BROWN BUTTER ROASTED TURBOT CONCORD GRAPE, CHANTERELLE & TUSCAN KALE	34
CORNISH ROCK HEN SPAETZEL, BRUSSELS SPROUT, CARROT & OMA CHEESE SAUCE	33
MILK BRAISED BERKSHIRE SHOULDER MILK CURD, RADISH TOPS & CRISPY SAGE	33
ROASTED LAMB SHANK BRAISED IN TOMATO WITH DANDELION & GRILLED POLENTA	37
DRY AGED RIBEYE FOR TWO BÉARNAISE & THRICE COOKED CHIPS	MP

SIDES

BROCCOLI ANCHOVY & CALABRIAN CHILI	9
18K POTATOES SAUERKRAUT, ROSEMARY & CRÈME FRAÎCHE	10
CAULIFLOWER ROASTED GARLIC & CHERMOULA	10
CURRIED DELICATA & KABOCHA SQUASH CANDIED KAFFIR PUMPKIN SEEDS & LIME YOGURT	10
RADISHES AGED BALSAMIC VINEGAR & MARJORAM	9

CONSUMING RAW OR UNDERCOOKED MEATS, POULTRY, SEAFOOD, SHELLFISH OR EGGS MAY INCREASE YOUR RISK OF FOODBORNE ILLNESS

with which they can be assembled and delivered.

Hence the obvious positioning of the bar snacks at the top of The Spotted Pig's menu, which serves 800 customers a day, and the same, as well as the terrine board, at The Breslin, which serves 500. These comprise a series of dishes that may take some time to prepare – her favourites are the chicken liver toast and the Scotch egg that she asserts must be 'porky, full of flavour and runny in the middle' – but can swiftly assuage the hunger of her 'time-poor' customers. The terrine board (guinea hen with morels, rabbit and prune, liverwurst, head cheese and chicken liver parfait) is a not inexpensive dish at $34, but has been a tremendous success and one that gives her great pleasure to see ordered frequently by a table as a first course.

At The Spotted Pig, inevitably perhaps, the most popular dish – the burger with Roquefort cheese and a small mountain of shoestring potatoes – is also the one that takes the longest time to cook, 20–25 minutes. First courses must take no longer than 8–10 minutes from order to pickup. And no menu must be too long: 5–6 first courses, at most 8–10 main courses and 5 desserts. 'Rustic' and 'tight' were the adjectives she most frequently used to describe The Pig's menu.

Making this restaurant – with its menu full of dishes she likes to eat – a success was crucial as she needed to convince sceptical New Yorkers of her credentials. But the setting of her next opening at The Breslin gave her culinary imagination far more room to breathe.

'Once I saw the design of this space, which is much richer and more luscious than The Pig's compact corner site, I wanted a similar approach but to imbue the menu with a much more medieval feel. The dishes here have to be more grand and substantial in scale, to give the cooks more scope. That is the reason for the whole roasted suckling pigs and the ducks cooked with balsamic vinaigrette that have to be pre-ordered, dishes that up to 14 customers could enjoy in a restaurant and I want to be as perfect as can be.'

If medieval England is the unlikely inspiration for these dishes, planning lies at the heart of their execution. 'I know what I like and I plan the service in my head so that the food can be produced logistically. There is nothing worse than wasted

space, and smaller kitchens – which we will all have to get used to in this city given the soaring rents – can be as efficient as larger ones once they are laid out correctly.' This, incidentally, is a sentiment echoed by most leading chefs today.

Bloomfield remains very British at heart and extremely grateful that she fell into a profession (she was considered too small for the police force, her initial career choice) that has allowed her to travel, and one in which she has met colleagues only too happy to share their recipes and where she has encountered no discrimination. 'I've pushed every day, kept an eye on what I would like to do, aimed for success and tried, above all, not to fuck up. Every time I fry an egg I think of how my mother used to do it, so that it is crisp round the edges and runny in the middle. It is vital when you are cooking never to forget where you come from.'

It came, therefore, as little surprise to hear that her style of writing a menu as well as the dishes Bloomfield considers most representative encompass her years at the stove.

'Although I never worked for him, I do admire the simplicity of Fergus Henderson's menu writing at St John, Smithfield, the pared back way in which just the principal ingredients are collated. You don't want customers to read too much into any dish; that way only disappointment lies. And anyway, I like my customers to be wowed after they have eaten my food, not to be wowed while they are reading the menu.'

The two dishes she would never be without are much more in keeping with New York, her adopted home. At The Spotted Pig it is the ricotta gnudi – small balls of ricotta and Parmesan finished with sage, which reveals the city's strong Italian influence – while at The Breslin it's Caesar salad, which she describes as 'well balanced, with good acidity and served just cool enough'. 'They bring my customers too much joy. Why would I ever take them off the menu?' she asks me quizzically.

But, like many chefs, Bloomfield does dream of a small restaurant without any menu at all. 'It would be small, I would be cooking on a wood-fired range, and maybe there would be room for two tables.' Pigs may fly first.

HESTON BLUMENTHAL

THE FAT DUCK

The menu at Heston Blumenthal's The Fat Duck in Bray, Berkshire, reveals itself like no other.

As you arrive at what was built as a 16th-century pub, you enter a mirrored vestibule where the receptionist politely informs you that you are about to go on a journey. Once you have sat down in the dining room, which can seat a maximum of 40, you are handed a menu and a magnifying glass.

The latter is to inspect the inside of the menu (*pages 70–71*), a seemingly random amalgamation that incorporates figures from Lewis Carroll's *Alice Through the Looking Glass*: a multi-coloured ice lolly; two symbols signifying the sound of the sea; a comfortably laid up table for two; and the moon and stars under a clock that reads 11.30pm. In the bottom right-hand corner is the coat of arms designed by David McKean for *The Fat Duck Cookbook* that reveals a duck holding a magnifying glass above an apple that is a reference to Sir Isaac Newton's experiments that led to the discovery of the laws of gravity.

The actual menu (*pages 68–69*) is on the other side, broken down into sections which Blumenthal presents as the itinerary for a journey over the course of a day. He ends, as all good chefs do, by wishing you sweet dreams.

I met Blumenthal in his office, above the staff canteen that feeds the 150 staff currently employed to run not only The Fat Duck and the five kitchens that support it, but also his two local pubs, The Hinds Head and The Crown at Bray. There are also The Perfectionists' Café in Terminal 2, Heathrow, and two branches of Dinner: in the Mandarin Oriental Hotel in London and the Crown Plaza, Melbourne. Initially, we talked about our children; how he managed to damage his right hand while punching a pane of glass after having yet again lost the key to his front door; and for over 90 minutes about how he had finally redefined what constitutes his menu at The Fat Duck.

The timing of my visit was propitious, he explained, as it came at the end of what had proved to be the hardest period in over 12 years. But the recent reopening of The Fat Duck in Bray, with the kitchens fully modernised, had allowed him to rethink his style of food again. There were other symbiotic avenues to consider, too. He was working on a Channel 4 programme on cooking food for the first British astronaut on a British mission and smiled at the pleasure of seeing him eating a bacon sandwich and drinking a cup of tea in space. And, more relevantly, he is involved in the Oxford, Cambridge and RSA Examinations' new GCSE cookery course that will, he hopes, lead to more creative cooking.

'At the heart of the problem is that perfection in cooking comes at the expense of creativity, a fear of failure that leads to a sense of failure. Kids clam up and, as a result, confidence issues develop around what they are prepared to eat. We need to replace the word perfect with the word discovery. Then we can make some progress,' he adds. And when I point out that his café in Terminal 2 is called The Perfectionists' Café, he explains the difference between being in search of perfection and assuming that there is a perfect, finished dish. 'What I want to establish is the process of getting my chefs to say that there is no bad idea in cooking. And what I dream of establishing is that one day my team can establish their own photo album of dishes.'

Blumenthal's own CV reinforces this sense of the narrow line that separates success from failure. He left after a week in the kitchen of the only formal restaurant he ever worked in; he took over a dilapidated pub and converted this into The Fat Duck; he paid the price with the break-up of his marriage; and he has a very clear idea of how certain dishes he created en route helped him to establish his own photo album of dishes.

The first dish to have this effect was the crab ice cream Blumenthal created in 1997. According to Professor Barry C. Smith, founder of the Centre for the Study of the Senses in London and one of the many collaborators who has worked alongside Blumenthal, this was such an important dish because it changed the

customer's perception of a dish from 'cross-modal', in which two or more senses are alerted, to 'multi-sensory', in which all our senses are integrated into the nervous system. Then came a massive 92 page, all IP protected, discourse on a multi-sensory dining table in 2005.

The second was a series of dishes based on 'nostalgia cards', flavours and sensations Blumenthal recalled while watching his own son Jack watching a Pink Panther cartoon. These cards were, until the new menu appeared, handed out to customers to prompt feelings of their childhood, where they had first encountered different tastes and ingredients, and invariably their, very personal, reactions to them.

But the dish which proved to be a 'game changer', to quote Blumenthal, was his creation of what is billed on the menu as 'The Original Sound of the Sea', his extraordinary box set that comes with its own iPod, playing the sound of waves breaking on the shore. This proved not only to be multi-sensory but also a catalyst for many customers' memories of their initial family holidays, of their first trips to the seaside, of peaceful days just spent being together as a family.

His precise recipe details also highlight the risks involved. One of the ingredients for the 'sand' is a tapioca specially developed by National Starch whose volume of dry mixes allows the fats to absorb the oils, while another is the oysters that were a cause of the outbreak of the norovirus that caused the restaurant to close for two weeks in February 2009.

Much of this was 'going on in my head' as he began to travel to Australia at the beginning of 2015, he explained, and he began to piece the elements together. The context and narrative of the *Alice in Wonderland* story appealed to him for several reasons: because it is so fundamentally British; because of the heroine's sense of discovery; because her dreams are so episodic; and because of the sense of playfulness and fun that are so much a part of it.

The Fat Duck
heston blumenthal

The Fat Duck
heston blumenthal

ITINERARY

2. Morning: Rise and shine, it's breakfast time

EXCUSE ME, THERE SEEMS TO BE
a RABBIT in MY TEA.
Hot and cold velouté of rabbit with tarragon and mustard

WHY DO I HAVE TO CHOOSE BETWEEN
a VARIETY PACK and a FULL ENGLISH?
Truffled egg mousse, jellied tomato consommé, bacon and toasted bread cream, cereals

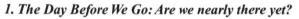

1. The Day Before We Go: Are we nearly there yet?

A CHANGE-of-AIR
Aerated beetroot macaroon

JUST THE TONIC
Smoked cumin Royale, Jerusalem artichoke ice cream

A WELCOME DRINK
Paloma, Campari soda, Pina Colada, Vodka Lime Sour

3. Mid-morning: First one to see the sea...

"SOUND of the SEA"

CAN I HAVE SOME MONEY FOR
THE ICE CREAM VAN?
Waldorf salad "Rocket", Salmon, avocado and horseradish "Twister", Crab and passion fruit '99

THEN WE WENT ROCKPOOLING
Cornish crab, smoked caviar and golden trout roe, velouté of white chocolate and sea vegetables

4. Afternoon: If you go down to the woods today...
(...and we did)

DAMPING THROUGH
the BOROUGHGROVES...

Mushroom, beet and blackberry, scented with fig leaf, meadowsweet, melilot, oakmoss and black truffle

...WE DISCOVERED
the MOCK TURTLE PICNIC

Mock turtle soup and egg, toast sandwich

6. Bedtime: Off to the Land of Nod

COUNTING SHEEP

Malt, orange blossom, tonka, milk, meringue, crystallised white chocolate, pistachio

5. Evening: Are you ready for dinner?

Starter
Main Course
Dessert
Digestif

(serious enough for the kids, fun enough for the adults)

7. And then to dream...

LIKE a KID in a SWEETSHOP

Oxcho , Caramel in edible wrapper Queen of Hearts jam tart, mandarin scented aerated chocolate

Lee Hall, who wrote *Billy Elliot*, helped Blumenthal to establish what he refers to as the 'anchors' of the menu: the seven episodes that carry the diner through, from the excitement of setting off to bedtime. Each table has its own lighting system to nudge the customers into a sense of nostalgia, while opportunities will increase, Blumenthal assured me – with their £150,000 sweet trolley, two liquid nitrogen ice cream makers and the creative input of the illusionist, Derren Brown – to personalise the final sweet courses to each customer's tastes.

Blumenthal turned 50 in 2016. Whether this will signal a slow down in his creativity is anyone's guess. I, for one, doubt this very much indeed.

MASSIMO BOTTURA

OSTERIA FRANCESCANA

Massimo Bottura agreed to meet and to talk menus with me at 6pm on a Saturday evening in the Champagne Room of the Connaught Hotel, Mayfair, London, because there they make the very best Bloody Mary, in his opinion.

What emerged was an impressive, tall drink, and while Bottura – dressed in a very chic, grey Issey Miyake pleated top – was fascinated by the celery foam that covered the top of the glass, I could not help but notice that the green of the celery and the dark red of the vodka and tomato juice mix beneath represented the colours of the Italian flag. Did Bottura know this already? Was he trying to be funny or ironic, or was he simply being patriotic?

He is, after all, all of these things, as anyone who calls his book *Never Trust a Skinny Italian Chef* surely has to be. Bottura has achieved the fame he has since opening his first restaurant, Osteria Francescana, in Modena in 1995. Subsequently, he has opened a second in Modena and one in Istanbul, and he ran an admirable soup kitchen during Expo Milan 2015.

He is also a chef, possibly *the* chef, who most ably maximises the vibrancy, artistic potential and sheer fun of a menu. It is impossible not to be excited as the large-format, four-page menu unfolds.

The print is extremely clear, a simple grey font on a white background. Then a journey begins that takes the customer from the *aperitivi* in the top left-hand corner to the final flap with Proust's famous quote – about the effect of soaking a morsel of madeleine in a spoonful of tea – above a large, colourful *pizza napoletana* with the signature of the artist, Giulliano della Casa, and the date.

En route, Bottura takes us to Langhirano for 36-month-aged Parma prosciutto; from Boston, USA, to Hokkaido, Japan, by way of Goro, a town by the mouth of the Po River in Emilia-Romagna, for his crab dish; then, off to his native Modena for a taste of its rare 44-year-old balsamic vinegar; and finally up the river where the eel for another dish once swam.

Watercolours of a lobster, the outline of Mt Vesuvius above the word Napoli and the name of Georges Cogny (the French chef to whom Bottura was once apprenticed) accompanied by a heart, also grace the page. No fewer than nine tortellini, the dish cooked by his grandmother that excited Bottura's palate as a boy, hover above the seven other pasta courses because, as he added, they are always floating in his mind. There is intrigue too: what is the 'crunchy' part of the lasagne or veal 'not flame grilled'? And how could one not order a dessert described as 'Oops! I dropped the lemon tart'?

Bottura's menu, his culinary canvas, has to be as large and as broad as this to accommodate not just the many dishes he and his team create but also how he thinks about writing his menus. 'There are several layers that may help you understand. There is my brain, how I think about food. Then there is my culture, as a citizen of Emilia-Romagna and of Italy. There is my conscience, my fight for a fairer world. Then there is my sense of responsibility, not just as a chef but also as an employer, as a husband and as a father. All of these combine to shape my point of view when it comes to writing our menus, and often I have to reset my brain to accommodate all these factors.'

It is the tension between Emilia-Romagna and Italy that is most obvious and constant. Bottura has managed to achieve for his native country what his friends René Redzepi and Heston Blumenthal have done for Denmark and England respectively. He has arguably done for Italy what Ferran Adrià did for Spain, but in certain respects Bottura's task has been even more difficult. The reputation of the other three countries' cooking was hardly glorious before these chefs emerged, whereas Italian food has been popular for decades.

And within Italy there has been a constant reluctance to change. 'Every Italian believes that their family makes a magic sauce and the perfect pasta. There is an inbuilt nostalgia that goes back to our walled cities,' he explains. 'There is a rigidity here that is very difficult to change, but that is what I am trying to do.' As I listen, I am conscious that Bottura's latest menu is only a work in progress, although he does add that with each menu this brain-crunching

becomes more and more difficult. 'The words get harder and harder,' he sighs.

The person responsible for allowing Bottura to reach this stage with his menus is his American-born wife Lara (whom he met while working in a New York kitchen) and whom he cites immediately as his constant inspiration. 'She is not afraid to be critical but most importantly she is never nostalgic. She makes me think, and when that happens two people are always more effective than one.'

Hence his now-famous dish 'tortellini walking on broth': half a dozen tortellini fixed to a bowl with gelatin so that when hot broth is added they appear to move or 'to walk as Christ once did on the water'. 'I like this dish because as you dig into it with the spoon it allows my customers to stop and think and not to lose themselves completely in everyday life,' Bottura explains.

And it was the construction of something as simple as the tortellini that allowed Bottura to cite three very different examples of what still excites him about writing menus. The first was pretty basic: judging the quality and quantity of the prosciutto ham, mortadella and Parmesan so that the umami level was absolutely correct in these pasta shells. The second was the joy in his voice as he explained how recently two producers of buffalo mozzarella from Naples had come to show him their cheese and how he had found the quality to be so amazing that he felt compelled to create a new dessert involving the sour cherries of Modena especially for them.

Finally, perhaps when the Bloody Mary had worked its magic, he started to describe another dessert he was working on. 'Red Camouflage' incorporates smoked chocolate, has the brown/green colouring of a jugged hare, and is a savoury dish that takes its name from Andy Warhol's painting *Camouflage*. Even Bottura admitted it sounded 'crazy'.

OSTERIA FRANCESCANA

APERITIVI

Annamaria Clementi Ca' del Bosco

Champagne Marie Noelle Ledru Gran Cru

OUR SELECTION OF CURED MEATS

42-month aged culatello from Zibello produced by Spigaroli,
selected for Massimo Bottura

36-month aged Parma prosciutto by Fratelli Galloni in Langhirano,
finished in barrique

Served with warm focaccia, local honey and Campanine apple mostarda

ANTIPASTI

Terrine of lightly smoked cauliflower with red shrimp and caviar

Crab from Boston to Hokkaido by way of Goro

An eel swimming up the Po River

Eggplant, cherry tomatoes, burrata and anchovies

Five ages of Parmigiano Reggiano in different temperatures and textures

Ambrosie of foie gras with award winning Traditional Balsamic
Vinegar from Modena, aged 44 years

FIRST COURSES

Spaghetti cetarese:
pesto of anchovies, capers, pine nuts, and anchovy juice

Guitar string pasta with charred Amberjack and smoked green tomato

Passatelli in marinara sauce with shellfish

Polenta and rice in praise of pizza

Ravioli of foie gras, leek and truffle

Modenese tortellini in a broth of everything

Emilian tagliatelle with hand-chopped ragù

MAIN COURSES

Branzino with an infusion of fragrances from the Gulf of Sorrento

Fish soup

Lobster served with double sauces, acidic and sweet

Cod in Emilia

Milk-fed baby pork with a reduction of marinade
and Traditional Balsamic Vinegar from Modena

Ox rib-eye served with pickled vegetables, bone marrow,
black truffles and cream of potatoes in red wine sauce

La Cina è vicina: lacquered duck with oriental spices

Bollito, not boiled: variety meats (cotechino, veal tongue, tail, cheek, and belly)
prepared sous-vide and served with salsa verde and peperonata

OUR TASTING MENUS

SENSATIONS

Twelve seasonal plates from our experimental kitchen

Wine pairing

TRADITION IN EVOLUTION

Croccatino of foie gras

An eel swimming up the Po River

Caesar salad in Emilia

Five ages of Parmigiano Reggiano in different temperatures and textures

The crunchy part of the lasagne

Spin-painted veal, not flame grilled

La torta di riso

Oops! I dropped the lemon tart

Vignola

Wine pairing

We recommend selecting one menu for the entire table

... in una Madeleine, nel tè, ho trovato il ricordo del passato della madre
che da bambino mi serviva la merendina e da lì un nuovo mondo si spalanca...

LE SOSTE

OSTERIA FRANCESCANA
MODENA

www.osteriafrancescana.it

DANIEL BOULUD

BAR BOULUD

The first time I discussed menus with Daniel Boulud we only got as far as the first course.

Born in Provence, Boulud today runs 17 restaurants that stretch from New York to London and Singapore in a uniquely delineated business: his Christian name is reserved for his three-star Michelin restaurant, his surname for his more relaxed bistros.

Like many chefs, Boulud finds creating first courses the most exciting and he explained why: 'Seventy per cent of first courses are cold and typically half the size of the main course, so you can concentrate the flavours more. Also, as in desserts, there is usually more complexity, more contrast, more layers of texture and taste because they are cold. There is more acidity and more seasoning, which suits the spicier white wines that customers usually order with the first courses – chefs cannot be that adventurous with the seasoning on main courses because they are usually enjoyed with red wine. And finally because first courses are served cold or lukewarm, chefs have more time to play with the final dish. There are limitations on just how much a chef can influence a main course because it has to be served hot and you have to plate it that much faster.'

Boulud added one further insightful note, a reflection of more than 40 years in the kitchen: 'First courses have the other advantage of being served when we are most hungry. They generate more vibes for the palate.'

We met again at 2.30pm in the private dining room of Bar Boulud in the Mandarin Oriental Hotel, London, over a *salade lyonnaise* and a glass of burgundy. Boulud had just finished service in this basement restaurant that serves 900 customers a day, in what was formerly a mattress warehouse. He began by saying how much he enjoyed this particular service, an opportunity to cook with his team while New York was still waking up.

Boulud then focused on how he writes the whole menu – a process that begins

with two very different maps – before reminiscing about the conversations that took place amongst the chefs in the kitchens of Roger Vergé and Michel Guérard in France in the 1970s that were to inspire his subsequent career.

'The process begins, whichever city I am to open in, with the suppliers. Whenever a chef asks what can they do to make me welcome in their city, I reply "introduce to me your suppliers". I go and visit as many of the meat, fish and vegetables suppliers to make sense of the city. Then I will add in the secondary suppliers of wild mushrooms, salads and herbs so that I have a picture of what is available locally and nationally.'

Boulud cited the potential variation in the quality of the pork and crab as examples. The former will determine the recipes for the charcuterie, while it is the varying textures of the crab that are available that will ultimately determine how they will appear on the different menus. 'The peekytoe crab that we receive on the US East Coast is a very different texture from the Alaskan or Dungeness crab on the West Coast, and the Cornish crab available here is different again.'

Then Boulud drew a map of his kitchen, something he referred to as a series of grids that take in all the sections necessary to execute the menu. The more sections there are, the larger the menu can be (there are nine in London) but it is an essential aspect of his job to ensure that no section is overloaded. 'The section that handles the braised dishes, for example, will have a lot of preparation to do beforehand but it will never be that busy during service. Writing a menu that has this balance is an important responsibility of the chef. This is as crucial as ensuring that the menu has the correct balance of textures and flavours.'

So too is consulting with his fellow chefs and taking some account of the mood they are all in. But Boulud was clear on who is in charge. 'They will all have some input but I am the veto.'

Boulud's menus are also inspired by a unique worldliness. He was one of the few chefs to take advantage of Michel Guérard's offer of sponsored English lessons and this opportunity led him to cook in Copenhagen, where he can still recall the taste of 'the most wonderful, tiny, brown shrimps'.

FOR THE TABLE

SPINACH & ARTICHOKE DIP £8
CREAMY & CHEESY SPINACH DIP
BAGUETTE CROUTONS

HOUMOUS £6
CUMIN & CORIANDER
HUMMUS, PITA BREAD

GOUGÈRES £5
GRUYÈRE CHEESE PUFFS

CALAMAR £9
CRISPY CALAMARI &
BEER-BATTERED ONION RINGS
AÏOLI DIP

SAUCISSES

TASTING OF TWO £15 • THREE £24 • FOUR £36

BOUDIN NOIR £8 / £12
BLACK PUDDING, CELERIAC PUREE, FRESH APPLE

BOUDIN BLANC £12 / £21
WHITE PORK SAUSAGE, TRUFFLE MASHED POTATO

TUNISIENNE £9 / £17
LAMB MERGUEZ, HERBED COUSCOUS, PEPPERS, YOGHURT

KÄSEKRAINER £9 / £17
BEEF & PORK SAUSAGE, SMOKED SWISS CHEESE

CHARCUTERIE MAISON
WITH SOME CLASSIC RECIPES OF GILLES VEROT FROM PARIS

DÉGUSTATION
SMALL BOARD £15 | LARGE BOARD £30
SELECTION OF HOUSE SPECIALTIES
SERVED WITH HORS D'OEUVRES, PICKLES & MUSTARDS

TERRINES ET PÂTÉS

PÂTÉ GRAND-MÈRE £8
CHICKEN LIVER, PORK, COGNAC

PÂTÉ GRAND-PÈRE £10
FOIE GRAS, PORK, TRUFFLE

JOUE DE BOEUF £8
CONFIT BEEF CHEEK, PEARL ONION
PISTACHIO

TAJINE D'AGNEAU £9
BRAISED LAMB, MOROCCAN SPICES

FROMAGE DE TÊTE £8
PORK HEAD CHEESE TERRINE

PÂTÉ EN CROÛTE £11
FOIE GRAS, CHICKEN, PORK
BUTTON MUSHROOM

SAUCISSONS ET JAMBONS

JAMBON DE PARIS £8
HOUSE-MADE COOKED HAM

JAMÓN IBÉRICO £19
JUAN PEDRO DOMECQ IBERICO 30
MONTHS AGED HAM

COPPA £10
ITALIAN CURED PORK

SAUCISSON "JESUS" £10
DRY CURED PORK SAUSAGE

WARM SPECIALITIES

RILLONS CROUSTILLANTS £9
CRISPY PORK BELLY, PEPPER
FRISÉE, DIJON

CERVELAS £9
LYON SAUSAGE, PISTACHIO
& TRUFFLE IN BRIOCHE

SOUPES

SOUPE À L'OIGNON £8
ONION SOUP, BEEF BROTH, WHITE WINE, GRUYÈRE

SOUPE DE POISSON £15
FISH SOUP, SEA BREAM & SHELLFISH, SAFFRON, ROUILLE

SALADES

SALADE DE ROQUETTE £9 / £17
ROCKET SALAD, BUFFALO MOZZARELLA, TOMATO & OLIVES

ENDIVE ET BETTERAVES £8 / £16
ENDIVE SALAD, BEETROOT, DEVON BLUE CHEESE
CANDIED WALNUTS & SHALLOT DRESSING

SALADE LYONNAISE £12 / £22
FRISÉE, POACHED EGG, LARDONS, CHICKEN LIVERS, SHERRY

SALADE DE CREVETTES £15 / £26
CHILLED PRAWNS, BIBB LETTUCE, FRENCH COCKTAIL DRESSING

ENTRÉES

AÏOLI CLASSIQUE
PETIT £19 | GRAND £32
CHILLED CRUDITÉS, LOBSTER & PRAWNS, MUSSELS, GARLIC DIP

TERRINE DE FOIE GRAS £18
FOIE GRAS TERRINE, CLEMENTINE CHUTNEY
TOASTED GINGER BREAD

CORNISH CRAB ROLL £14 / £22
HAND PICKED CORNISH CRAB MEAT, BRIOCHE BUN
YUZU MAYONNAISE, TOBIKO ROE, PICKLED CUCUMBER

ESCARGOTS DE BOURGOGNE £9 / £17
BURGUNDY SNAILS, GRILLED BREAD, PARSLEY & GARLIC BUTTER

TARTARE DE BŒUF À LA BETTRAVE £15 / £26
HAND CUT RAW BEEF SIRLOIN, BEETROOT & APPLE PUREE
MUSTARD EGG YOLK DRESSING, CRISPY SWEET POTATO

EXECUTIVE CHEF – THOMAS PIAT

POISSONS

CREVETTES £15 / £26
SEARED PRAWNS, LEMON & GARLIC SAUCE

MOULES À LA CRÈME £9 / £17
STEAMED MUSSELS, WHITE WINE, PARSLEY, CRÈME FRAÎCHE

SAINT-JACQUES £26
SEARED SCALLOPS, BRUSSELS SPROUT & BACON
SWEET POTATO PUREE

MAIGRE A LA PLANCHA £24
STONE BASS, CREAMY PEARL BARLEY RISOTTO
CUCUMBER & POTATO FRICASSÉE, FRESH DILL

SOLE LIMANDE £28
ROASTED LEMON SOLE, CROUTONS, GRENOBLOISE SAUCE

VIANDES

COQ AU VIN £25
CHICKEN LEGS, LARDONS, KING OYSTER MUSHROOM
ONIONS, HAND-MADE FARFALLE, RED WINE SAUCE

VOLAILLE RÔTIE £24
ROASTED CHICKEN BREAST, LEEK FONDUE, GLAZED BABY VEGETABLES
CRISPY LEEK, CREAMY CHICKEN JUS

PALERON CARBONNADE £24
ALE BRAISED BEEF FEATHERBLADE, SPÄTZLE
CHESTNUT MUSHROOMS, BABY GEM LETTUCE

CROQUE MONSIEUR £12 / MADAME £13
WARM HOUSE-MADE HAM & CHEESE SANDWICH

RIBEYE £32 • SIRLOIN £34 ~USDA 10oz /283GR
SERVED WITH MIXED SALAD, BÉARNAISE OR PEPPERCORN SAUCE

CÔTE DE BŒUF POUR DEUX £72
28 DAY DRY AGED BLACK ANGUS RIBEYE TO SHARE
CHOICE OF TWO SIDE DISHES

SIDE DISHES £4

GREEN BEANS	POMMES FRITES
MIXED LEAF SALAD	SAUTÉED BABY SPINACH
POMMES LYONNAISES	TRUFFLE MASHED POTATO

GRILLED BEEF BURGERS

100% UK BEEF, GROUND DAILY IN-HOUSE SERVED ON
A HOME-MADE BUN WITH POMMES FRITES

YANKEE £17
BEEF PATTY, ICEBERG, TOMATO, ONION, PICKLE, SESAME BUN
ADD CHEDDAR CHEESE SUPP, £1

FRENCHIE £19
BEEF PATTY, CONFIT PORK BELLY, TOMATO, DIJON, MORBIER, PEPPERED BUN

PIGGIE £19
BEEF PATTY, BBQ PORK, JALAPEÑO MAYO, CABBAGE, CHEDDAR BUN

"BB" £24
BEEF PATTY, FOIE GRAS, SHORT RIBS, HORSERADISH MAYO
CONFIT TOMATOES, BLACK ONION SEED BUN

FROMAGES
~ EUROPEAN CHEESES ~
SERVED WITH SEASONAL GARNISH

I CHEESE £5
2 CHEESES £9
3 CHEESES £14

FRENCH
COULOMMIERS
COW, ILE DE FRANCE, FRANCE
UNPASTEURISED

...

FRENCH
LE COUSIN
COW, SAVOIE, FRANCE
UNPASTEURISED

...

ENGLISH
COLSTON BASSETT STILTON
COW, NOTTINGHAMSHIRE, ENGLAND
PASTEURISED

DESSERTS

ENQUIRE ABOUT OUR DESSERT DU JOUR

GÂTEAU BASQUE £7
CLASSIC FRENCH CAKE, BRANDIED CHERRY JAM
VANILLA ANGLAISE

LE MIRLITON AU BEURRE DE POMME £9
PUFF PASTRY, ALMOND CREAM, SPICED APPLE BUTTER
RICE CRISPIES, SALTED BUTTER CARAMELISED FRESH APPLE
SPECULOOS ICE CREAM, CRANBERRY COULIS

MARGUERITE DES ÎLES £10
WHITE CHOCOLATE MOUSSE, TROPICAL ESPUMA
CARAMELISED BANANA, COCONUT SORBET, HONEYCOMB

LE ROYAL £10
HAZELNUT DACQUOISE, MILK CHOCOLATE MOUSSE
PRALINÉ FEUILLANTINE, CARAMELISED HAZELNUTS
CHOCOLATE SHERBET

LE CITRON £11
LEMON CURD, CRUMBLE, CRISPY MERINGUE
VANILLA & LEMON MARSHMALLOW, DULCE MOELLEUX
BROWN BUTTER SNOW, LIMONCELLO CHOCOLATE
PASSIONATA SORBET

LE 'FRENCH COFFEE' £12
DARK CHOCOLATE SPHERE, LIGHT VANILLA CHANTILLY
ARMAGNAC & KAHLUA SAUCE, CRISPY PEARLS
COFFEE ICE CREAM

GLACES ET SORBETS, £3 PER SCOOP

GLACES
VANILLA • CHOCOLATE •
SPECULOOS
PISTACHIO • COFFEE

SORBETS
BLUEBERRY-YOGHURT • RASPBERRY
COCONUT • PASSIONNATTA

PETITS SUCRÉS

FRESHLY BAKED MADELEINES £5
ASSORTMENT OF MACARONS £6
COCONUT TRUFFLES & CRUNCHY NOUGAT LAYERS £7
PRALINÉ & CARAMELISED PUFFED RICE TRUFFLES £4

HEAD PASTRY CHEF ~ QUENTIN GIUDICELLI

He then moved to Le Cirque, New York, where, as Head Chef at the age of 31, he was responsible for the first time for the menu, the organisation of the kitchen and managing the personnel.

This experience has influenced Boulud's menus in two distinct ways. The first is that he has come to appreciate that with his customers coming from increasingly diverse cultural and ethnic backgrounds, there must always be certain dishes on his menus with which they feel completely comfortable.

The second is how well the dishes go with wine. 'It is crucially important that my menus give our sommeliers the opportunity to do their job properly, to recommend a suitable glass of wine. I always enjoy writing an à la carte menu but my fondest memories will always be of writing menus for wine dinners, menus that will lift the wines. Shortly after I had arrived in New York, numerous amateur food and wine lovers challenged me to create special menus for these dinners. I will always be very grateful for those opportunities.'

ARNAUD DONCKELE

LA RÉSIDENCE DE LA PINÈDE

Virtually every chef has a streak of masochism. This characteristic has to be there from the minute an interest in the profession is initially kindled, followed by the realisation, and acceptance, of the long and anti-social working hours that will ensue.

And all this has to happen before any chef arrives at a position in which it is possible to write their own menu: a piece of paper that goes on view to the general public twice a day, to be analysed, commented upon and even criticised by an unforgiving readership.

There are chefs, however, who, in pursuit of even higher goals, reveal an even deeper masochistic streak.

One example is Kevin Aherne at Sage Restaurant in Midleton, a 30-minute drive from Cork in Ireland. Disillusioned by terms such as national and regional, which he believes have today lost their relevance, he has imposed on his kitchen a 12-mile radius for the majority of his suppliers (excluding his dry goods and wine, although there is a renowned whiskey distillery in the town). On every table is a list of their 14 local suppliers that culminates in a credit to those on the Sage team who gather the foraged ingredients.

Such rigour will appeal to many chefs but can be realised by only a few. One of the preconditions of such an approach is that the restaurant must be close to its suppliers but at the same time not so remote that it cannot attract good staff. One chef who has been able to pull off this seemingly difficult task is Arnaud Donckele, who has gained three Michelin stars for his cooking at La Résidence de la Pinède in St Tropez in the south of France.

It would be difficult not to feel envious of Donckele's location. The restaurant faces the beach. He is surrounded by the bounty of Provence. And the hotel attracts only those who are able to pay Michelin three-star prices, which elsewhere adorn painstaking but relatively static menus. But in Donckele, the

strain of masochism obviously runs deep.

This manifests itself in his menu 'Fugue en Provence' that sits within his more expansive à la carte menu; fugue, in this instance, means 'having nothing to do with' the rest of his menu.

This five-course menu, which changes every day, is Donckele's expression of being 100 per cent local, of using ingredients only from the Var, the department in which St Tropez is located, eschewing even those from around Nice and Marseille at the eastern and western limits of Provence.

Donckele begins writing the menu at 11am when he sees what his suppliers have delivered, although on the day I stood opposite him in his kitchen this was supplemented by artichokes and *haricots verts* that he had picked himself en route to the kitchen. He rattled off the names of his suppliers with pride as though they were close friends. 'There is Yann Menard in Grimaud for vegetables, Nadia in La Môle for saffron, ingredients that I believe are most typical of the Var. Then there are cheeses and vegetables from Monsieur de Salneuve.'

Then there are the fish, so fresh that they are still in rigor mortis. Donckele showed me seven red mullets, just delivered, each weighing between 120 and 150 grams. These, he explained, would be filleted, covered with a thin scale of potato alongside a lively mixture of its liver and the meat of the local crab, *araignée de mer*.

The daily composition of the 'fugue' menu begins once lunch is over. Donckele formulates the ideas that emerge as they prepare the ingredients, and at 2pm he begins to write down the potential dishes in conjunction with Thierry Di Tullio, the restaurant manager. By 3.30, 80 per cent of the dishes are finished and they are finalised any time between 5.30 and 7pm, just in time for the waiting staff to be briefed on them.

The idea for this menu came to Donckele (born in 1977 in Normandy) when in 2008 he was staying at a Provençal inn that offered a different menu every evening based on what was available in the market. But transferring this fundamentally local and small-scale approach to a bigger, more international

stage – one that is under intense professional scrutiny and is expensive to boot – is not easy.

'Writing a menu requires personal and solitary research, and yet I cannot deliver this menu without the full backing of my team. This particular menu relies heavily on personal instinct and our reward is obviously the pleasure it generates for our customers. The challenges arise from getting the team who cook alongside me every day to share the same values.'

Cooking is not really learnt, it is something you live,
Something that gives you joy by the act of giving.

To be a cook is a simple act of love and sharing
Between the people that cultivate, raise or fish the produce.

Nature burst with heavenly tastes and flavours.
It is important to understand that behind each product
There is a face and a terrain that helps.

My cooking tells my past, my region, my desires.
Our only aim is to give of our best, and during the process of learning
To be worthy of these products and the people who produced them.

Arnaud

The sea
To begin with....

'Chopin' of jackfish, a homage to the author. Victor Petit,   75€
Served with wild rocket leaves,
Fresh garden tomatoes and grilled tiny new potatoes,
A creamy tuna and Lambrusco sauce served at your table.

Amberjack fish and crabmeat marinated in local mandarin oranges,   78€
Thyme leaves, raw baby vegetables and tender plant shoots.

Baby lobster and sea mullet in two services: 115€
Cold service: Finely sliced cuts in aspic,
                       Lobster coral cooked in yuzu lemon

Hot service: Pearled and cooked in their own natural sea water,
                       Crunchy pearls of caviar,
                       Salicornia salad and fresh verbena.leaves infused in shellfish broth

La Borgne, the traditional Fish soup « Soupe d'œuf » in Provence.   68€
Orange flavored toasted bread, poached egg in rock fish soup.
Tome of cow from Taradeau.
Rainbow wrasses and red mullets tempura served with a rouille sauce

And to follow by......

Turbot in sea salt of Camargue crust flavoured lemon grass and seaweed   108€
Simple mix of baby abalone, wedge molluscs, squids, barnacles and rock samphire.
A whole potato baked in broth and shellfish

Dover Sole in summer truffle shell braised .   112€
Olivette tomatoes with fennel heart
The juice scented with Riviera vegetables

Sea bass, in scales of squill-fish just braised   104€
Topped on stewed tomato, pearls of vegetables, clams, lime,
smoked zucchini and oregano

Cod fish petals and 'Léiume en Boui-Abaisso' "when the Mistral wind blew so strong" 98€
Garden vegetables cooked in a country style "Mona Lisa" potato and rock fish broth
A saffron infusion, orange peels and laurel leaves

Land and Sea

Langoustine and Pigeon in two services: 102€
First service: Ravioli filled with the claws and pigeon legs served in a broth

Second service: Breast and langoustine just roasted in rosemary butter
Chanterelle mushrooms, potatoes in scampi and chestnuts honey velouté

Silky broth of blue lobster and farm guinea fowl   98€
Vegetables, herbs and marinated ginger.
Prepared like a stew.

Provençal Gardens
To begin with...

A joyful summer meeting between marjoram and lemon herbs,   75€
Pearled early vegetables, enlivened with a pure juice sorbet of black tomatoes
Finger food beignets, a choron sauce with citrus.

The Farm
And to follow...

Sisteron lamb in two services: 104€
First service: Baron of lamb with wild thyme, a juice flavoured with argan oil,
Sicilian eggplant, purée of tomato and mild onion.

Second service: Lamb" pieds-paquets" (tripe and sheep trotters)
Shoulder of lamb with sweetbreads and kidneys,
A strong juice and a pimientos/ wild savory liquor

Zitone pasta:
'In gratitude to a chef who taught me so much'

As a starter, delicately filled with black truffle and foie gras,   94€
Violet artichokes prepared in three textures and flavoured with Thai basil.

Or

As main course, served with a velvety, milk-fed chicken supreme,   125€
First service: Slowly cooked in a bladder and truffle juice
Second service: Patties of thigh meat, the 'oyster', wing and a touch of fillet,
Flavored with cebette onions and broth

All our meats are guarantoeed of French origin by our producers

The dairy

Cheeses from the countryside I love,   32€
Beautifully produced by our local cheesemakers.

A Rove Brousse goat cheese, soft sheep milk cheese and Caillolais from Marseille   30€
Pear prepared in two textures,
Saffron honey from "La Môle" region and Bouteillan olive oil.

From the orchard to the dessert table
Sweet ideas from Guillaume Godin

(Order at the start of the meal)

A seductive, simply presented romance between very dark chocolate and raspberries.   39€
Composed naturally with a touch of bergamot orange.

Melting strawberry and lime topped on a thin jelly crispy tart   38€
The soufflé on the side with grated lemon
An infusion scented with basilic citrus water

An artistic assembly of grapefruit and wild aloe vera,   38€
Crunchy biscuit lightly flavoured with lemon mint,
Hassaku japanese pomelo fruit lemonade served at your table.

Green apple, refreshed by kaffir lime,   35€
The lightness of a hot soufflé. An apple and rhubarb spin dried juice.

A smart casual dress code is required (Shorts and beach sandals forbidden)
We do not accept cheques
Taxes and service are included in the prices

The 'Neptunia by Residénce de la Pinède' knife   135€ each
Your male or female evening companion,   250€ the Duet

Provence escapade

Prélude:
Amberjack fish and crabmeat marinated in local mandarin oranges,
Thyme leaves, raw baby vegetables and tender plant shoots.

'Chopin' of jackfish, homage to the author, Victor Petit,
Served with wild rocket leaves,
Fresh garden tomatoes and grilled tiny new potatoes,
A creamy tuna and Lambrusco sauce served at your table.

"Sea" potato baked in broth and shellfish with Caviar

Sea bream with Mediterranean scampi
Smooth clams and juice of the heads
The whole scented with absinthe and coriander

Thyme sherbet ice, Florentine fennel heart sorbet.
A touch of absinthe at your table

Perch in truffle shells
Vierge dressing with truffle, fennel celery and basil

A seductive romance between very dark chocolate and raspberries.
Composed naturally.

245€

An Epicurean Adventure

Prelude :
Amberjack fish and crabmeat marinated in local mandarin oranges,
Thyme leaves, raw baby vegetables and tender plant shoots.

Baby lobster and sea mullet in two services
Pearled and cooked in their own natural sea water,
Crunchy pearls of caviar,
Salicornia salad and verbena. Leaves infused in shellfish broth

Zitone pasta delicately filled with black truffle and foie gras,
Violet artichokes flavoured with Thai basil.

Sea Bass dressed with thin slices of carabineros lightly braised,
Vierge dressing of Roma tomato and clams with lime
Violon zucchini like a rose slightly smoked and wild oregano

Thyme sherbet ice, Florentine fennel heart sorbet.
A touch of absinthe at your table.

A gentle nuance of a blue lobster and farm guinea fowl stew
Vegetables, herbs and marinated ginger.

Rove Brousse goat cheese, soft sheep cheese and Caillolais from Marseille
Pear prepared in two textures,
Saffron from "La Môle" region honey and Bouteillan olive oil.

Green apple, refreshed by kaffir lime,
The lightness of a hot soufflé. An apple and rhubarb spin dried juice.

295€

PETER GILMORE

QUAY

The setting of Quay, Peter Gilmore's original restaurant in Sydney, could not be more expressive of the city or, in fact, of Australia itself.

It is housed in the Ocean Passenger Terminal, whose many windows allow every customer full views of the city's famous harbour bridge, and across the water – when no cruise ship blocks the way – of the inspiring Sydney Opera House, which is home to Bennelong, Gilmore's other restaurant.

Nor could Gilmore's menu be any more expressive of the country. We ate there in March 2016 and a dish of muntries was one of the choices among the four first courses. These sweet little fruits are only in season for about six weeks of the year and are served there with pistachios, ewe's milk curd, sour herbs and white cucumber. It makes for an excellent entrée, the cool temperature at which it is served astutely whetting the appetite for what is to follow.

This encompasses numerous dishes that include many other indigenous ingredients. There is a combination of mud crabs and tapioca in a mud crab congee; whiting from King George Island alongside white turnips and *hatsuka* radishes; native coastal greens and a Lebanese cucumber that has been sliced and then grilled, a combination that adds piquancy to a grilled and marinated duck breast; and, finally, Gilmore's signature dessert, his white nectarine Snow Egg that is ordered by a good half of the restaurant's 200 daily customers.

An emphasis on local ingredients has become de rigueur for any top chef today. And yet for Gilmore – an extremely jolly chef who at the age of 47 has been cooking for more than 30 years – this emphasis on his own country's ingredients came about as a reaction to the process that chef Ferran Adrià initiated in the 1990s, many miles away in El Bulli.

'This was my very personal response to the rise of molecular gastronomy,' Gilmore explained when we met, 'a movement I didn't want any part of. Instead,

I found that its spread forced me to rethink my whole approach to cooking. I wanted my menu to be more expressive not just of nature but also of just what was available here in Australia.'

This thought process coincided with a new direction in Gilmore's personal pastimes and in particular his discovery of gardening – a hobby that he has now expanded to four 10 by 1 metre beds raised on railway sleepers that must consume a large part of the garden of his home by the city's northern beaches. And it was from his newfound scrutiny of the gardening catalogues that Gilmore began to appreciate just how much he and his fellow Australian chefs were missing: pea flowers, purple onions, multi-coloured radishes – ingredients that embraced not just diversity but also a large palette of colours that had hitherto been ignored and whose charms were therefore not being made available to their customers.

'This realisation seems obvious today but it certainly wasn't the case back then. And I feel fortunate that I picked a winning horse, as this emphasis on foraging has been recognised by the chefs at Noma in Denmark, by Mugaritz in Spain and at many other restaurants around the world. It will be seen, in my opinion, as the second movement in modern cuisine after nouvelle cuisine.'

The numerous growers and farmers with whom Gilmore now works are acknowledged on the opening page of his menu, most notably Tim and Elizabeth Johnstone, who grow many of the herbs and vegetables in Hawkesbury, an hour west of Sydney, and Yan and Heather Dizcballs, who are responsible for the palm hearts that are finely sliced and served on top of the mud crab congee.

Gilmore spoke enthusiastically, in particular, about Mike Quamby, the man responsible for our muntries dish and whose company, Outback Pride, has become a major supplier of fresh ingredients 'from the bush' to Gilmore's kitchen, and to those of over 100 chefs across Australia. This relationship began four years earlier with an initial phone call from Gilmore enquiring as to whether these products – previously available only dried – could be delivered fresh. The consequence has

seen Quamby growing increasingly large amounts of fresh herbs and fruits – and here Gilmore rattled off names such as lemon aspen, mountain lilly pilly, river mint, saltbush and wattleseed – that are now being incorporated by chefs, not for their novelty but for their flavour.

This refocusing on indigenous ingredients has been a great boon for Australia as it has drawn numerous food journalists, TV crews, and the increasing number of those interested in good food and wine to the continent. So too has the country's wide climatic variation, which in early March produces simultaneously ripe mangosteens up in Queensland and crisp heritage apples ready to be harvested in Tasmania, 2,300 kilometres to the south.

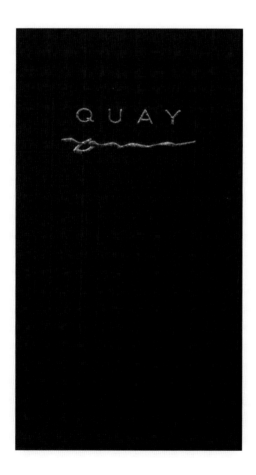

Panel 1

Sashimi of south coast crayfish,
squash seeds, cultured cream, tapioca,
white cucumber, green almonds

Mud crab congee
(est. 2003)

Raw smoked Blackmore wagyu,
horseradish soured cream,
fermented rye crisps,
raw funghi

Salad of ox heart tomatoes,
sheep's milk feta, sherry caramel, herbs

Panel 2

Uni, koshihikari rice,
salted yolk, fish maw,
sweet prawns, umami broth

Slow cooked abalone,
smoked confit pig jowl,
fermented shiitake chawanmushi,
bamboo, koji cultured grains

XO, XO, XO

Slow braised quail,
brioche, grains, hazelnuts,
coco button mushrooms

Panel 3

Tasting Menu

Sashimi of south coast crayfish,
squash seeds, cultured cream, tapioca,
white cucumber, green almonds

Raw smoked Blackmore wagyu,
horseradish soured cream,
fermented rye crisps, raw funghi

Uni, koshihikari rice,
salted yolk, fish maw,
sweet prawns, umami broth

Slow cooked abalone, smoked confit pig jowl,
fermented shiitake chawanmushi,
bamboo, koji cultured grains

Steamed King George whiting,
sea scallop, southern squid, white turnips,
hatsuka radish, citrus anchovy butter

Roasted masterstock duck,
black rice miso, orach,
black garlic

Optional cheese course $25

White nectarine Snow Egg

Cream, prune, oloroso caramel,
sugar crystals

Coffee, Tea & Quay Petits Fours

Tasting menu $235
Classic wines pairing $105
Premium wines pairing $195
Non alcoholic drinks pairing $75

Tasting menu available 12pm - 1.30pm & 6pm - 9pm

Panel 4

My aim is to embrace nature's diversity
to achieve a sense of balance
and purity through produce, technique,
texture, flavour and composition. P Gilmore

We would like to acknowledge some of the
passionate farmers, growers and providores
who support us in our endeavour to bring our
guests unique and beautiful produce.

Tim and Elizabeth Johnstone
Johnstone Kitchen Garden
Bespoke vegetables and greens

Wayne Hulme
Seafood providore (Joto)

Paul Lee
Artisan Asian Ingredients

Yan and Heather Diczbalis
Palm hearts

Anthony Puharich
Vic's Meat
Beef and Poultry

Executive Chef - Peter Gilmore
Chef de Cuisine - Rob Kabboord

Panel 5

Steamed King George whiting,
sea scallop, southern squid,
white turnips, hatsuka radish,
citrus anchovy butter

Roasted masterstock duck,
scorched pickled cucumber,
native coastal greens, orach, barletta onions

Blackmore wagyu,
black rice miso, white maitake,
black garlic

Stone pot organic green rice,
silken tofu, mountain spinach,
cabbage stems, seaweed

Panel 6

Cherries, white chocolate,
nougat, coconut

White nectarine Snow Egg

Cream, prune, oloroso caramel,
sugar crystals

Eight textured chocolate cake

A selection of cheese,
raisin and walnut sourdough

Menu $175 per person

Coffee, Tea & Quay Petits Fours $10
Quay Signature Blend by Single Origin Roasted Coffee
Tea by World Par Tea

Aside from his ever-growing focus on nature, Gilmore explained that there are three other considerations necessary in the final composition of any dish and the structure of his menus. The first is the contrasting texture of the ingredients; the second is the innate harmony of the flavours involved; and finally, and most importantly, there is the overall balance of the dish.

These elements have to fit into a very busy restaurant and two very different menus that are presented to each customer once they have sat down. The first, at the back, is a tasting menu of eight courses that is made up of a range of dishes from the à la carte menu, which itself comprises four different choices for each of the four courses. Why, I wondered, does he still offer both?

'Until seven years ago there was just the à la carte, then tasting menus became more popular and I wondered whether we should move in that direction. Then I thought about my customers, those who are coming quite a long way in many cases to eat my food, and I thought I should give them the choice. And in many ways, I find the four-course option more alluring. It gives us the option of writing three savoury dishes with less protein in each instance; it has become a more interesting format for the kitchen to work with, and the overall balance of the two menus, which is split equally, shows that both continue to be popular.'

Gilmore described Quay as a 'real working restaurant' that has to justify its food costs and its wage costs. And Gilmore seems in no hurry to move on or upwards – after our interview I spotted him scurrying down the service stairs in his whites at 4.30pm. Gilmore struck me as a chef very much in love with his profession and his customers. 'Being a chef,' he explained to me, 'allows me the joy of being at the centre of a creative art form, one that engages all the senses and provides the customer with very positive memories.'

SHAUN HILL

THE WALNUT TREE INN

If menu-writing were an academic discipline, then those written by Shaun Hill, the chef/proprietor of The Walnut Tree Inn outside Abergavenny in Wales, would be required texts, documents that should be read and studied by any aspiring chef.

Hill's menus are models of clarity and distinction. Written in lower case, he foregoes any possible confusion by using capitals only when they are essential, such as in the name of a supplier or a place name.

These menus may mix languages but no spelling mistakes are allowed to creep in. And most particularly, each dish is described without flamboyance. Each sentence is grammatically correct. And, as a result, the overall effect is extremely appetising. That Hill manages to achieve all this despite the fact that he claims to finish writing these menus just as the first customers are being shown to their tables bears testimony not just to his experience but also to his upbringing.

Hill, 69 at the time of writing, has been cooking since he was 21, initially at the Capital Hotel, Blakes and the Gay Hussar in London; then in the countryside at Gidleigh Park in Devon and The Merchant House in Ludlow, before finally settling at The Walnut Tree Inn. But Hill's father was a journalist and scriptwriter who impressed on his son the importance of clear, correct English. 'That's the way I was taught,' he explained. 'I get infuriated when I see the s missing from petits fours.'

Years at the stove, interspersed with travel, have introduced Hill's fertile mind and taste buds to many new dishes and ingredients that he has made his own, but it is the initial menus in any restaurant he has opened that are, in his opinion, the most difficult. 'These will set the tone for the restaurant you want, the customers you want and those who want you. Put on prosciutto and melon or prawn cocktail, and those are the customers you will attract. And I have always

Menu

goats cheese tortellini with tomato consommé	£10
new season asparagus, jersey royals, morels and hollandaise	£12
skate with cucumber and mustard sauce	£9
monkfish with tomato, chilli and ginger	£13
turbot and scallop bourride	£15
Robert Carrier's pâté aux herbes and pear chutney	£9
a board of Spanish meats with tomato and olive salad	£12
veal sweetbreads with sauerkraut and warm dressing	£16

*

cod with mussels, pancetta and brown butter sauce	£23
dover sole with spring vegetables and parsley dressing	£25
halibut with wild garlic bubble and squeak	£27
calf's liver and bacon with cassis sauce	£21
guinea fowl and kiev with fondant potato	£22
skirt of beef with braised shin and red wine sauce	£23
saddle of rabbit with kidney, liver and pudding	£23
loin of middle white pork, belly, cheek, and black pudding	£24
spring vegetable risotto	£16

puddings @ £9

orange and almond cake

walnut, rum and quince trifle

chocolate and pear tart with stracciatella ice cream

vanilla cheesecake with rhubarb

pistachio crème brûlée

mango kulfi with lime and ginger sorbet

white chocolate, cherry and pistachio torte

baked treacle and pecan pudding with custard

cheese @ £12.

a selection of British cheeses

(Wigmore, Bosworth Ash ,Golden Cenarth, Double Barrel, Stinking Bishop and Crozier Blue)

coffee - tea – tisane and petits fours £4.50

digestif cocktails £8.50

brandy Alexander
cognac, crème de cacao, cream

espresso martini
espresso, vodka, Kahlúa

manhattan
bourbon, sweet vermouth, angoustora bitters

believed that it would be very silly not to cook what you like to eat, because how else can you tell whether it is right or not?'

In Hill's particular case, this means that his menus are never devoid of his two favourite ingredients – offal and shellfish – with the former appealing because of its versatility, the latter for its sweetness, especially scallops, his particular favourite.

Scallops sautéed with a lentil sauce is a dish that will forever be associated with Hill but it has its origins in a visit to the late Hans Stucki's restaurant in Basel, Switzerland, where Hill ate a langoustine dish that precipitated what he refers to as a 'light bulb moment'. 'I went back to Gidleigh Park, substituted scallops, then started to combine cardamom, cumin, coriander and then dhal until the dish finally came together.' Hill's fascination with India has also chimed with his customers' growing interest in all things spicy. 'I saw a lovely dish in Tuscany, a soup that combined lobster, chickpeas, olive oil and bread, and when I came home I put it straight on the menu. It didn't sell. I changed the combination, added coriander, called it curry and it flew out of the door.'

Hill reads a lot of menus, principally from a desire to discover what may be missing from his own, but he has learnt that the location of his own restaurant is a hugely important factor too. 'I understand the emphasis on foraging, local and seasonal, but in the heart of Wales from the end of January, when the game season is over, there is nothing local or seasonal to be had around here until May. And bavette from a Welsh cow is tough as old shoe leather, whoever is cooking it, while that from the US is much cheaper and cuts like butter.'

The composition of Hill's dishes never changes. 'I think of the protein alone first. If it's a piece of lamb then it has to be pink, hot and juicy, then I will add the vegetables and potatoes to make it into a dish.' But the input into his menus is far more varied. 'Talk to everyone in the kitchen. Find out what is coming in. And, perhaps most importantly, find out what was on yesterday's menu and did not sell. The great advantage of being in a restaurant kitchen is that the chef does not have to sit down with the customers, as happens at home, so you are in control until the very last minute the dish is to be served.'

BRUCE POOLE

CHEZ BRUCE

I have talked menus on two very different occasions with Bruce Poole, the 51-year-old founder of Chez Bruce, the Michelin-starred restaurant he opened in Wandsworth, south London, in 1995.

The first occasion was over a dish of cassoulet, the second over a cup of Earl Grey tea. But in both instances I was struck by the sense of insecurity that appears to be an inherent part of being a chef and writing a menu, what Poole refers to as 'any restaurant's beating heart'.

'What you have to understand about chefs is that we are all insecure. We want our customers to like our food and in deciding whether they do or they don't means forming an opinion about us. It is that personal. If someone says they don't like my food then I know we cannot be friends, that I couldn't go down to the pub and buy them a drink. Conversely when I see a menu that I enjoy, I know it could only have been written by someone I would enjoy spending time with.'

But in getting to that stage, Poole acknowledged that any good chef must face up to two sets of limitations, the first personal, the second physical.

The first is that every chef is limited by what they can cook well. 'I enjoy playing the guitar,' Poole explained, 'but I am no Eric Clapton. I cannot play whatever I want. Now in many respects that is a nice restriction to have. It is difficult to have a voice, but that is what every menu must have and knowing what to leave out, a style of cooking that you have not been able to master, can be an advantage.'

Poole cited the absence of soufflés from his menu as an example of this. 'I have never really enjoyed eating them so I've never taken the time to learn how to cook them properly.' And then, illustrating the insecurity he sees in every chef, he continued, 'But does that make me a bad chef? Why spend time perfecting something you don't like eating? But I do enjoy iced soufflés, *nougat glacé* for instance, and the ones I make I think are pretty good.'

Then there are the physical constraints of delivering the menu and the dishes you want to cook, in spite of the layout of the restaurant, the equipment, the experience of your staff and the brigade at your disposal, which can change should one member of the team call in sick at the last moment. 'We will serve 150 on a Saturday night and our intention is that they always leave here in a happier frame of mind than when they came in.'

Poole also gives considerable thought to the temperature at which dishes are to be served, a hugely important factor but one that remains largely beyond his control. 'Kitchens are never as well ventilated as you would like. In the summer, when you would like to serve more cool starters, the larder section is invariably quite hot.'

Like most chefs, Poole enjoys the challenge of conceiving first courses more than main courses because the protein element is less significant. There will always be a pasta first course on the menu because he enjoys making it so much, and he acknowledges the growing importance of vegetables – an ingredient all chefs will have to embrace more fully in the future, as fish become more scarce and meat becomes more expensive.

A new menu will evolve over the course of a week – with the exception of perennial favourites such as the cod with olive oil mash and the hot chocolate pudding – with the inclusion of rabbit, a white meat, ruling out chicken on the same menu, for example, and then pairing it with the most suitable garnish. The three fish dishes will depend more on his fishmonger, with the garnishes for these dishes being more interchangeable than those for meat, with the exception that there would never be an oily vinaigrette served alongside an oily fish.

But whether out of all of these possible permutations a happy chef will emerge is a debatable point. Poole, the son of painters who met while teaching at the same art school, and who were never satisfied professionally, may not be the most appropriate person to pass judgement. But it is because he has grown up in such an environment that he can see the chef's role, and the menu that represents him, in perspective.

Chez Bruce

C h e z   B r u c e

Lunch Sunday 24th January 2016

Please let a member of staff know if you have any allergies or food intolerances.

Rhubarb Bellini £ 10
Apple & dill Cooler £ 5.00

Chestnut soup with bacon, sage and onion
Foie gras and chicken liver parfait with toasted brioche
Devilled lamb kidneys with semolina gnocchi, crisp shallots and red wine
Sairass ricotta with blood oranges, grilled fennel, iberico chorizo, basil and marjoram
January salad with enoki mushrooms, puffed wild rice, sprouting beans and avocado
Scallop sashimi with pickled rhubarb, pink peppercorns and ginger (+£4.00)
Creamed cod brandade with Cornish mussel kievs, basil oil and garlic
Broccoli tagliatelle with sausage, garlic, chilli and almonds

Cassoulet of duck with garlic sausage, confit and magret
Glazed pig's cheeks with parmesan polenta, pickled celery, gremolata and chilli
Anjou pigeon with sauce grand veneur, calçot onions, grilled pears and spelt (+£5.00)
Truffled wild mushroom and fontina arancini with pumpkin velouté and Jerusalem artichokes
Shetland salmon with pickled cucumber, brown shrimps, roast fennel, crème fraiche and sorrel
Roast cod with truffle mash, porcini sauce, hazelnut crumble, leek hearts and chanterelles
Crisp fillet of sea bream with black rice, shellfish, ginger, garlic and soy

Crème brûlée
Hot chocolate pudding with praline parfait
Bramley apple crumble with vanilla ice cream
Pot au chocolat with kirsch chantilly, griottine cherries and toasted almonds
Poached Yorkshire rhubarb with lemon poppy seed cake, mascarpone, bergamot and macadamias
Butter pecan ice cream or passion fruit sorbet
Calvados camembert with truffled hazelnut pesto, apple and raisins
Cheeses from the board (+£6.00)

£35.00 for three courses.

Coffee: £3.95, Mineral water: £3.95 (75cl btl.)
A discretionary gratuity of 12.5% will be added to the total bill.

Whilst we will do all we can to accommodate guests with food intolerances and allergies, we are unable to guarantee that dishes will be completely allergen-free

C h e z   B r u c e

Dinner Saturday 22nd August 2015

Please let a member of staff know if you have any allergies or food intolerances.

Strawberry Bellini £10.00

Gazpacho Andaluz with salted marcona almonds
Foie gras and chicken liver parfait with toasted brioche
Pappardelle with duck leg ragoût, girolles and parmesan
Burrata with fresh peaches, Kentish cobnuts, sweet fennel and rocket
Salad of pork belly and runner beans with tonnato dressing and crackling
Charred sprouting broccoli with Ortiz anchovies, crisp egg, pine nuts, garlic and chilli
Cornish mackerel with warm potato and smoked eel salad, redcurrants and pickled shallots
Crisp fishcake with fennel purée, grilled baby squid, sauce vierge and pea shoots

Côte de boeuf with béarnaise sauce and hand cut chips, for two (+£6.00pp)
Chicken lasagne and ballotine with wild mushrooms, truffle velouté and peas
Roast new season's Yorkshire grouse with creamed spelt and damsons (+£7.50)
Rump of veal with fresh coco beans, morteau sausage, meatballs and mustard
Courgette and ricotta cakes with sweetcorn relish, spring onions, beetroot and mint
Poached Cornish skate with razor clams, young leeks, charlotte potatoes, samphire and rouille
Wild sea trout with herb crust, cauliflower purée, beurre noisette and almonds
Roast cod with olive oil mash, Provençale tomato and gremolata

Crème brûlée
Hot chocolate pudding with praline parfait
Strawberry, pistachio and blackcurrant mille-feuille
Warm fig financier with whipped mascarpone and port (baked to order)
Gâteau Basque with blueberry compote, yoghurt sorbet and lemon curd
Baked cheesecake with apple & cinnamon doughnuts, crème Normande and blackberries
Sour cherry stracciatella ice cream or lychee sorbet
Gorgonzola dolce with pickled cherries, walnuts and rosemary
Cheeses from the board (+£6.00)

£47.50 for three courses

Coffee: £3.95, Mineral water: £3.95 (75cl btl.)
A discretionary gratuity of 12.5% will be added to the total bill.

Whilst we will do all we can to accommodate guests with food intolerances and allergies, we are unable to guarantee that dishes will be completely allergen-free

Please note our game dishes may contain shot.

RENÉ REDZEPI

NOMA

René Redzepi chose to meet at what sounded, to me at least, like a not-very-Danish rendezvous, a taco stand in Torvehallerne, a series of modern glass food stalls and shops in the centre of Copenhagen. But in the end, everything about it and what followed over the next two hours proved to be distinctly Danish.

The stand, Hija de Sanchez, belongs to Rosio Sanchez, who cooked at Noma for five years. Well fed, Redzepi bundled me into the children-carrier on the front of his bicycle and then pedalled me 15 minutes across town to his home, a five-minute walk from the restaurant. My lasting image of Redzepi is of him starting to prepare an organic roast chicken supper around his kitchen table for his wife Nadine and their three blonde daughters.

In between we talked Noma non-stop. Of how, at 38 years old when we spoke, he has spent almost half his life cooking. Of how, during its 13 years, the restaurant has never made a loss but has never made a gross profit of more than six per cent on turnover whereas most restaurants with Noma's reputation would expect to make ten per cent. Of how he does not want to cook at a different quality level to the one he has already established. Of how he would like to generate more profitability to reward and to hold on to his team, particularly his restaurant managers who continuously face tempting offers to go and work in hotels. And of how the menu at the new Noma, due to open nearby in spring/summer 2017, will be radically different from those of the past.

With jazz playing softly in the background and autumn sunlight streaming in through the French windows, Redzepi modestly acknowledged his two most significant contributions to the menus of the world. The first is the attention now paid to foraging – a technique he insists many others have practised before him and concedes that it was his doing it at the right time and in an unlikely environment that captured the world's attention and imagination. The second, and perhaps even more significant, is the idea of using past methods

of preservation – fermentation, drying and storing – as the building blocks of today's menus. Both these approaches feature on so many menus around the world today and, he added with pride and pleasure, seem to be here to stay.

I asked him how, after Noma's weekly closure on Sunday and Monday, its chefs would be preparing for Tuesday's service, when the maximum 40 covers would be occupied at both lunch and dinner, and they would be serving 20 courses to each diner, a total of 1,600 dishes. 'We started planning these menus last week and they will have been finalised by Saturday lunch. There is a team in the kitchen preparing the ingredients today (Monday), even though we are closed, and a kitchen manager who works to a harvest plan alongside our one full-time forager. Over 99 per cent of what we serve and prepare now comes from within a 70-kilometre radius of the restaurant.'

He continued, 'In an effort to shape our way of cooking, we look to our landscape and delve into our ingredients and culture, hoping to rediscover our history and shape our future.' Landscape and culture are as integral to the menu at Noma as foraging and fermentation, factors that have led to the entire restaurant team decamping for three months, initially to Tokyo in spring 2015 and then to Sydney in spring 2016.

All 87 individuals travelled to Tokyo, over 100 to Sydney (the number boosted by new spouses and more children), with both cities chosen for their very different relevance to culture and to landscape. 'Being in the centre of Tokyo was similar to being in Copenhagen but the food culture there is so very different: their obsession with food, from ramen noodles to a *kaiseki* menu, is so developed, the very opposite of that in Denmark at the moment. In Australia, the attraction is of its role as a melting pot of immigrants, the wildness of its countryside as well as its indigenous ingredients.'

These moves have also stimulated Redzepi's fertile brain into creating what he believes will be even more relevant menus for the new Noma, which will open not that far from its original location, overlooking a lake and, most importantly,

surrounded by a hectare of land on which they will be able to grow and harvest their own ingredients.

He has been focusing on how to break away from an obviously seasonal menu that is constrained by a predictable format of nibbles, fish, and then a meat main course that essentially has to be a crowd-pleaser, and so is pork, chicken, lamb, beef or squab. He began by asking himself 'where in nature does the energy flow?' for these ingredients, and particularly where is this the case in the challenging winter months?

The answer, he realised, lies in the ocean, as it is in winter that the water is at its coldest, the fish are therefore at their fattest and the shellfish at their richest. These ingredients, rather than meat, will dominate Noma's future winter menus. As the world turns green, so will the next seasonal menu, with more raw dishes alongside the cooked ones, more seeds, roots and fruits, more vegetarian dishes. Finally, there is autumn, clearly Redzepi's favourite cooking season, but here again he anticipates creating a new menu, one that concentrates on different interpretations of the wild game that still abound in this part of the world, rather than on a sequence of different, contrasting ingredients.

While philosophically Redzepi has a clear vision for Noma's future menus, he is also growing aware – almost daily – of how increasingly difficult these menus are becoming to write, for three very different reasons, two of which affect all other restaurateurs too.

The first is the customers' use of social media. 'At our first service in Tokyo, the first table arrived 10 minutes early and one of the party had a significant following on Twitter. Within minutes all our dishes were out there and we had lost that WOW element for all those who came subsequently. Fortunately, I still believe that the words on a menu are as critically important in creating the dream as the images.'

The second is how many different menus Redzepi has to write each service to cope with his customers' increasing range of allergies, intolerances and dislikes. 'On Saturday night for our 40 covers we had to write seven or eight different

menus to please everyone. There has been an explosion in what customers are allergic to and this really puts a strain not just on me but on the whole team.'

Finally, there is a very particular and emotional challenge, one that Redzepi has unthinkingly created for himself by making Noma and its menu so exceptional. But this is one challenge, he stressed, that he and his team are happy to rise to.

'About ten times a year, we receive a request from someone saying that they are dying and that one of their final wishes is to eat at Noma. We obviously do our very best to accommodate them. There was one man from Iceland who wanted to eat here but was told even the journey was risky. He came anyway and he had a good time, and after he passed away his family came back here to eat so that they could remember where he had last been so happy. When we hear from the family that this person has passed away but did so with one of their ambitions fulfilled, all of us in the kitchen find this very touching.'

Our conversation ended on a happier note. What has also surprised and delighted Redzepi is how the physical menu at Noma has become totemic for the new millennials who book into the restaurant to celebrate a birthday or an engagement, or to make a marriage proposal. 'They want the menu and they want to keep it with them for the rest of their lives. We are extremely proud of this.'

Malt flatbread and juniper
Moss and cep
Seabuckthorn leather and pickled hip roses
Smoked mussel
Cookie with lardo and currant
Rye bread, chicken skin, lumpfish roe and smoked cheese
Pickled and smoked quails egg
Radish, soil and herbs
Toast, herbs, smoked cod roe and vinegar
Æbleskive

Razor clam and dill
Buttermilk and horseradish

Scallops and beech nut
Watercress and grains

Chestnut and löjrom
Cress and walnut

Langoustine and sol

Onions and chick weed
Onion bouillon and thyme oil

Vintage carrot and truffle

Pickled vegetables and bone marrow

Beef cheek beets and apple

Sheepsmousse and sorrel

Walnut and berries

Øllebrød and skyr

NV Champagne "Terre de Vertus"
Pierre Larmanedier
Vertus

2009 Bourgogne Aligoté
Fanny Sabre
Pommard

2009 Arwen
By Noma
Lillø

2006 Riesling "Steinmassl" Magnum
Fred Loimer
Kamptal

2004 Riesling "Berg Schlossberg" Magnum
Georg Breuer
Rheingau

2008 Côtes du Jura "Margerite" Chardonnay Magnum
Domaine Ganevat
Jura

2006 Saumur Blanc "Brezé"
Clos Rougeard
Saumur

2008 Chambolle-Musigny
Domaine Roumier
Bourgogne

1950 La Mission Haut Brion Magnum

2008 Riesling Spätlese "Wolfer Goldgrube"
Daniel Vollenweider
Mosel

1989 Riesling Beerenauslese "Urziger Würzsgarten"
Karl Erbes
Mosel

RUTH ROGERS

THE RIVER CAFE

Ruth Rogers sat smiling in the sunshine across the table from me on the terrace of the River Cafe in Hammersmith, west London. Thirty years earlier, with her partner, the late Rose Grey, she laid down the culinary model for what has proved to be a highly distinctive and successful restaurant.

On the table between us lay a thick, well-thumbed chef's diary, whose cover had worn away, that contained lists of ingredients and suppliers with large ticks through them in pink, light green and blue ink. There were also two thinner, dark blue folders on the table and next to them, most importantly, was that lunchtime's menu that had just been printed in the office upstairs. Rogers pushed her empty espresso cup to one side, threw a sachet of sugar next to the menu, and looked up at me before adding, 'That, I hope, encapsulates the style of what we have always hoped this restaurant will be.'

It is a particularly uncluttered and unchanged style, as far as the menu is concerned. For its first 10 years the menu was handwritten for every service by the manager on a smaller, square piece of paper. When the restaurant became so much busier (its roots were originally as a staff canteen rather than a commercial business) the restaurant switched to an A4 sheet, printed on both sides, using a font that many believe is still based on someone's handwriting. The menu is a flimsy, insubstantial piece of paper, stylistically in keeping with the paper tablecloths, and it probably constitutes the menu where the difference between its cost of production and the menu prices on display is most extreme (first courses hover around £20, main courses around £40).

But this simplicity belies this menu's effectiveness on two very different fronts. The first is how easily anything can be added into the sales mix. This ranges from a summer cocktail, to the details of how many the private dining room can seat, to the publication of a new River Cafe cookbook, to the proposal of a plate of their extremely moreish *zucchini fritti* with the main course.

Rogers said she couldn't remember whether it was from New York restaurateur André Balazs or Danny Meyer that she had first learnt quite how irresistible customers find anything advertised in the top right-hand corner of any menu, before adding that she has always been extremely grateful for such advice.

The simplicity and directness of this menu also mean that the two founders' original goals have never had to be compromised. 'From the outset,' Rogers explained, 'we always thought of our menu as the welcome, an incarnation of the pleasures to come. It is in essence a letter to our customers. Here we are, we want to take care of you and these are the ingredients about which we are most excited today.'

Then continuing with typical female insight, she added, 'The menu has to be a combination of information and restraint: this is the main ingredient and what will be served alongside it, with due emphasis given to the vegetables, the right-hand side of any dish. But there must never be too much detail, nothing that smacks of "let me introduce you to the carrot" or means that our customers' conversations need to be unnecessarily interrupted. Every time I come back from Italy it is with the feeling that we still put too many ingredients on the plate.'

Softly spoken but resolute (and a Jewish mother and grandmother who asked me twice during our interview whether I wanted something to eat), Rogers continued, 'And I think it would be the scariest thing for me to ever have to do, or even to have to watch any chef having to write the menu on their own. I need at least a couple of chefs by my side to finish the writing process. They provide the sounding board, the dialogue and so much of the input.'

These sentiments are the connection between the menu and the chef's diary, which the customers never see, and the clock projected on to the far wall of the kitchen behind the wood-fired oven which no customer can miss as they move past the bar and into the dining room.

At the River Cafe no menu lasts more than one service. At the end of the lunch service the staff finish off any food that is left over and the cooks begin

again, with inspiration for the dinner menu resting with the chef in charge, following collaboration with the team.

As a result, the same main ingredients can appear in two completely different forms at lunch and dinner, as Rogers has experienced herself. 'I was working one lunch and we cooked the turbot from Dorset in the wood-burning oven and served it with capers, marjoram, anchovies and braised yellow beans. It was so good, I recommended it to the Mexican friends we were entertaining here for dinner that night without paying close attention to the menu. When it arrived it was completely different, it had been baked in salt because that is how Danny, the Head Chef on duty that night, had chosen to cook it when he came into work at 3pm.'

This approach means they have to keep track of what their suppliers are offering and have to ensure that, particularly for the chef on duty in the morning, a record is kept in this diary of what will be coming in and what has to be immediately incorporated on to the next menu. It involves a lot of creative independence that explains, in turn, why so many chefs stay here for so long; why the gross food margins are lower than normal here despite the menu prices; and why the whole system relies on the clock, an unusual feature in any restaurant, and one that was part of the original £25,000 investment in the nascent restaurant.

Because the menus change every service, it has never been possible to justify a computer-based programme for processing the orders between the waiting staff and the kitchen, which is the norm elsewhere. Instead, the waiters hand their orders to the kitchen and write down the time as they do so, working on the basis of a maximum of 10 minutes for the first course to be served once the order is taken and 20 for the main course once the first course has been cleared. Here, it would appear, the old systems are still the best.

The River Café

Monday 7th December – Lunch
Antipasti

Puntarelle alla Romana £20

Calamari ai ferri – chargrilled squid with fresh red chilli & rocket £21

Mozzarella di Bufala – with grilled Violino pumpkin, black olives and
leaves from the Milan market £20

Culatello di Zibello – with chicken liver & Vecchia Romagna crostino £25

Capesante in padella – seared Scottish scallops with Castelluccio lentils,
fresh chilli, parsley & red wine vinegar £21

**Carne Cruda – finely chopped beef fillet with mâche & Parmesan £22

Pizzetta – with Taleggio, radicchio, thyme and 2g white Truffle £44

Primi

**Zuppa – pumpkin, chestnut & faro soup with pancetta and rosemary £18

Risotto Nero – with Cuttlefish cooked in its ink & Pieropan Soave Classico £20

Taglierini al Pomodoro – fresh fine pasta with slow-cooked tomato £20

Ravioli – with buffalo ricotta & spinach, sage butter and Parmesan £20

Rigatoni – with pheasant & duck slow-cooked in Cortona Vin Santo £21

Taglierini Bianchi con Tartufo Bianco 5g £75 or 10g £135

Secondi

Sogliola al forno – whole Dover Sole wood-roasted with fresh marjoram
with cicoria and whole artichokes with breadcrumbs £40

Branzino in cartoccio – wild Sea Bass baked in a bag with trevise & vermouth
with braised Swiss chard and coco blanc £40

Coda di Rospo ai ferri – chargrilled Cornish Monkfish with cima di rape
and anchovy & rosemary sauce £38

Coscia d'Agnello ai ferri – chargrilled leg of Lamb with large leaf rocket,
Florence fennel 'parmigiani' and fresh horseradish £38

Piccione al forno – whole Anjou pigeon wood-roasted on a Fontodi Chianti
bruschetta with Lardo and Cavolo Nero £38

Costoletta di Vitello al forno – roast thick-cut Veal chop with lemon & sage,
Tuscan roast potatoes and salsa verde £40

The River Cafe has a
Private Dining Room
For up to 18 people

Gelati del River Cafe
Caramel
Roasted Almond
Hazelnut
Stracciatella
Sicilian Orange & Campari Sorbet
Selection of 2 Ice Creams £8
Selection of 3 Ice Creams £12
Affogato with: Grappa £14 Vin Santo £16 or Espresso £10

Dolci £10
Chocolate Nemesis
Lemon Tart
Pear & Almond Tart
Hazelnut & Espresso Cake
Pannacotta with Grappa & Pomegranate
River Cafe Panettone with a glass of Selvapiana Vin Santo £18

Formaggi - from our Cheese Room
Caprino Fresco – fresh, goats milk, Piemonte
Alto But Vecchio – cow's milk cheese, Lombardia
Pecorino Sardo D.O.P – pasteurised sheep's milk, Sardegna
Castellino Caciotta – unpasteurised cow's milk, washed rind, Veneto
Blu di Bufala – unpasteurised blue buffalo milk, Lombardia
Selection of 3 cheeses £13 Or 5 cheeses £23

Wine suggestions for Cheese:
Sweet: Recioto della Valpolicella, Allegrini 2010 £15
White: Verdicchio dei Castelli di Jesi, Riserva, Bucci 2012 £17
Red: La Serre Nuove, Tenuta dell'Ornellaia £19

CHAPTER

4

THE EVER-EXPANDING MENU

In outline, at least, today's menu has barely changed from that which first emerged in Paris over 200 years ago.

It is a single piece of paper with a list of dishes and prices, a bill of fare. And while the style of cooking has changed considerably, the biggest single change has been the figures down the right-hand side of the menu – the prices that are charged today for dinner would in certain instances be enough to buy an entire 19th-century restaurant with change to spare.

Even in its contents, not that much has changed. I don't believe it would take too long for one of the more revered chefs of yore – Auguste Escoffier or Alexis Soyer, for example – to understand how today's chefs write their menus and to appreciate the combination of flavours they work so hard to create for their customers' pleasure.

And yet over the past five years, there has been significant change, not so much in the menu's overall contents but rather in the make-up of its constituent parts. Today, menus proliferate more than ever before as they become more specialised, more focused on how the customer uses any restaurant at different times of the day and for many different purposes.

This chapter focuses on four different styles of menu, three of which have

emerged only recently: the breakfast/brunch menu, the afternoon tea menu and the cocktail menu. The fourth, the separate dessert menu, is more a matter of the restaurateur's choice, taste and style but one I very much appreciate. As a restaurateur in the 1980s I implemented a separate dessert menu initially for purely personal reasons: as a customer, I much prefer to contemplate my choice of dessert without having to look again at the list of starters and main courses. I quickly appreciated its commercial advantages: it not only boosted sales of desserts and glasses of dessert wine but it also encouraged those in the pastry section, who, by virtue of having their own menu, now stood on a more equal footing with the rest of the kitchen. And perhaps the essential secret of being a successful restaurateur is to look after your staff so that they can, in turn, look after your customers.

The emergence of the other three menus – breakfast/brunch, afternoon tea and cocktail – reflects more the changing rhythms of our working lives and of how we use restaurants. Ten years ago breakfast meetings mainly took place in the US; afternoon tea was only served in the stuffy grandeur of a hotel; and cocktails were far more limited in their range, style and flavour patterns.

These four styles of menu constitute the hitherto unexplored regions of the genre where considerable innovation has been made. Far more, I believe, will follow.

THE BREAKFAST & BRUNCH MENU

Of all the menus currently on offer, the breakfast/brunch menu is without a doubt the fastest growing of them all and probably the one read and enjoyed by more customers than any other.

More restaurants are now opening for breakfast, and serving brunch at the weekends, to take advantage of their customers' changing working lives and habits. More and more customers now enjoy what can best be described as a 'menu of convenience', one that both sides benefit from (except perhaps for those who have to get up even earlier to prepare and cook them) but that neither side excessively profits from.

Prices on these menus have to be reasonable because they are by and large offering the kind of dishes we can all cook at home and whose raw ingredients we all know the cost of. There is very little alcohol sold, other than a jug of Bloody Mary at the weekend with the papers, so the average spend is low – even lower than that at afternoon tea. And most working breakfasts last no more than 45 minutes. If longer than this, it usually means that the service has been so slow the customer is unlikely to return. Breakfast/brunch, unlike lunch or dinner, is invariably a one-course affair.

For any restaurant of size to be busy at breakfast, three different aspects of its location need to align. The first two – proximity to public transport and to an office hub – are obvious and by far the most important, so that customers do not have to take too long to arrive at their breakfast meetings before 8am and so they can be en route to their desks before 9am. The final factor, proximity to hotels, is a luxury but nevertheless a welcome one for the restaurateur, as this can provide a further source of customers for the early morning breakfast meeting as well as a second wave of business somewhat later. It is interesting to note that less than a generation ago, breakfast meetings only used to take place in hotels, a business they kissed goodbye to when their management accountants forced them to replace their à la carte waiter service with the invariably disappointing and dreary 'breakfast buffet'.

From a purely financial perspective, this was probably a correct strategy. To succeed, a breakfast/brunch menu has to be a high volume/low margin affair, and the biggest challenge for any restaurateur – even those blessed with the best of locations – is labour, as Terry Coughlin, Managing Partner of Maialino (where my wife is addicted to the caramelised brioche for her breakfast) and Marta restaurants in New York, explained. Both of these restaurants are on the ground floor of stylish hotels and close to offices and the subway, yet running the breakfast service is not easy.

'During a busy breakfast shift, you can do a similar number of covers as at a busy dinner, and to provide a great service experience you need to staff the restaurant with a generous amount of bodies. The issue is that the average bill is so much lower at breakfast that it really impacts your overall labour numbers in a negative way.' And Coughlin continued that a waiter at breakfast will probably have to work even harder than at dinner but earn a lower tip. In the evening, a customer will order a cocktail or a glass of wine and they are usually more than happy to wait two or three minutes for that drink to hit the table. At breakfast when a customer orders a coffee, they want that cup to be touching their lips within 45 seconds. That is why in diner-style restaurants, the cups are pre-set and the waitress will greet the customer with a pot of coffee in hand. Customers expect their food at breakfast, because it is seemingly less complicated, to come out of the kitchen much faster than at lunch or dinner. Customers start to get very anxious for their breakfast if they have to wait more than eight minutes, in Coughlin's experience.

Examples cited by two chefs, Jonathan Arana-Morton and Miles Kirby – who have both made their breakfast/brunch menus so successful in London over the past five years – reveal how these menus are now not only deeply entrenched in our way of life, and work, but also how they reflect the somewhat more sensitive mood we are in at this early time of the day.

Arana-Morton opened the initial The Breakfast Club, with its bright, egg-yolk yellow frontage in Soho five years ago, and there are now half a dozen

branches around the capital. He is the first to admit that his food is not 'rocket science' (one reason that they have struggled to come up with enough recipes for a cookbook, he confessed). And at the beginning he was very concerned about price and possible comparisons with the nearby 'greasy spoon' cafés that have been around for years – but this concern was overcome by adopting a policy of offering a higher quality of ingredients in both the food and drink to minimise any price discrepancy.

But what the popularity of the various Breakfast Clubs has revealed is how differently we use the breakfast/brunch menu during the week. Any place needs what he refers to as Monday–Thursday dishes, ones that are fairly guilt-free so that we can get on with our work afterwards. The champion of all these at his restaurants is their version of avocado on toast which incorporates lime, fresh red chillis and a poached egg.

Breakfast/brunch on a Friday is a different matter as this menu takes on the role of a hangover cure after a Thursday night, the night that is the busiest night of the week for London's restaurants, bars and clubs (London loves a Thursday night, he was delighted to report). No other meal has such a close association with a possible medical cure and it is to take advantage of this that his customers keep his tables full for breakfast/brunch on Fridays.

Then there is the weekend, when, in his experience, this meal takes on another distinct aspect. 'Everyone is aware that they are more than capable of cooking eggs, making toast and coffee and squeezing a few oranges. But brunch at the weekend has come to represent free time and customers seem more than happy to let us get on and do all that for them and pay us for the pleasure.'

Yet because the psychology of how we feel early in the morning is so varied and so complex, it is perhaps not surprising that it has been an Australian and a New Zealander chef who have had such a singular impact on these particular menus. After all, if the sun is shining at 8am, as it invariably is Down Under, then there is a reasonable chance we will all be in a better mood for the rest of the day.

Miles Kirby is the New Zealander chef at Caravan, King's Cross, which has achieved great success with breakfast/brunch, serving up to 200 most weekday mornings and 600 between 10am and 4pm at the weekend, as a result of its location, its excellent coffee and its menu. The latter incorporates my particular favourite breakfast dish, coconut bread with lemon curd, the recipe for which he first came across when he used to visit a Pacific Island market in Wellington as a child with his mother.

Kirby was quick to outline the limits any chef has for manoeuvre within a breakfast menu. Firstly, such is demand and the need for speed, that while the fashion for small plates now appears all-pervasive, this style of service would be what he described as 'professional suicide at breakfast'. Then because we all seem to be creatures of habit at this time of day, the brunch menu can be changed far less frequently than other menus. There has been public outcry and virtual hate mail at Caravan when certain dishes have been withdrawn; and it is somewhat disappointing for any ambitious chef that – despite everything that has seemingly changed in our approach to our food, our diet and our well-being – the most popular breakfast/brunch dish still remains 'the fry up', that plateful of eggs, sausage, bacon, tomatoes and the rest.

And because the kitchen is dealing with dishes with which customers have grown up, the breakfast chef faces issues none of his colleagues would come across at lunch or dinner. 'Nobody likes their granola like they like their mother's, it would appear,' Kirby commented drily, 'and we have actually had customers bring in their mother's recipe and ask that my chefs prepare that version instead.'

Kirby's experience of cooking breakfast and brunch for an average of 2,000 a week has also led him to the conclusion that this number is split into two different types of customer: those who want to be there and those who have been dragged along by people who want to be there. And, as Coughlin would confirm, what they have in common is that they are generally desperate for food and coffee and if either are not delivered immediately, there may be tears. Breakfast/brunch customers, unlike those the rest of the day, are often tired, hungry and in a hurry

to be somewhere else. The particular consequences of this customer profile are twofold, in his experience. 'Firstly, if we do not deliver, we risk really upsetting them, and secondly, brunch customers, particularly at the weekend, are the most indecisive of all those we deal with. The waiters have to keep going back to their table to get their order far more often than they do at lunch or dinner.'

And yet a successful, invigorating and slightly unusual breakfast/brunch menu can sow the seeds for the future success of the restaurant in one particular way that no other menu at any other time of the day can match. That is not my opinion but that of Australian Bill Granger, who has scrambled more eggs to greater good fortune than anyone else via his 15 cafes that currently stretch from Australia to Japan, South Korea, Hawaii and the United Kingdom. His restaurants use 3 million eggs a year and his ricotta pancakes have become such a success in Japan that they've been turned into a key ring.

This is all because of the very specific commercial role these menus play and the fact that we are all creatures of habit. It is Granger's belief that most people only really have five or six favourite restaurants: those that they come to rely on and return to regularly for business, to socialise, to impress and to have fun in. And those restaurants that are open and are busy for breakfast have an opportunity to win these customers over in a way that other restaurants whose menus only begin with lunch simply cannot match. 'This is the message I impress on my teams all over the world,' Granger explained. 'Look after our customers as well as you can first thing in the morning and they will return as loyal customers at lunch and dinner.'

To help in this process, Granger also stressed quite how clear and easy to navigate the design of the breakfast menu has to be, and in this he attributed great credit to Mary Libro, its designer and fellow Australian.

The inspiration for her design came initially from stripping back the old, tried-and-trusted diner menu and then refining that – a process that led to a design that feels comfortable, something that a customer will feel he has seen before but not in such an elegant fashion. It says that the restaurant is established,

trusted and classic but simultaneously simple and contemporary.

Then it is all about directing the customer to what they need as swiftly as possible. The healthy dishes are separated out at the top right of the page. If you are fighting a hangover – for which the breakfast menu is a universal remedy, it would appear – then you would avoid that section and cast your eye immediately down to 'Big Plates' or 'Bill's Classics'. The drinks section takes up the left-hand side of the page, with the cross shape for a cold, hydrating smoothie or juice, and the round cup rim shape for what she described as the hot fuel, coffee or tea. Overall, Libro hopes the approach is quiet yet strong, and communicates efficiently in a clear voice with a contemporary style. The success of Granger & Co. in the UK (*page 133*) and its sister restaurants, which trade under the name of Bill's in the rest of the world, appear to be a testament to that.

But as these breakfast/brunch menus proliferate seemingly to everyone's benefit, their ubiquity is also testimony to a bigger social change than even the more expensive, more rarefied, more elaborate and more luxurious menus now available at lunch or in the evening exemplify.

Until perhaps as little as a decade ago, what we ate for breakfast was a symbol of national character and represented a fundamental difference in our eating habits. Scots ate kippers and porridge; the French dunked croissants in their coffee sitting at a table; the Italians stood at the counter drinking an espresso and eating a piece of cake, at most; the English tucked into a 'Full Monty'; the Chinese had a variety of different-flavoured congee; while the Japanese ate a breakfast predominantly based on fish and rice that can still challenge even the most adventurous Western palate.

Today, these dishes seem to have become harder to find. More and more of us enjoy bacon, scrambled eggs, pancakes and waffles, croissants and toast with our morning cappuccino. The ubiquity of the breakfast/brunch menu is another representation of the globalisation process under way in so many other different forms, albeit one writ relatively small.

GRANGER
&Co.

BREAKFAST UNTIL 12PM

JUICES & SMOOTHIES

freshly squeezed orange juice 3.30

bill's greens - green apple,
cucumber, ginger, silver beet, chia
& coconut water 4.80

bill's beets - beetroot,
carrot, fennel & apple 4.80

bill's raw - almond milk, lsa, raw cacao,
banana & honey 4.80

pineapple, kale, coconut water & coriander 5.20

COLD DRINKS

homemade lemonade - hibiscus & lime soda
- elderflower cordial 3.50

watermelon & lime frappé 4.50

acai & raspberry frappe 5.00

iced oolong tea 4.20

iced allpress cold drip 3.50
(with or without milk)

espresso & avocado frappé 5.00

FROM 8AM

white peach bellini 9.50

bill's spiced bloody mary - clamato,
wasabi, lime & coriander 9.00

billecart-salmon brut reserve
nv champagne 13.00

HOT DRINKS

coffee by allpress espresso 2.80
(soy or double .60)

tea by rare tea company
breakfast, afternoon, chamomile,
rooibos, rosehip 3.00
jasmine silver tip, china green leaf,
cornish earl grey, chai, lemon verbena,
lemongrass, genmai 3.50

fresh mint tea 2.50

bill's hot chocolate 3.50

FRUIT & GRAINS

red fruit bowl, greek yoghurt 8.00

almond milk chia seed pot,
berries, pomegranate
& coconut yoghurt 5.00

bircher muesli, granny smith apple,
medjool date and almonds 6.75

bill's granola, coconut yoghurt
& fruit compote 7.50

BAKERY
DAILY SCONES, BUNS, MUFFINS & TRAY BAKES

toasted coconut bread, butter 4.50

st john's organic sourdough, rye toast
or our brioche with marmalade, jam,
vegemite, honey or almond butter 3.50

toasted rye, avocado, lime & coriander 6.75
+ poached egg 2.00

jasmine tea smoked salmon, cream cheese, dill,
pea shoots, edamame and toasted rye 12.00

chilli fried egg & bacon brioche roll,
spiced mango chutney & rocket 8.00

BILL'S CLASSICS

ricotta hotcakes, banana & honeycomb butter 11.80

sweet corn fritters, roast tomato,
spinach & bacon 13.50

fresh aussie - tea smoked salmon, poached eggs,
greens, avocado & cherry tomatoes 13.80

scrambled eggs & sourdough toast 8.20

EGGS & SIDES

two sunny fried, poached or soft boiled eggs,
sourdough toast 6.00

avocado - avocado salsa - wild greens - kim chee
- cremini mushrooms - roast tomato 2.80
chorizo - grilled ashdale bacon 3.80
jasmine tea smoked salmon 4.80
rose harissa 2.80

BIG PLATES

bone broth, wild greens, poached egg,
fennel kraut, pickles & kelp noodles 11.50

buckwheat bowl, poached egg, kefir goats milk,
rose harissa, avocado & alfalfa sprouts 11.00

chicken fat fried rice - raw vegetables,
brown rice, arame, pickles,
chilli fried egg & sprouting seeds 12.50

• a discretionary service charge of 12.5% applies to each bill •

please inform your waiter if you are allergic to any food items
before you order - we cannot guarantee the absence of allergens in our
dishes, due to being produced in a kitchen that contains allergens.

From our Kitchen

Crowe's Rashers
Jack McCarthy's Sausages 9, 11
Mushrooms and Tomatoes 2
Roscarbery Black and White Pudding 8, 11, 13
Ballymaloe Free Range Eggs – Boiled, Poached, Scrambled or Fried 1, 2

~

Seasonal Omelette 1, 2

~

Crêpes with Sugar & Lemon 1, 2

~

Sally Barnes' Kippers

~

Fresh Fish from Ballycotton when available 2

~

Fresh Herbal Teas when available – Mint, Lemon Verbena, Lemon Balm

~

Green Tea
Barry's Breakfast Tea
Earl Grey Tea
Coffee*

1 Eggs	9 Sulphur dioxyde	
2 Milk	11 Cereals containing gluten	
8 Soya	13 Mustard	

*Our coffee comes from The Golden Bean coffee roaster on the farm. The beans come from single estates in South America.

Ballymaloe, Shanagarry, Ireland

This merely for the breakfast dishes that emanate from the kitchen, just in case the groaning buffet of poached fruits, porridge made from Macroom oats, and fresh Irish sourdough bread and jams are not sufficient. Note the hen on the right.

CECCONI'S

BREAKFAST

Coffee	Tea	Juice	Smoothie
£2.50	£2.50	£3.50	£5.00
Espresso	English Breakfast	Orange	Passion fruit
Cappucino	Peppermint	Pink Grapefruit	Blackberry
Caffelatte	Fresh mint	Apple	Strawberry
Americano	Assam	Pineapple	Banana
Mocha	Darjeeling	Carrot & Ginger	Pear
Hot Chocolate	Lapsang Souchong	Pear	Raspberry

Pastries	each £3	Egg white omelette	£5
Wheat free toast, soya spread	£4	Granola with mixed berries, natural yoghurt & honey	£6
Cereals & muesli	£4		
All bran, skimmed milk	£4	Porridge with banana	£6
Wheat free muesli	£4	Seasonal fruit with natural yoghurt	£7
Pancake with strawberries & almonds	£7	French toast with mixed berries	£8
Bacon sandwich	£7	Black truffle scrambled eggs	£10
Pan toasted tomato & fontina sandwich	£7	Smoked salmon & scrambled eggs	£11
Mushroom or ham & cheese omelette	£8	Eggs any style with cumberland sausage, streaky bacon, mushrooms, roast tomatoes & toast	£12
Eggs Benedict/Florentine/Royale	£9		

There is a discretionary 12.5% service charge added to your bill
All of the above prices are inclusive of VAT

Cecconi's, London

A very different breakfast menu aimed at a clientele of businessmen and women in a hurry and watching their weight. Note the coffee top left and a long list of non-fattening ingredients such as soya spread, skimmed milk and an egg white omelette.

THE AFTERNOON TEA MENU

The afternoon tea menu is proliferating. The website www.afternoontea.co.uk lists over 250 different places in central London alone that offer this very British mixture of sweet and savoury, a number that seems set to increase.

For customers, still predominantly female, there are a wide variety of reasons to indulge in an afternoon tea. It can provide a restful interlude while shopping, a sense of occasion, a celebration, the thrill of a guilty pleasure, or just an excuse for a good gossip.

Afternoon tea appeals to anyone with a sweet tooth, and the popularity of *The Great British Bake Off*, and the many other TV baking programmes it has spawned, suggests that means almost everyone. The consequence of all these factors is that today afternoon tea has become a mealtime in its own right, something that many will miss lunch for and which some see as an alternative to dinner.

It is equally attractive to restaurateurs and hoteliers, for whom the afternoon tea service now provides a healthy financial fillip to what used to be the quiet trading period between lunch and dinner. And it appeals to many with the long-cherished idea of opening a café or restaurant who believe that this seemingly uncomplicated menu – one that can, after all, be quite successfully reproduced in a domestic kitchen – provides the easiest route to fulfilling their dreams.

This is not, in fact, the reality, and to learn about the harsh facts that lie behind the compilation of a top-class afternoon tea menu, I went to meet ace pastry chef Claire Clark. Our rendezvous took place in the highly unromantic setting of her production kitchen, two floors below ground in a modern, anonymous building – albeit in a very British location, 200 metres from Westminster Abbey.

Clark has honed her skills with a rolling pin over more than 30 years. During that period she has written numerous afternoon tea menus; she worked as the Head Pastry Chef for The French Laundry in California for five years; she has been awarded an MBE for her commitment to her craft; and she most recently

appeared as one of the three judges on *Bake Off: The Professionals*. With her partner and fellow pastry chef Sarah Crouchman, Clark launched Pretty Sweet, a high-end patisserie catering service in 2014.

Such is the demand for what they produce that instant success has followed, and as I waited for Clark in a spotless kitchen full of the tools of her trade – whisks, mixers and plastic tubs full of chocolate, sea salt flakes, mini marshmallows, chocolate and gluten-free flour – I could begin to appreciate the essential discrepancy between the large, cool spaces required to produce the ingredients for an afternoon tea menu and the intimate, plush surroundings in which so many are enjoyed. This subterranean kitchen, devoid of any natural light, provides the patisserie for the afternoon teas in the Georgian Room at Harrods and the cakes for those attending the annual garden parties on the lawns of Buckingham Palace.

Clark arrived, clutching a symbolic mug of tea, and began to talk passionately about the menu that has brought her so much renown and her customers so much pleasure, although, regrettably, she rarely meets them face-to-face.

'The afternoon tea menu is essentially a very simple affair,' she began. 'It's three items: a scone, a sandwich or a savoury item, and a cake. The scone, that has to be fluffy inside and crisp on the outside, is, in effect, simply a vessel for the jam and the cream. The bread for the sandwiches has to be moist and the filling must not be too dry either. The cakes have got to be enticing but not overly sweet because the menu has to be in balance. The best afternoon tea menus are more than the sum of their constituent parts, rather than a preponderance of either the sweet or the savoury. A good afternoon tea menu must have this trinity of ingredients in equal balance.'

Clark acknowledges that there is plenty of scope for initiative, in terms of texture, flavour and presentation, but that there has been a tendency to overcomplicate this menu recently, a tendency that she would like to see reversed. Acquiring and reproducing the classic, basic skills are the essential tools, in her opinion.

This is particularly the case with the afternoon tea menu because so many of its key elements are very different from those required to produce a lunch or dinner menu.

Firstly, everyone agrees that pastry chefs are very different from other chefs. In Clark's opinion, they are more experimental, linear and methodical, and they are perfectionists who hate any last-minute changes. They are often considered to be the kitchen's equivalent of goalkeepers in a soccer team: indispensable, perhaps unpredictable, but capable of great things.

Secondly, and most importantly, they require very different working conditions: lots of cool space away from the heat of the main kitchen. This is the main logistical challenge facing anyone aspiring to specialise in afternoon teas. A production kitchen soon becomes essential but it is usually only affordable in an industrial unit quite a distance from where the tea is served. Fortunately, scones, quiches and cakes are light and, when well packaged, easily transportable – while the small, extra additions such as the petals and the delicate cake toppings are freeze-dried and wrapped separately in bubble wrap so that the whole cake can be assembled before service. Just as flour, water and sugar seem to combine magically to produce the most delicious cakes, so too there is a certain amount of illusion in the service of the afternoon tea menu. While the host and the customer would like to believe that the cakes and scones are the creation of a series of talented pastry cooks working away on the other side of the swing door, this is rarely the case today.

Instead, Clark works in a highly specialised market that, while growing so rapidly, is also developing along very particular lines.

The first, and most pronounced, is the increasing emphasis on ingredients for the afternoon tea menu that are gluten-, dairy- and nut-free as well as vegan. 'This is the biggest expanding sector of the market, and in certain respects I absolutely welcome this because, as a pastry chef, I just love mastering the science to make it happen, the challenge of it all. But as a businesswoman trying to protect my gross profits, it is an enormous challenge because all these alternative ingredients,

such as coconut flour, coconut blossom sugar and egg replacers, are currently so much more expensive than the ingredients we have normally used. And gross profits do vary considerably anyway. You have to make sure there is a decent margin on the scones, for example, to compensate for the more complicated and expensive cakes. And once you become busy there is a natural tendency to want to use more expensive ingredients, particularly chocolate. You have to be very self-restrained because we can only charge so much.'

Demand for afternoon tea has its own particular rhythm, too. The busiest days are not surprisingly Friday to Sunday, with Monday to Wednesday often only half as busy, but recently Clark has seen a big rise in demand on Thursdays. This, she believes, could be due to the increasingly common practice in London of 'business afternoon teas' held by companies in restaurants and hotels where what is not enjoyed *in situ* is then taken home.

Clark is inevitably extremely fussy when it comes to recommending anywhere for afternoon tea but her recent experience at Fortnum & Mason had left her very happy, not just because of what she ate but also because it reveals how flexible the afternoon tea menu has become. Here afternoon tea comprises three menus in total: a traditional menu, a savoury menu with more unusual dishes, such as lobster bisque and Omelette Arnold Bennett, and a separate à la carte menu.

Clark argues that this is an example of why the afternoon tea menu remains a source of pleasure for the customer and the pastry chef – and constitutes a menu that has yet to be fully explored.

Menu

Tea Salon
FORTNUM & MASON

Fortnum's High Tea

A CHOICE OF:

Smoked Haddock Kedgeree, Quails Egg & Curry Mayonnaise

OR

Eggs Royale, Benedict, Florentine

OR

Lobster Omelette Victoria, Lobster Bisque & Truffle

OR

Beef Wellington (please allow 20 min)

OR

Welsh Rarebit, Oven Dried Tomato & Caramelised Shallots

OR

Scotch Egg with Mango Chutney

OR

Spinach & Ricotta Pithivier, Beurre Blanc

FORTNUM'S SCONES

Plain & Fruit Scones

Presented with Somerset Clotted Cream
& a choice of Fortnum & Mason Preserve:

Lemon Curd, Raspberry,
Strawberry, Wild Blueberry

AFTERNOON TEA CAKES

Individual Pâtisserie

Selection from the Cake Carriage

Offered with your choice of:

Fortnum's Classic Blend Tea £46.00 per person

OR

Fortnum's Single Estate Tea £50.00 per person

Fortnum's
Afternoon Tea

FINGER SANDWICHES
Fortnum's Smoked Salmon
Coronation Chicken
Cucumber with Mint & Cream Cheese
Smoked Turkey, Mustard & Honey
Rare Breed Hen's Egg, English Cress

FORTNUM'S SCONES
Plain & Fruit Scones

Presented with Somerset Clotted Cream
& a choice of Fortnum & Mason Preserve:

Lemon Curd, Raspberry,
Strawberry, Wild Blueberry

AFTERNOON TEA CAKES
Individual Pâtisserie
Selection from the Cake Carriage

Offered with your choice of:
Fortnum's Classic Blend Tea £44.00 per person

Fortnum's Single Estate Tea £48.00 per person

Fortnum's Savoury Afternoon Tea

FINGER SANDWICHES

Fortnum's Smoked Salmon

Coronation Chicken

Cucumber, Mint & Cream Cheese

Smoked Turkey, Mustard & Honey

Rare Breed Hen's Egg, English Cress

FORTNUM'S SAVOURY SCONES

Wild Blackberry Scone with Stilton Cream Cheese

Lobster Scone with Brandy Cream Cheese & Caviar

AFTERNOON TEA SAVOURIES

Brown Crab Muffin & White Crab Mayonnaise

Wild Mushroom Turnover

Oeuf Drumkilbo

Smoked Duck on Shortbread, Orange Grand-Marnier Purée

AFTERNOON TEA CAKES

Selection from the Cake Carriage

Offered with your choice of

Fortnum's Classic Blend Tea £46.00 per person

Fortnum's Single Estate Tea £50.00 per person

Fortnum's Vegetarian Afternoon Tea

FINGER SANDWICHES

Cucumber and Mint Butter

Cox's Apple, Celery & Chicory, Blue Cheese Dressing

Grilled Courgettes, Red Onion Marmalade

Rare Breed Hen's Egg, English Cress

Barber's Vintage Cheddar, Tomato Chutney

FORTNUM'S SCONES

Plain & Fruit Scones

Presented with Somerset Clotted Cream
& a choice of Fortnum & Mason Preserve:

Lemon Curd, Raspberry,
Strawberry, Wild Blueberry

AFTERNOON TEA CAKES

Individual Pâtisserie
Selection from the Cake Carriage

Offered with your choice of:
Fortnum's Classic Blend Tea £44.00 per person
OR
Fortnum's Single Estate Tea £48.00 per person

THE DESSERT MENU

The dessert menu presents the chef and the restaurateur with a particular psychological challenge: how best to induce the customer to order.

At lunch, this is an extremely difficult, often impossible, task with time pressure the most immediate inhibitor. As a result, dessert sales can be no more than 20–25 per cent of main course sales. In the evening, desserts are offered when the customer is often well fed, has had more than a little to drink and has one eye on their watch. It is to capitalise on this situation that restaurants now increasingly offer a combination of petits fours with a cup of tea or coffee.

But the correct handling of the dessert menu can bring considerable rewards. Almost everyone has a 'sweet tooth' so the opportunity is ripe for the pastry chefs to impress. As the final course, desserts also represent what will be the customers' parting and, every chef hopes, most long-lasting and favourable impressions of any meal. Handled appropriately, this stage of the meal allows the host to appear magnanimous, while for the restaurant these extra sales can be a significant boost to profits. Finally, the pastry section is inevitably the last to leave the kitchen so it is much better for morale if they can be kept busy.

It was to find the possible solutions to these issues that I sat down one sunny morning across the table from Sally Clarke in her restaurant Clarke's in Notting Hill Gate (*pages 148–149*). For more than 30 years Clarke has been noted for her bread, cakes and patisserie for which she also has a separate bakery nearby with a weekly production of 9,000 kg of bread and 2,000 kg of *viennoiserie*, plus cakes and tarts of the highest standard. But it is her restaurant's desserts that I find impossible to resist, alongside her chocolate truffles, possibly the world's finest (all handmade, rolled and dipped, she confessed, to an unchanging recipe).

As we talked, it became obvious that the creation of a successful dessert menu requires a very different set of skills from those needed to write the rest of the menu.

For 20 years, Clarke followed in the path of her mentor, Alice Waters of Chez Panisse in Berkeley, California, and in the evening only offered a set, four-course

dinner, of which the last two courses were a cheese plate and dessert. This process required her to think about the balance of her menu from the outset.

'This is the aspect of being a chef that I like the most, sitting down early in the morning, writing and styling my menus, ensuring that the balance is correct. There must not be too much cream, too much olive oil, nor too many dishes that require a lot of chewing. Everything has to be thought out carefully and by this I mean not just every comma but the wording of each dessert, whether the ice cream comes before the fruit ingredient or afterwards, where the word madeleine sits. This is all incredibly important because it sets the scene. That's what I most enjoy, as well as answering the phone – it's important that customers hear the voice of la patronne.'

And although there is now a full à la carte menu at Clarke's, it is the experience of writing the set menus that dictates the quantity of what is served towards the end of the meal. The cheese plate must never be too large that it leaves the customer feeling unable to finish either this or the dessert, both of which are included in the price. And Clarke underlined this point by explaining how on certain nights she can come to realise that the pastry section has not sold as many desserts as expected because the senior sous chef in charge of the main courses has been overgenerous with the fish or the meat. If that is the case, customers will simply settle for an espresso and a chocolate truffle.

To entice them further, Clarke explained the most obvious, and perhaps the easiest, path to follow is to cover the whole spectrum of tastes. Over the summer months, when English desserts are at their best, that will mean two bowls of different fruit; one dessert that is light and fresh; something creamy, a posset or a panna cotta; one dessert with nuts and another with chocolate; a tart or cake; and, finally, an ice cream or sorbet. And even in January and February when there is no fresh fruit readily available, there is always inspiration for the pastry chef in the shape of dried fruits, nuts and chocolate.

To get the best from the pastry section and allow it to deliver the best to the customer requires understanding two aspects of this part of the menu – the first

explained by Clarke, the second by Paul Baldwin, her experienced restaurant manager and partner.

The first and universal aspect is that pastry chefs are very different from the other chefs in the kitchen. They like to start work early when the ovens are cool and they can only leave at the very end. And while the rest of the kitchen can often cook by taste and feel, 75 per cent of what any pastry chef produces, according to Clarke, is to strict measurements. Clarke had recently been asked by Meryl Streep (who coincidentally played the food writer Julia Child in the film *Julie and Julia*) after dinner in her restaurant, how many chefs she had met in her 30 years who had been able to cross over from the pastry section to the rest of the kitchen. Clarke can only recall one who managed to do so.

In 2014 there was a significant change in the restaurant's approach when, instead of the desserts being listed on the reverse of the first and main courses, they were put on to a separate sheet of paper. Although more cumbersome and expensive, this is highly preferable, in my opinion, for the customer who is now no longer confronted by a long list of what they could have ordered – and may have been better than what they did.

This new layout has led to a significant boost in sales, Baldwin reported, of both the cheese plate and desserts. The cheeses have always been listed before the desserts to allow the customer to enjoy them with the red wine ordered with their main courses. And because of this layout, a table of two will order a plate of cheese to share before moving on to the sweeter stuff.

Because this dessert menu reads so well, the arrival of a separate, fresh menu allows Baldwin and his team to show it off to best effect. The removal of the main course plates, then the side plates, then the salt and pepper signals almost a fresh start, Baldwin explained. 'Then the dessert menu goes down and it is up to us to judge how long to leave the table to enjoy it. Maybe five minutes, never too long, and it always depends on the size of the table and any signals from the host. Then we can move in and sell a menu that deep down everyone loves. For me, it's the icing on the cake.'

— 147 —

CLARKE'S

CHEESES

Comté, Ragstone and St. James cheeses,
oatmeal biscuits, pickled cherries and celery £ 11

DESSERTS

Glass of *vin d'orange* with 2 Clarke's chocolate truffles £ 9

Bowl of French cherries over ice for the table

Plate of English strawberries with crème fraîche and brown sugar

Soft vanilla meringue with strawberry ripple ice cream
and strawberry sauce

Raspberry and apricot trifle with *crème Anglaise* and sugared almonds

Lemon posset with poached cherries and shortbread

Tiramisu with mascarpone, Marsala and chocolate shavings

Dark chocolate roulade with poached cherries and cream
... All £ 8.50

Monmouth Coffee - Espresso, Americano, Cappuccino, Latte,
pot of Rare Tea Company tea, fresh mint or ginger *tisane*
- all served with dark chocolate truffle £5

CLARKE'S

CHEESES

Cashel Blue, Caerphilly and Ragstone cheeses with
oatmeal biscuits, chutney, celery and radishes £ 11

DESSERTS

Glass of *vin d'orange* with 2 Clarke's chocolate truffles £ 9

Plate of white peaches, purple figs and black grapes

Lemon curd meringue 'bombe' with damson sauce and strawberries

Warm plum and blackberry tart with sugar almonds
and crème Anglaise

Apple Brown Betty with spiced crumbs and cinnamon cream

Baked greengages and purple figs with polenta cake
and vanilla ice cream

Chocolate, raspberry and coconut cake with chocolate sauce
... All £ 8.50

**Monmouth Coffee - Espresso, Americano, Cappuccino, Latte,
pot of Rare Tea Company tea, fresh mint or ginger *tisane*
- all served with dark chocolate truffle £5**

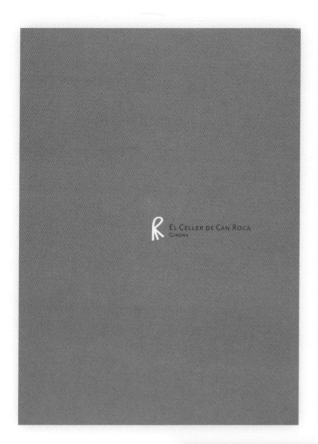

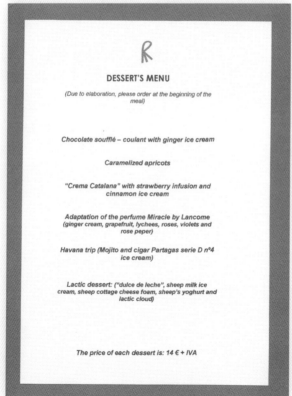

El Celler de Can Roca, Girona, Spain

This restaurant belongs to three brothers, Joan, Josep and Jordi, and it is the latter's pastry menu that is on show here. I can still recall the flavours of the lactic dessert that I ordered.

THE COCKTAIL MENU

Cocktails – whether a caipirinha, a Bloody Mary or just a seemingly straightforward and relatively easy-to-prepare gin and tonic – make a great and colourful start to any meal. And increasingly they play an important role in the success of any restaurant.

This is due in part to cocktails' considerable alcoholic strength (and the late James Thurber's comment that 'one martini is all right, two are too many and three are never enough' is as true today as it ever was) but even more to their broad appeal.

They are easier to understand, as well as more potent, than wine (no names of any grape varieties or foreign words to remember) so immediately delight younger drinkers, while the classic cocktails continue to remain almost a romantic standard for anyone above a certain age. They appeal equally to both sexes. And their impact can be immediate: cocktails generate more emotion per square foot than any other drink.

Appreciating their importance is also vital for a restaurateur in understanding customers' changing drinking habits. Few drink at lunch these days (in my day as a restaurateur it was unusual for a table not to order wine at lunch) but so many are in need of a drink straight after work. This is a time when relatively few customers want to eat, but any initially empty space can be quickly transformed – thanks to the theatrical appeal of an elegant bar, and perhaps even more by the presence of an elegant barman – into a space that will now generate a higher spend and, more importantly, set the tone for the rest of the night. If the first customers only order glasses of house wine, however excellent the quality, then an opportunity has been wasted. Far more inspirational would be a selection of low alcohol cocktails.

That is the considered opinion of Robbie Bargh, who has been devising cocktails, designing bars and acting as a consultant on such matters to hotels and restaurants around the world for the past 20 years. And when I met him to discuss what he refers to today not as 'cocktail lists' but as 'cocktail menus', he was dressed as colourfully as a newly created drink, in a cerise-coloured shirt

and multi-coloured trousers with an elasticated waist that were, he added, highly suitable for getting around London on a bicycle.

This outfit was almost as unusual as the piece of thin wood we were handed at the Artesian Bar in London's Hotel (*page 153*). On the wood were engraved their 19 original cocktails underneath the names of the two barmen, Alex Kratena and Simone Caporale, who are in charge. The theme behind these cocktails (their classic cocktails appear on a more staid piece of paper) was surrealism and in particular a connection to the artist Salvador Dalí, although, in a 21st-century twist, each of these drinks had its own Instagram hashtag.

When our two drinks arrived, their presentation was as striking as that which many must have found confusing in many of the original surrealist artists' paintings. 'Join the Colony' is served in two cups that are placed on the back of a large copper ant, legs splayed, while 'Anti Hero' is served in one cup that takes the place of a mahout above an elephant made of Lego (which the waiter explained can and does go in the dishwasher). Bargh audibly sighed, 'The guys here have gone beyond glasses for their cocktails, they are now into vessels.'

This redefining of the cocktail has been going on for a couple of decades – Bargh cited the late chef Charlie Trotter in Chicago and Ferran Adrià at El Bulli, then Grant Achatz at Alinea, also in Chicago, as the first chefs to appreciate what Bargh refers to as the need for the bar chef and the head chef to work together. This has now become a worldwide phenomenon, best exemplified in the annual bartenders' shindig that now takes place in New Orleans, aptly entitled Tales of the Cocktail (www.talesofthecocktail.com).

Regardless of the location of the bar and its size – and in fact this movement initially set in motion by great chefs in large kitchens is now being embraced by young bartenders and chefs working cheek by jowl in much smaller establishments which Bargh refers to as 'gastrobars' or 'drinking restaurants' – the key ingredient is a much closer collaboration between the bar and the kitchen.

'The kitchen and bar staff need to be talking to the same suppliers, both to be taking advantage of all that is available in the dry stores, the condiments, the

ARTESIAN | Alex Kratena & Simone Caporale

SECONDS BEFORE AWAKENING #FeelingCurious
Mortlach Old Rare, Aquavit, Ylang Ylang, Jasmine, Cypress

SNAKE CHARMER #FeelingAdventurous
Carrot, Sesame, Elderflower, Orange Blossom

SPRING DRIFTING INTO SUMMER #FeelingAwesome
Ketel One, Shochu, Artichoke, Coffee, Yuzu, Passion, Coriander

ANTI HERO #FeelingLikeARockstar
Don Julio Reposado, Muscat, Gentian, Verjus, Smoke, Blood Orange

SUSPENDED IN TIME #FeelingPretty
Star of Bombay, Lime, Niaouli, Yarrow, Palmarosa

JOIN THE COLONY #FeelingExcited
Absolut Elyx, Wheat, Almond, Juniper, Bergamot

FAST MONEY COMES AT A DANGEROUS PRICE
#FeelingSurprised
Johnnie Walker Gold, Chamomile, Vetiver, Sandalwood, Kombucha

NO MORE COLADA! #FeelingSarcastic
Bacardi, Coconut, Pineapple, Cinnamon

DREAMQUEST #FeelingIndulgent
Cashew, Caramel, Dulse, Verjus, Tonka

CHAMELEON CRYSTALS #FeelingAmazing
Tanqueray No Ten, Pisco, Lime, Perilla, Chilli, Soy

YOUR ROOM, OR MINE? #FeelingNaughty
Glenfiddich 15 Year Old, Becherovka, Pineau des Charentes

HEAVEN IS FOR SINNERS #FeelingMischievous
Zacapa 23, Furikake, Pineapple, Mango, Tonka, Saison

YOU'RE SO GANGSTA #FeelingLikeABoss
Grey Goose, Yuzu, Lychee, Ginseng, Juniper, Rose

BEDROOM ESCAPADES #FeelingSexy
Geranium, Sherry, Lime, Coriander, Patchouli, Argan

LAST WISH #FeelingAnxious
Bulleit Rye, Calvados, Armagnac, Amber, Essensia

ALWAYS PRINT THE MYTH #FeelingWitty
Hendrick's, Aquavit, Sherry, Cucumber, Lemon Balm, Cedar

HOW NOT TO BE SEEN #FeelingRelaxed
Martell Cordon Bleu, Caju, Sauvignon Blanc, Agave

MEZCAL PAPARAZZI #FeelingCrazy
Martini Rosso, White Rhino Rye, Mezcal, Leather, Bitter

DEATH OF THE HIPSTER #FeelingSilly
Workshop Coffee, Jasmine, Tonic, Oak Smoke, Elderflower

All cocktails £18. All non alcoholic cocktails £16

All prices are in £ sterling and include VAT.
A discretionary 12.5% service charge will
be added to your bill.

Food allergies and intolerances
If you are allergic or intolerant to any
food or beverage products, please advise
a member of the service team.

The Langham, London
1C Portland Place, Regent Street
London, W1B 1JA

T 44 (0)20 7636 1000
E info@artesian-bar.co.uk
   artesian-bar.co.uk

ARTESIAN | Alex Kratena & Simone Caporale

spices and the dried fruit, so that they can continually innovate. For example, I am extremely excited when I see a Bellini of the day on a brief cocktail menu regardless of the fact that the wonderful white peach is only in season for three weeks of the year. And as long as it is well balanced – with a champagne cocktail, a sour, white and dark spirits – no cocktail menu today has to be longer than the food menu.'

Everyone will benefit, in Bargh's opinion. The customer, most obviously, as the cocktail menu can now be more flexible and adapt to a world that, thanks to climate change, has shorter seasons that change more rapidly than in the past.

And for the restaurateur – to work towards a similar level of understanding and cooperation between the chef and the bartender as significant as that between the chef and the sommelier – it will bring benefits on two fronts. The first and most obvious is what a strong, initial impression can be made, as the cocktail menu is delivered as soon as the customer walks through the door. The second, and more hidden, is the commercial benefit that such an approach can deliver at the end of every month when the management accounts are prepared. A cocktail menu can deliver a gross profit of at least 80 per cent, 10 per cent higher than is the norm for a kitchen or a well-managed wine list.

But – and here for the first time the smile disappeared from Bargh's face – it is in his opinion vitally important that those in charge finally appreciate that the art of bartending depends critically on the discipline of tending the bar. 'The name mixologist is nonsense,' Bargh added, almost interpreting the word as a personal insult. Training is vital, and he swiftly rattled off the most important steps between neophyte and barman: as a barback, learning the layout of the bar, its set-up and how to make the essential syrups; as a drinks runner, having to memorise the contents of each drink, to be able to explain them to the customers face-to-face; as an assistant, learning to control the five essential elements of any cocktail – the glass or increasingly the vessel, the ice, the garnish, the non-alcoholic element, and, of course, the essential (and most costly if wasted) alcohol. Then, finally, comes the graduation to bartender when an appropriate balance has to be struck between creativity, those cocktail combinations waiting to be conceived, and making those classic cocktails that the world seemingly and justifiably will never tire of.

COCKTAILS

Monteleone	30	Vermouth	30
Vieux Carre	40	D'Aquiri	40
Jack Rose	40	West India D'Aquiri	35
Dry Martini	30	Alexander	45
Sweet Martini	30	Ojen	35
Manhattan	30	Clover Leaf	35
Bacardi	40	Stinger	40
Bronx	30	Side Car	45
Brandy	45	Navy	30
Dubonnet	30	Champagne	55
Old Fashion	30	Red Lion	45
President	40	Pink Lady	40
Coffee	40	Creole	30

FIZZES

Plain	30	Silver Fizz	35
Sloe Gin Fizz	35	Golden Fizz	35
New Orleans Fizz	35	Royal Fizz	40

MIXED DRINKS

Gin Rickey	30	Orange Blossom	30
Gin Buck	35	Sloe Gin Rickey	30
Tom Collins	35	Cold Eggnog	40
Rum Collins	40	Sherry Flip	40
Mint Smash	35	Whiskey Toddy	30
Mint Julep	40	Milk Toddy	30
Claret Lemonade	40	Tom & Jerry	40
Brandy Flip	45	Lemonade	25
Sherry Cobbler	40	Orangeade	25
Suissez	40		

PUNCHES

Claret	40	Milk	35
Brandy	45	Planters	40
Whiskey Sour	30	Whiskey	30

RUMS

Bacardi	40	Carioca	30
Jamaica	40	Ron Rico	30
Don "Q"	30		

MISCELLANEOUS WHISKEYS

Tom Hardy	30	G & B Black Label	30
Paul Jones	30	Gibson Rye	30
Four Roses	30	Park and Tilford Private	
Seagrams 5 Crown	30	Stock	30
Seagrams 7 Crown	30	Bushmill Irish	40
Crab Orchard	30	Three Feathers, Silver Label	30
Glenmore	30	Old Quaker	30
Calvert Reserve	30	Cream of Kentucky	30
Calvert Special	30	Mattingly & Moore	30
Calvert Private Stock	30	G & B Bourbon	30
Cascade	30	Old Lewis Hunter	35

BONDED WHISKEYS

Tip Top, 17 Years	55	Seagram's V. O., 6 Years	40
I. W. Harper, 16 Years	55	Walker's Bourbon DeLuxe,	
Special Old Reserve,		6 Years	40
15 Years	55	Seagram's American Bour-	
Early Times, 12 Years	40	bon, 5 Years	40
Seagram's Pedigree, 8 Years	40	Mount Vernon Rye, 5 Years	40
Kentucky Tavern, 4 Years	40	Old Forester, 4 Years	40
Am. G. & W Bourbon,		Old Grand Dad, 4 Years	40
7 Years	40	Bond and Lillard, 4 Years	40
Father Time, 7 Years	40	Old Taylor, 4 Years	40
H. W. Canadian Club,		I. W. Harper, 4 Years	40
6 Years	40		

GINS

Gordon's Dry	35	Burnett Dry	30
Sloe Gin	30	Milshire Tom	30
Lloyd's Dry	30	Milshire Dry	30
Gilbey's Dry	30	Fleischmann's Dry	30

SCOTCH WHISKEYS

Johnny Walker Black Label	45	Grant's	30
Johnny Walker Red Label	40	Sandy McDonald	35
Haig and Haig Pinch	45	Teacher's	35
Haig and Haig 5 Star	40	DeWar Ne Plus Ultra	45
Plus Four	40	DeWar White Label	40
White Horse	40	King's Ransom	45
Vat 69	40	Martin, V. V. O.	35
Ballantine's	40	Highland Queen	40
Peter Dawson	35	Grand MacNish	35
Old Angus	30	Black & White	40

LIQUEURS AND CORDIALS

Benedictine	40	Apricot, Imp.	45
Prunelle	40	Apricot, Dom.	40
Cointreau	40	Blackberry Brandy	40
Creme De Menthe Green	40	Peach Brandy	40
Creme De Menthe White	40	3 Star Hennessy Brandy	40
Creme De Cocoa	40	Martel Brandy	40
Creme De Yvette	40	Remy Martin Brandy	40
Chartreuse Green	40	Grand Mariner Cognac	40
Chartreuse Yellow	40	Grand Mariner, Orange	40
Anisette	40	Grand Mariner, Cherry	40
Curacoa	40	Kummel	40
		Pousse Cafe	50

BEER AND ALES

Budweiser	25	Regal	20
Schlitz	25	Falstaff	20
Pabst Blue Ribbon,		4X	20
Can or Bottle	25	Dixie	20
Blue Ribbon Ale	30	Old Union	20
Burke's Ale	30	Wirthbru	20
Drewry's Ale	30	Bass Ale, Split	40
Jax	20	Bass Ale, Pints	55
		Pilsner, Imp.	55

30c Highballs with Ginger Ale, White Rock or Coca-Cola 5c Extra
NO DRINKS SERVED AT TABLES FOR LESS THAN 25c

The Monteleone Hotel, New Orleans

Cocktails will forever be associated with New Orleans and nowhere more so than this hotel at the foot of Royal Street. The French Quarter is reputed to begin in the hotel lobby.

PORTLAND

COCKTAILS

HOUSE SPECIALITIES - ALL £9

Red Pepper Caipiroska
Vodka, fresh bell pepper and Campari
Hay Breeze
Lime, honey and hay infused vodka
Caramel Margarita
With caramel infused tequila and Liquor 43
Rose Chamomile Martini
Rose petal vodka with chamomile vermouth
Chili Raspberry Martini
Gin and Lillet Rouge with chili, lime and fresh raspberries
Spicy Basil Gin Sour
With fresh basil, tabasco & nutmeg
Old Fashioned
With forced rhubarb marmalade

CLASSICS - ALL £9

Portland Bloody Mary
Infused with chili & horseradish
Martini
Sipsmith Gin or Vodka, made however you like it
Negroni
Aged on fruit peels & spices

Portland Restaurant, London

For a restaurant that opened in January 2015, when its list of non-alcoholic cocktails were popular, their cocktail list has now grown to encompass the weird, the wonderful and the classics. Importantly, each is priced under £10.

DESIGNING THE MENU

First win the eye… then the heart… then the mind.

This approach has been the leitmotif behind the success of graphic designer Mary Lewis over the past 40 years. As the founder and managing director of her company, Lewis Moberly, she and her team have won great acclaim in the distinctive fields of branding and packaging design. And although this opening sentence may not mention the word 'stomach' – after all, everyone is aware that we eat with our eyes – this instruction should be at the forefront of all chefs' and restaurateurs' minds as they sit down to write a menu.

While her award-winning designs – for bottles of Moët champagne, Johnnie Walker Scotch and the Waitrose Essential cooking range, as well as the iconic blue lettering of St Pancras International station – are cool, clean and eye-catching, Mary Lewis herself is a softly spoken, gentle, blonde woman who is fascinated by all aspects of design.

We met early one evening in her London office, the walls and sideboards of which are covered with the vast number of design awards her company has garnered. She confessed that her experience with menu design was relatively limited – her biggest job in this field had been setting out the design rules for 15 different restaurants Grand Hyatt opened in a hotel complex in Dubai – but

she expressed her fascination with the opportunity to talk about menu design. Design, she firmly believes, is life.

I began with what I believe to be a very specific example of excellent, inexpensive menu design that many restaurateurs still fail to acknowledge or to take advantage of.

For many years the late Mark Birley was the most elegant London restaurateur who never was. Although he ran numerous restaurants, these were all within his private clubs, such as Annabel's, George, Mark's Club and Harry's Bar. The son of a painter, Birley had a remarkable eye for detail and a very distinctive way of writing the Harry's Bar menu (*pages 160–161*). This was a traditional Italian menu, broken down into the normal sections of antipasti, primi and secondi. But while most of the dishes were printed in black ink, within each section one or two dishes were printed in red.

On one occasion, I summoned up the courage to ask Birley, a formidable man in many respects, why he did this. His reply was in retrospect utterly simple and highly perceptive. Customers' eyes get tired and they need to be continually stimulated, he explained. Faced with the customary mass of black ink on a menu, they will lose focus and not bother reading the menu in any detail. Rather than exploring the menu, and invariably in a hurry or with a waiter hovering expectantly over their shoulders, they will simply choose what they had before or the same as their host.

Lewis nodded in agreement. She explained that this vital aspect of good design is all about breaking the pace and setting the pace. In this instance, the red ink does this very effectively but she added that there are other tools, such as boxing off certain sections or using different typefaces for the menu's various sections.

This relates back to a basic design fact of life: the importance of signposting. This works well in newspapers to allow readers to find easily what they are looking for on the page, and it is the same technique that architects use to guide visitors around new buildings. 'Many menus fail this test,' Lewis continued, 'and confuse diners instead.'

Clarifying choice becomes increasingly important as we plunge inexorably into the digital age. During the working day most people's eyes face information overload. 'People don't see any more,' Lewis said with a sigh, 'and this is increasingly the case at the end of a weary day.'

Although writing a stimulating menu has therefore become increasingly important, the choice of tools at the restaurateur's disposal is today wider and less expensive than ever before. Colour laser printers are widely available. Everyone seems delighted with a daily changing menu. And the shorter the menu, the wider its appeal, a feature that particularly entices Lewis whenever she hosts a client lunch. 'There is no excuse today for anyone to write a dull menu,' Lewis said, in the tone of a benign design headmistress.

Before moving on to her principles for successful design, Lewis cited one example of how several restaurateurs had tried to incorporate technology into restaurants, something she had found unfortunate and that had, in the end, proved short-lived. They had usd an iPad for the wine list – a novel toy that ultimately failed to allow the customer to find his way round the restaurant's cellar because it made a comparison of the wines on offer virtually impossible. The design of the iPad may be extremely elegant but in this role it was not fit for purpose.

This example allowed Lewis to elaborate on the similarities between good design and the creation of enticing dishes, both of which share similar roots in an individual's memory. Whenever Lewis is challenged to come up with a new design she always finds herself going through the mental files of all that she has designed before, in the same way that any chef looks back over his or her memory bank of flavours and tastes that in certain instances go back to their childhood.

Then comes the intellectual rigour, the process that in both professions is probably the most significant factor that divides the very good from the very best. 'As soon as I think of an idea for a design, I become very excited. I love it. Then I try as quickly as possible to fall out of love with it, to become extremely critical of

HARRY'S BAR

A PRIVATE CLUB

LUNCHEON

Zuppa di Cereali Bianca, Castagne e Pancetta £9.00
Borlotti and Cannellini Bean Soup, Chestnuts and Pancetta
Passata di Asparagi Calda, Granchio, Olio Crudo £12.00
Asparagus Soup, Crab and Olive Oil
Prosciutto 'Pio Tosini' e Pere £12.00
'Pio Tosini' Parma Ham and Pear
Carpaccio di Manzo Piemontese, Pecorino e Lattughe £16.00
Beef Carpaccio, Pecorino Cheese and Lettuce
Cipolla Rossa di Tropea Farcita con Granchio, Crema di Lenticchie £18.00
Warm Crab with Slow Cooked Red Onions, Lentil Cream

*

Ravioli di Carciofi e Taleggio Piemontese, Emulsione al Dragoncello £16.00
Artichoke and Taleggio Ravioli, Tarragon Sauce
Stracci di Pasta al Limone in Bianco, Granchio e Rucola £18.00
Stracci with Lemon, Crab and Rocket
Risotto Mantecato con Sedano di Verona e Gorgonzola £14.00
Celery and Gorgonzola Risotto
Vermicelli Classici alla Carrettiera £14.00
Spaghetti with Olives and Oregano
Tagliolini Verdi Gratinati al Prosciutto £16.00
Spinach Tagliolini Gratin with Prosciutto

*

Spiedino di Capesante, Prosciutto Crudo, Gratinate al Forno £24.00
Oven Baked Scallops with Parma Ham
Merluzzo Cotto in Padella, Purea di Cavolfiore £24.00
Pan-fried Cod, Cauliflower Purée
Coda di Rospo con il Crudo Verze Stufate £30.00
Grilled Monkfish, Savoy Cabbage and Prosciutto
Filetto di Branzino D'Altura, Broccoli e Lardoni £28.00
Seared Fillet of Sea Bass, Broccoli and Bacon

*

Costolette d'Agnello al Rosmarino, Peperoni e Uvetta £24.00
Rosemary Crusted Lamb Cutlets, Sweet and Sour Peppers
Polleto Nostrano Aperto, Soffritto di Scalogno £20.00
Rosemary Roast Baby Chicken, Sautéed Shallots
Filetto di Manzo Grigliato, Porcini e Salsa Vino Rosso £32.00
Grilled Fillet of Beef, Ceps and Red Wine Sauce
Fegato Trifolato alla Veneta su Risotto al Rosmarino £24.00
Pan-fried Calf's Liver with Onions and Sage on Rosemary Risotto
Piccata di Vitello alla Plancia, Carciofi e Bufala Gratinata £30.00
Seared Veal Escalope, Artichokes and Buffalo Mozzarella

what I have created. Then I begin to ask myself: How little do I need of it? How many elements could I strip away? Then, and only then, does a good, finished design emerge, something that I feel proud of.'

This process relates strategically to another phrase that appears on the front of the Lewis Moberly website and applies with equal force to menu design today. It reads: 'Everything must earn its space.' There is a combination of increasingly tired customers' eyes, information overload and the fact that while restaurants can act as an oasis in their customers' working lives, so many customers are in a rush to enjoy them – all this means that continuous editing to refine what is necessary is an essential ingredient of a successful menu today.

Yet this process must not, and cannot, lead to bland design, and Lewis went on to divulge what, for her, are the six essential factors in successful design, factors which, she believes, restaurateurs can and must apply to their own menus. These are: relevance, distinction, intelligence, tension, aesthetic pleasure and fighting spirit.

After she had explained these vital traits, I began to relate them to the menus that I see on a regular basis. I then thought of how useful this advice would have been to me as I sat down to write my first menus over 30 years ago.

Fighting spirit and aesthetic pleasure struck me as elements that are invariably paid too little attention. The determination that is required to open any restaurant means that the restaurateur and/or the chef must possess the requisite stubbornness to overcome far more professional hurdles than they envisaged at the outset. Lewis's advice is to allow the menu to carry on expressing these qualities.

Intelligence is not meant in the IQ sense of the word but rather in its relationship to an element invariably overlooked in design: wit. The menu, on every single occasion it is presented to a customer, provides the restaurateur with an opportunity to bring a smile to a customer's face, to make them relax and enjoy the meal even more. Too few take advantage of this opportunity, in my opinion.

Distinction and relevance are perhaps the most subjective of the factors, elements that the chef and the restaurateur can only work out from their own priorities and, perhaps even more relevantly, from how their customers choose to use their menus. And anyone will make a grave mistake if they believe that what makes a menu distinctive and relevant at one period of the restaurant's life will last forever. The underlying design may never change, but the need to make small tweaks to continually improve the menu – a visible example of the practice of continuous innovation that is the trademark of the great restaurateur – should never be overlooked.

This brought us to Lewis's final point, her use of the word tension, which she spotted immediately brought a rather blank look to my face. 'Tension in this instance conveys the energy, the dynamism inherent either in the design of the product or in the restaurant – somewhere that abounds in energy, of which the menu is an example that any customer holds in their hands. The typography, the layout, the cover of the menu can all be used to convey this vital element.'

Fortunately, among the half-dozen menus I had brought along from my collection, Lewis immediately spotted one that exuded tension. This is the four-page menu from Compartir restaurant (*page 164*) in Cadaqués on the Costa Brava, north-east Spain, founded by Mateu Casañas, Eduard Xatruch and Oriol Castro after the closure of El Bulli. The front cover has the name of the restaurant in dark blue handwriting across the centre with the word Restaurant written in more formal lettering underneath. A juxtaposition of colour runs across the next two pages, with the dishes listed in French in black ink and their English translations alongside in blue. On the back page is a small black-and-white photo of the interior with the website listed underneath. Lewis was most impressed by the menu's honesty and clarity. 'It brings a smile to my face,' she added.

Next Lewis picked up the menu from London's River Cafe (*pages 122–123*) and while she warmed to the stylish lettering highlighting the restaurant's name at the top of the menu, she was disappointed in the long, unbroken list of courses underneath. 'It looks at first glance more like a shopping list than a menu,' she

Compartir
Restaurant

POUR PARTAGER / For sharing

POUR COMMENCER / Starting with...

o Gazpacho	6,50 €
Gazpacho	
o Tomates et fraises au parmesan et basilique	8,75 €
Tomato and strawberries with parmesan and basil	
o Endives au gorgonzola, noix et fruit de la passion	8,75 €
Endives with gorgonzola cheese, walnuts and passion fruit	
o Jambon ibérique Joselito	16,50 €
Iberica ham "Joselito"	
o Jambon cuit et fumé à l'Empordà au paprika et huile d'olive	9 €
Smoked ham in the Empordà with sweet paprika and virgin olive oil	
o Saumon et vinaigrette citrique	9,75 €
Salmon with citrus vinaigrette	
o Anchois truffées	14 €
Truffled anchovies	
o Sardines marinées, orange et olive verte	9,50 €
Marinated sardines, orange and green olives	
o Les huitres de Genaro: / *Genaro's oysters:*	
Nature / *Natural*	4 €/uni /each
Froides à la vinaigrette fumée / *Cold, with smoked vinaigrette*	4,75 €/uni /each
Chaudes, au "suquet" / *Hot, with "suquet" (Mediterranean fish sauce)*	4,75 €/uni /each
o Couteaux tièdes (de la plage de Langosteira) avec un peu de citron	13,25 €
Warm razor clams (from Langosteira beach) with a lemon touch	
o Gambas à la sauce crémeuse	9,75 €
Crispy king prawns with creamy sauce	
o Beignets de morue au miel	9 €
Cod "buñuela" (croquette) with honey	
o Œuf et crème de pomme de terre: / *Egg with potato cream.*	
o À la truffe / *With black truffle*	7 €
o Aux œufs de saumon / *With salmon caviar*	7 €
o Pain / *Bread*	2,50 €
o "Pa amb tomàquet" / *"Pa amb tomàquet" (Grilled bread with tomato)*	3,50 €

Pain élaboré par Triticum /*Bread made by Triticum*

Prix TVA comprise/ *VAT included*

POUR PARTAGER / For sharing

NOS RIZ / Rice

o Riz marinier	18,50 €
Shellfish rice	
o Riz moelleux de homard	26 €
Juicy lobster rice	
o Riz ibérique aux trompettes de la mort	17,50 €
Iberica rice casserole with wild mushrooms	

minimum 2 personnes, prix par personne / *2 people minimum, price per person*

NOS POISSONS / Fish

o Loup de mer avec garniture de champignons et algues	16,50 €
Sea bass with mushrooms and seaweed	
o Lotte avec poivrons du Piquillo confis à la vanille	22 €
Monk fish with Piquillo peppers cooked with vanilla	
o "Shabu-shabu" de saumon et asperges vertes	16,50 €
Salmon and green asparagus "Shabu shabu"	
o Homard sans travail au jus de poulet et anisés	moitié/entier 19 €/35 €
"Ready to eat" lobster with chicken aniseed sauce	half / whole 19 €/35 €

NOS VIANDES / Meat

o Côtelettes de lapin à l'aïoli de pomme	14 €
Rabbit ribs with apple "aïoli" (Catalan sauce made with garlic and oil)	
o Poulet aux crustacés et "ratafia"	17 €
Chicken and crustacean with "Ratafia" (Catalan spirit)	
o Entrecôte (de 400 gr)	29,50 €
Entrecôte (de 400 gr)	

Nous avons des plats pour les enfants
We also have special dishes for children

Prix TVA comprise/ *VAT included*

www.compartircadaques.com

offered, continuing it would have made her inclined to put it down and just say, 'I'll have what you're having.'

Lewis then picked up a menu from 28°–50°, a small group of wine-focused London restaurants that takes it name from the bands of latitude on either side of the equator that lend themselves to wine grape growing. Although her first reaction as she read this menu was 'nobody is trying to seduce me', she praised it for its directness and the clarity of the signposting she had referred to initially as so important to allow the busy customers to make their decisions easily. Sharing plates and the lunch menu were clearly boxed off; the starters were separated on either side of the menu from the main courses; and different typefaces were used throughout. 'This menu tells it as it is,' she concluded.

Two menus from further afield – Greens Restaurant (*page 166*), the long-standing vegetarian restaurant in the Fort Mason Centre, San Francisco, and The French Laundry (*page 167*), chef Thomas Keller's restaurant in Yountville, Napa County – both from March 2010 – share similar distinctions despite their very different price points.

The first is their use of an American paper size, ANSI size D, whose UK equivalent is most closely A1, a relatively long, broad paper size whose overall dimensions allow all the dishes to stand out and not to feel too cramped. Both menus struck Lewis as understated, lacking in pretension and using the typography to do a lot of the talking. In the case of The French Laundry, Lewis found the juxtaposition of the roman typeface for the name with contrasting italics for the explanation underneath each dish extremely effective.

Finally, we turned to the most expensively produced menu I had brought along, the extensive colour menu from Troisgros (*pages 169–171*) in Roanne, France, which contrasts the heritage of the restaurant, which is now over 80 years old, with an ultra-modern example of branding: on the light gold cover is printed a large blue 'T', followed by a black-and-white photograph of a chef at work and then gold and blue pages, on which are stuck the various menus.

Greens Restaurant

March 1, 2010

First Course

Grilled Artichoke Panzanella with ciabatta, tardivo radicchio, picholine olives, capers, arugula, frisee, manchego and champagne vinaigrette 11.50

Grilled Delta Asparagus with shaved Andante Dairy Etude, mache and meyer lemon vinaigrette 11.00

Fresh Spring Roll with grilled tofu, carrots, napa cabbage, jicama, Thai basil, rice noodles, mint and chili dipping sauce. Served with grilled oyster mushroom, watermelon radish and purple daikon salad 10.50

Toasted Olive Bread with warm Italian butter beans, County Line braising greens, Regina olive oil and shaved Lamb Chopper 9.50

Sampler – French lentil salad with lemon and mint; roasted broccoli romanesco and cauliflower with pine nuts and pepper flakes; grilled artichoke with lemon oil; golden and chioggia beets; olives; grilled Italian bread with Bellwether fromage blanc 16.75

Artisan Cheese Plate –Andante Dairy Minuet, Cypress Grove Bermuda Triangle and Cowgirl Creamery Mt Tam; fennel and Italian parsley salad; warm Italian bread 13.50

Wilted Spinach Salad with County Line chicory, red orach, feta, croutons, red onions, gaeta olives, mint, sherry vinegar and hot olive oil 11.00   Small Salad 9.50

Little Gems, Escarole and Tardivo Radicchio with avocado, page mandarins, oro blanco grapefruit, fukumoto oranges, pumpkin seeds and page mandarin vinaigrette 11.00   Small Salad 9.50

Minestrone with lacinato kale, Sevillano olive oil and herbs   Cup 7.50   Bowl 8.50

Main Course

Artichoke and Sunchoke Gratin with tomatoes, peppers, spring onions, manchego and goat cheese custard. Served with roasted pepper garlic sauce, grilled asparagus with lemon oil 23.50

Winter Roots Filo with roasted butternut squash, parsnips, turnips, rutabagas, leeks, gruyere and walnuts. Served on warm Italian butter beans and lacinato kale with pepper flakes 24.00

Indian Curry - Winter vegetables with tomatoes, coconut milk, chick peas, ginger, chilies and cilantro. Served with mustard seed basmati rice and Hamada Farm winter fruit chutney 21.50   Small 17.50

Pappardelle with chanterelle, hedgehog and yellowfoot mushrooms, savoy spinach, spring onions, green garlic, pine nuts, herb butter and grana padano 19.50

Pizza Provencal with tomato sauce, grilled fennel, picholine olives, manchego, fontina, Italian parsley 17.00

Mesquite Grilled Brochettes - mushrooms, yellow finn potatoes, peppers, red onions, yams, fennel and Hodo Soy tofu with charmoula and cherry almond quinoa 21.00
Single Brochette 17.00

Sides 6.50
French lentil salad with lemon, mint and feta
Warm Italian butter beans
Grilled Ridgecut Gristmills polenta with herb butter
Lacinato kale with pepper flakes
Grilled artichokes with lemon oil and mint
Grilled Fingerling Potatoes and Cipollini Onion with charmoula

Our beautiful private dining room is available for parties and events.
Speak with your server for details.

18% service charge for parties of six or more. $15.00 minimum charge per guest.

THE FRENCH LAUNDRY

MR. FRIERSON
CHEF'S TASTING MENU | 29 JUNE 2008

YUZU SORBET
with Hearts of Palm and Cilantro Shoots

———

CAULIFLOWER "PANNA COTTA"
with Beau Soleil Oyster Glaze
and Sterling White Sturgeon Caviar

———

WHITE TRUFFLE CUSTARD
with a Ragoût of Périgord Truffles

———

SALAD OF SACRAMENTO DELTA ASPARAGUS
Pine Nut Purée and Sweet Pepper

———

HAND-ROLLED RUSSET POTATO "GNOCCHI"
with Shaved Black Truffles from Australia and Castelmagno Cheese

———

SAUTÉED FILLET OF COBIA "CONFIT À LA MINUTE"
Summer Squash, Niçoise Olive, Vine-Ripe Tomato
and Lemon Verbena

———

"CAESAR SALAD"
Australian Rock Lobster Tail "Pochée au Beurre Doux" with Roasted Romaine Lettuce,
Garlic "Melba" and "Bottarga di Muggine"

———

PAN-ROASTED NEW BEDFORD SEA SCALLOP
Chanterelle Mushrooms, Savoy Cabbage and Ramp Emulsion

———

MOULARD DUCK "FOIE GRAS EN TERRINE"
Sunchoke Glaze, Jacobsen's Farm Crab Apple, Dijon Mustard,
Watercress and Caraway Streusel

———

GRILLED SIRLOIN OF KUROGE BEEF FROM SHIGA
"Matignon" of Summer Garden Vegetables, "Pommes Mazim's"
and Sauce Bordelaise

———

"OSSAU VIEILLE"
"Jamón Ibérico," Artichoke, Frisée and Caper Emulsion

———

CANTALOUPE SORBET
Compressed Melon and "Muscat de Beaumes de Venise en Gelée"

———

"COFFEE AND DOUGHNUTS"
Cinnamon-Sugared Doughnuts
and "Cappuccino Semi-Freddo"

———

"LINGOT DE CHOCOLAT EN MOUSSE DE MALT CROUSTILLANTE"
Candied Spanish Peanuts, Popcorn Sherbet and Caramel Corn

———

"MIGNARDISES"

6640 WASHINGTON STREET, YOUNTVILLE CA 94599 707.944.2380

Lewis was notably impressed and her first response was, 'Can the food live up to the design?' Once I assured her it did, she found that the use of the different coloured paper was an extremely effective method of creating interest for the eyes, but also for whetting the appetite. 'I want to turn these pages, I like the feel of the paper, and tactility is always an important factor. This is the kind of menu that would entice anybody.'

But what also struck Lewis about this menu was that, other than the 'T' and the restaurant's address on the final page, there was no sense of a personality inserting himself between the customer and the food. 'That,' Lewis concluded, 'is the ultimate test of whether its design is successful. It has to be graphically entertaining and encourage an enthusiastic response from the customer. The menu, after all, is the invitation to the dance.'

Les variations lactées

Fromages frais et affinés
Entre la fourme et la poire
Cannelloni tiède de chèvre aux herbes fines

Mes fantaisies sucrées
(à choisir au début du repas)

Pots de thé au jasmin, meringué
Dim sum au goût épicé, relevé de cassis
Galette aux fraises chaudes, glace au miel
Tarte sublime au chocolat, à la poire
Ali-baba à l'orange, punché d'une eau de vie au gingembre
Soufflé menthe chocolat et son granité à l'orange
Soufflé à la noix de coco et à l'ananas

Menu pour les enfants
TVA 5.5% et service 13% inclus

L'AUTOMNE PAR LE MENU

Le goût de l'artichaut à la sardine fumée
—

Nage d'écrevisses à la manoa
—

Noix d'huîtres à l'oseille et cumin
—

Plins à la truffe blanche et au cèpe
—

Rouget Barbet dans un fumet de tamarin
—

Homard bleu au beurre intimidé
—

Noisettes de chevreuil persillées, noques
—

Les fromages fermiers frais et affinés
—

Entremets au chocolat et aux prunes, glace au café
Tartelette au basilic
Mikimoto marron et cassis

Nous vous proposons également,

L'Automne par le menu & les accords du sommelier

Ce sont des notes fraiches, légères…

Mosaïque de légumes aux cèpes
Battuta de veau et de thon frais, aux amandes croquantes
Nage d'écrevisses à la manoa

à la nature vagabonde,…

Mezzaluna de potimarron, à la truffe d'alba
Foie gras poêlé, en persillade, au maïs
Langoustines, poivron doux et mangue, sauce fruitée

des goûts pointus, des complicités

Rouget « Julia », au fumet de tamarin
Saint-Pierre à l'aneth, gousses d'ail nouveaux et carottes aigrelettes
Tronçon de turbot poché, une nage à la bergamote fraîche

souligrant les textures et la mâche.
Noix du ris de veau, dorée au beurre, yuzu piquant

Carré d'agneau, brûlé-épicé, croque jardinier

Tête de cochon, mijotée avec des coings

Canette de Challans, caramélisée, à la figue et au pamplemousse (pour 2)

Noisettes de chevreuil, beurre de câpres aux raisins

Lièvre en effilochade, râble en aiguillettes

La nouvelle cuisine de Jean et Pierre
Coquilles Saint-Jacques « Pierre Boulez »

Navarin de homard à la crème *(créé dans les années 70)*

Pièce de bœuf de Charolles *(AOC)* au poivre blanc

Nos viandes bovines sont d'origine française

CHAPTER

6

THE MENU AS FUNDRAISER

Shaun Searley is the chef at our son Will's restaurant, The Quality Chop House, in Farringdon, east London. Like many in his profession, he is highly talented and creative. In addition, he is a keen cyclist and he is only too aware that he is in a position to benefit the many in this world who are less well off than him and who do not have enough to eat.

In September 2015, Searley joined several other chefs in a sponsored cycle ride across Myanmar (formerly Burma) to raise money for Action Against Hunger, a charity justifiably popular among those in the hospitality profession. While sponsorship via friends was the obvious route towards the £6,000 each chef had pledged to raise, Searley created a new dish for his menu, which meant by the time he flew off, having put in considerable hours off-duty training to be in a position to face the 250-mile cycle ride, the customers at his restaurant had happily contributed over £1,000 towards his target.

They had done so every time they ordered his hugely popular 'Burma Burger', a dish that was displayed prominently in a box on the restaurant's menu (*page 174*) and which cost £15, of which £2 per burger went directly to the charity. This proved to be a fundraising mechanism from which everyone benefited. The customers loved the novel twist on a dish of universal appeal (Searley's 'Burmese' twist included garlic crisps, garlic fried peanuts and lime mayonnaise). Searley and

Q

LUNCH MENU
Friday 2ⁿᵈ October

Marcona Almonds £4 | Nocellara Olives £4

Lardo di Colonnata £9.50
Charcuterie Board £15
'Nduja/ Montalcino Salame/ Coppa/ Jesus Salame

◆◆◆◆◆◆◆◆◆◆◆

Cauliflower Soup £6.50
Courgette, Boquerones, Goat's Curd, Watercress £7
Monk Liver, Sea Vegetables, Lemon £8
Blackface Lamb, Green Sauce, Rocket, Parmesan £8.50
Hansen & Lydersen Smoked Salmon £9.50

◆◆◆◆◆◆◆◆◆◆◆

Galloway Mince, Dripping Toast, Watercress £14.50
Delica Squash Tart, Girolles, Egg Yolk, Truffle £15
Cod, Puy Lentils, Sea Vegetables, Cockles £19
Lamb, Jerusalem Artichoke, Cavalo Nero £20

Lunch Plate £10
Somerset Kid Liver, onions, mash & a glass of red

Hereford Burma Burger £15
*£2 goes to support head chef Shaun Searley's Action Against
Hunger charity bike ride in Burma*
*Contains nuts

Watercress, Pickled Walnut, Shallot £4
Hispi Cabbage £4.50
Confit Potatoes £5.50

For allergen information please speak to a member of staff before ordering.
The Quality Chop House 92-94 Farringdon Road 0207 278 1452

his brigade got a thrill every time the dish was ordered. And those in Myanmar were the ultimate beneficiaries from these donations.

The practice of donating a certain amount of money from a particular dish to a specific charity is not new but it is an expression of just how flexible and effective the menu can be at fundraising for worthy causes.

In the UK, the most successful and long-term application has been via the Pizza Veneziana in what are today the many branches of PizzaExpress. This restaurant was founded after an initial visit to Naples in the 1960s by Peter Boizot, a far-sighted restaurateur who not only founded this restaurant chain but was also one of the first in London to introduce jazz as late-night entertainment. A subsequent visit to Venice alerted Boizot to the threat that beautiful city was facing from the rising sea levels and his response was remarkably simple and effective. In 1977 the new Pizza Veneziana was introduced on to the menu of the rapidly expanding number of PizzaExpress restaurants (*pages 176–177*), and 5p from each pizza ordered was donated to the Venice in Peril Fund. Over the years the sum was increased to 25p per pizza and the recipient became the Veneziana Fund, which then splits the proceeds between the Venice in Peril Fund and the restoration, repair and maintenance of buildings, fixtures and fittings of buildings, and works of art created before 1750. To date this humble pizza has raised the rather princely sum of £2 million.

However impressive this sum is, it is a shadow of the amount that menus in the developed world have raised, and will continue to raise, for good causes. This is, in my opinion, the menu's most distinct and undervalued achievement.

Menus manage to fulfil this role in various, varying forms. The most obvious is purely as a matter of record because the menu serves as the information board that brings together the worthy cause, the food, the wine, the speakers, the diners/donors, and the order in which they will appear over the course of the fundraising meal.

THE MAGIC STARTS WHEN YOU ORDER

What makes our pizzas so special? Each and every one is individually handcrafted, just for you, by our passionate pizzaiolos. All freshly stretched and tossed before your eyes, in our open kitchen. Only the best ingredients will do here. Our pizzaiolos prepare them with pride, dicing and drizzling to make your perfect pizza, your way. More peppers? Sure thing. Hold the anchovies? No worries. Just care, craft and quality – from order to oven.

PIZZAEXPRESS

ROMANA PIZZA

A bigger, thinner, crispier pizza, inspired by pizza from Rome

Margherita Bufala ⊘ £11.95
Buffalo mozzarella, tomato, fresh basil, garlic oil, oregano
and black pepper, finished with fresh tomatoes, torn buffalo
mozzarella, fresh basil and extra virgin olive oil

American Hottest £13.95
Pepperoni, hot green and Roquito peppers, fresh red chilli, spicy,
hot, soft 'nduja sausage, tomato and buffalo mozzarella, finished
with torn buffalo mozzarella, fresh parsley and chilli oil

American Hot £12.95
Pepperoni, mozzarella and tomato, with your choice of hot green,
Roquito, or jalapeño peppers

Padana £12.75
Goat's cheese, mozzarella, tomato, caramelised onion, spinach,
red onion and garlic oil
A discretionary 25p will be donated on your behalf to Macmillan
Cancer Support

Melanzane ⊘ £12.45
Marinated Italian aubergine, light mozzarella, tomato, chilli flakes
and garlic oil, finished with fresh basil, Gran Milano cheese and
fresh parsley

Pollo ad Astra £12.95
Chicken, sweet Peppadew peppers, red onion, mozzarella, tomato,
Cajun spices and garlic oil

Niçoise £13.45
Tuna, anchovies, surfine capers, black olives, tomato, free-range
hard-boiled egg, fresh tomatoes and mozzarella, finished with
rocket, lemon and fresh parsley

Diavolo £13.45
Hot spiced beef, pepperoni, mozzarella, tomato, green pepper,
red onion and Tabasco, with your choice of hot green, Roquito or
jalapeño peppers

Pollo Forza £12.95
Chicken with smoked chilli, garlic oil and dried chilli flakes with
red & yellow peppers, Roquito pepper, mozzarella and tomato,
finished with Gran Milano cheese, fresh parsley and chilli oil

---

CLASSIC PIZZA

*Our original, which hasn't changed since 1965.
All of our Classic pizza recipes are available as a bigger, thinner,
crispier Romana for an extra £1.65*

American £10.10
Pepperoni, mozzarella and tomato

Margherita ⊘ £8.45
Mozzarella and tomato

La Reine £10.45
Prosciutto cotto, black olives, closed cup mushroom, mozzarella
and tomato

Fiorentina ⊘ £9.95
Spinach, free-range egg, mozzarella, tomato, garlic oil and
black olives, finished with Gran Milano cheese

Pianta ⊘⊛ £9.75
Spinach, closed cup mushroom, pine kernels, artichoke, tomato,
chilli flakes and garlic oil finished with rocket, extra virgin olive
oil and fresh parsley. No cheese

Veneziana ⊘⊛ £9.25
Pine kernels, red onion, surfine capers, black olives, sultanas,
mozzarella and tomato
A discretionary 25p will be donated on your behalf to the
Veneziana Fund

Giardiniera ⊘⊛ £11.25
Artichoke, closed cup mushroom, red pepper, fresh tomatoes,
red onion, black olives, pesto, tomato, mozzarella and garlic oil

Sloppy Giuseppe £11.45
Hot spiced beef, green pepper, red onion, mozzarella and tomato

Formaggi ⊘ £11.25
Mozzarella and tomato with creamy buffalo mozzarella, baked
and finished with shaved Gran Milano cheese

Soho 65 ⊘ £11.75
Mozzarella and tomato with black olives and garlic oil finished
with rocket, shaved Gran Milano cheese, torn buffalo mozzarella
and extra virgin olive oil

Add a finish of cured Italian meats for £1.85

DESSERTS & GELATO

Chocolate Fudge Cake * ⊘ £5.25
Moist rich chocolate cake, baked in-house

Honeycomb Cream Slice * ⊘ £5.75
Sweet honeycomb and chocolate pieces in a light cream
topping on a layer of salted caramel and crunchy biscuit

Vanilla Cheesecake * ⊘ £5.45
Our New York-style vanilla cheesecake on a crumbly biscuit
base, served with fruit coulis

Tiramisu ⊘ £5.75
Made by La Donatella, using traditional methods and ingredients:
layers of ladyfingers, mascarpone cream, marsala wine,
coffee and cocoa

Leggera Tartufo Limoncello ⊘⊞ £5.75
UNDER 230 CALORIES Full of southern Italian flavours:
creamy Sicilian lemon and Fior di Latte gelato with a liquid
centre of limoncello

Leggera Raspberry Sorbet ⊘⊞ £4.95
UNDER 200 CALORIES Two scoops of dairy-free raspberry
sorbet, served with a chocolate straw and fresh mint

Chocolate Glory ⊘ £6.25
Vanilla gelato, chocolate sauce, chunks of chocolate
fudge cake, served with a chocolate straw

Coppa Gelato ⊘⊞ £3.75
Your choice of two scoops of vanilla, chocolate, strawberry or
salted caramel gelato, served with a chocolate straw

*Served with your choice of cream, gelato, or mascarpone

DOLCETTI

*Our Dolcetti are perfectly sized mini desserts to be served
alongside your choice of tea or coffee*

Salted Caramel Profiteroles ⊘ £5.25
Profiteroles with a sweet caramel coating, filled with
a delicately salted caramel cream

Chocolate Brownie ⊘⊞ £5.25
Made using gluten-free flour, topped with fresh strawberry
and icing sugar

Leggera Raspberry Sorbet ⊘⊞ £4.95
UNDER 100 CALORIES One scoop of dairy-free raspberry
sorbet served with a chocolate straw and fresh mint

Caffè Reale ⊘⊞ £4.75
Figs in a cinnamon and white wine spiced syrup
with mascarpone

Lemon Posset Crunch ⊘ £4.95
A creamy lemon posset on a ginger biscuit base

*Enjoy any of our Dolcetti with a liqueur coffee
for an additional £1.45*

(PERSONALISE *your* PIZZA)

Add extra flavour with jalapeño peppers, red & yellow peppers or pepperoni. Choose from these or any of your favourites for £1.65
If you are unable to find one of your favourite recipes, please just ask; if we have the ingredients, we will happily make it for you

---

CALABRESE

Our iconic rectangular pizza is inspired by the food of Calabria

Calabrese ⊛ £13.95
Fiery, soft 'nduja sausage and spicy Calabrese sausage D.O.P with
fresh red chilli, Roquito pepper, roasted red & yellow peppers,
mozzarella and tomato, finished with light mozzarella, rocket, pesto
and Gran Milano cheese

CALZONE

*Folded pizza dough baked with Gran Milano cheese
inspired by the classic dish from Naples.
Served with a fresh salad garnish, finished with house dressing*

Calzone Classico £13.95
Four meats: Coppa, Finocchiona, Milano salami and pepperoni; with
light mozzarella, fresh tomatoes, fresh parsley, fresh basil, garlic oil,
baby spinach, tomato and Gran Milano cheese

SIDES

Coleslaw 'PizzaExpress' ⊘⊞ NEW £3.75
Our best yet. A crunchy coleslaw of white cabbage, carrot and
onion with a chipotle spice in a rich and creamy dressing

Superboost ⊘⊞ NEW £4.95
A superfood mix of green lentils, black rice, edamame beans,
red quinoa, chickpeas, cranberries, pumpkin seeds and kale
with rocket, roasted red & yellow peppers, parsley and our
light house dressing

Mixed Salad ⊘⊞ £3.95
Seasonal mixed leaves, fresh tomato and cucumber with our
house dressing

Potato Nocciola ⊘⊞ £3.25
Golden fluffy potato balls, baked in our ovens, finished with
Gran Milano cheese and fresh parsley
We love these with a splash of truffle oil, if you do too, please just ask

Polenta Chips ⊘ £3.95
Italian polenta chips with rosemary, oven-baked and finished with
Gran Milano cheese, served with a honey & mustard dressing dip

But most fascinating is how, over the past 20 years, many in the hospitality business around the world have finessed various aspects of the menu to benefit many more individuals than could ever have been accommodated in any single restaurant.

These beneficiaries are wide-ranging. In 1998 William Sieghart and Mary-Lou Sturridge created StreetSmart and conceived of a mechanism which adds £1 to every bill in the participating restaurants during November and December – a donation that goes directly towards the homeless. And, of course, there would be no bill without a menu. StreetSmart is now supported by over 500 restaurants in the UK every year, and its simplicity and effectiveness has allowed it to spread to India, Ireland, New Zealand, Australia, Canada, and San Francisco and Nashville in the US.

Chris Corbin, the highly respected London restaurateur, has taken the opposite approach in raising funds for Leuka, an organisation that conducts invaluable research into leukaemia, from which Corbin himself happily recovered. Every year, in a different London hotel, he arranges a dinner for 200 people, at which 20 top chefs each create a different menu for the table of 10 they will cook for on the evening. But the real fundraising only starts after the meal when an auctioneer sells to the highest bidder dinner at home cooked by one of the participating top chefs.

Share Our Strength was the aptly named charity founded by Bill and Debbie Shore in the basement of their house in Washington, DC, in response to the famine then raging through Ethiopia in 1984. Its aim was simple: to unite the strength of the US hospitality industry to raise funds to help those in greater need of food and nourishment. Its achievements have been spectacular, and en route this particular charity has morphed into the considerably broader, and even more aptly named, No Kid Hungry (www.nokidhungry.org).

Chefs, restaurateurs and sommeliers still join together to raise funds, as evinced by the menu (*opposite*) from a dinner organised at North End Grill, Battery Park, New York, in September 2015, at which chef Eric Korsh was joined

AUTUMN
HARVEST
DINNER

22nd ANNUAL

September 28th, 2015

Hors d'oeuvres
Brussels Sprouts, Spicy Bacon & Citrus • Savory Pumpkin Beignets
Marinated Tuna, Olive & Capers • Epoisses Tartlet, Pomegranate & Rosemary
Pork Terrine, Pickled Grape • Grilled Octopus, Panisse & Romesco • Sea Urchin Custard & Corn
Rosé Champagne, Philippe Gonet, Brut, Le Mesnil-sur-Oger
Chef John Karangis, **Union Square Events**

_____

House Smoked Sable, Russ & Daughters Hackleback Caviar
Crispy Potato & Cream
Dezi Verdicchio, Solagne, Marche 2013
Chef Eric Korsh, **North End Grill**

_____

Artichoke Heart, Lobster & Brown Butter
Château Coussin Sainte-Victoire Rosé, Côtes-de-Provence 2014
Chef Eric Korsh, **North End Grill**

_____

Ox Tongue, Bread & Green Sauce
Boulevard Napoléon Grenache Noir, Le Pujol, Vin de Pays de l'Hérault 2011
Chef Fergus Henderson, **St. John**

_____

Pigeon & Trotter Pie
Boulevard Napoléon Carignan, L'Angely, Vin de Pays de l'Hérault 2011
Chef Fergus Henderson, **St. John**

_____

Tumbleweed Cheese & Eccles Cake
Chef Fergus Henderson, **St. John**

_____

Dr. Henderson Ice Cream
Chef Fergus Henderson, **St. John**

_____

After Dinner Confections
Key Lime Bites • Mini Doughnuts • Mini Pumpkin Whoopie Pies
Apple Cider Sorbet and Cookies & Cream Mini Ice Cream Cones
Pastry Chef Tracy Obolsky, **North End Grill**

_____

by Fergus Henderson and Trevor Gulliver from London's St John restaurant. That evening raised $250,000 for the charity.

But the single person who can most point to the efficacy of the menu, highlighting the role of good food and wine in opening wallets to raise significant sums of money for the particular charity he founded, is someone who grew up appreciating neither. John Wood is from the Midwest where beer is the drink and, I know personally, he still likes his meat cooked well-done. Having started his career at Microsoft, Wood's subsequent travels to Asia made him realise how many young people, particularly young girls, were being denied an education, and he founded the subsequently highly successful, and equally effective, Room to Read (www.roomtoread.org).

An encounter with John Ridding, CEO of the *Financial Times* then based in Hong Kong, led to the first wine dinner hosted by my wife, Jancis Robinson MW, as a fundraiser that was to prove a highly successful blueprint for the future. Subsequent dinners have taken place in Tokyo, Sydney, San Francisco, New York and London – and the total raised to provide libraries and schools is now close to $30 million. Grapes grown in Bordeaux, Burgundy and the Napa Valley continue to benefit the eager-to-learn young children of Sri Lanka, Nepal, Tanzania and Zambia.

It is a simple enough mechanism. Good food brings those round the table together. The excellent wine makes everyone feel more magnanimous and it readily releases the credit card. Then John Wood gets up and talks about the need to educate young children, which yanks at the heartstrings. The London Wine Gala dinner, held at the Honourable Society of Lincoln's Inn on October 1st 2015, as per the menu (*opposite*), raised $2.8 million.

But at charity events such as these, and the many others that take place around the world with such regularity, it is the menu that holds the whole event together.

The Honourable Society of

Lincoln's Inn

Wines

Montes, Outer Limits Sauvignon Blanc 2014 Zapallar

Errázuriz Chardonnay 2013 Aconcagua Costa

Clos des Fous, Pucalán Arenaria Pinot Noir 2012 Aconcagua Costa

Santa Rita, Floresta Cabernet Franc 2012 Pumanque, Colchagua

Aresti, Family Collection Cabernet Sauvignon 2001 Curico

Menu

Marinated Sea Trout with Pea Purée
Soft Boiled Quails' Egg
Red Pepper Jelly & Pea Shoots

~~~

Pan-fried Gressingham Breast of Duck, Lemon Thyme Infused Jus [A]
Braised Duck Leg & Potato Boulangère
Sautéed Broad Beans & Peas
Butternut Squash

~~~

Cheese Plate
Tunworth Soft, Cashel Blue
Driftwood Goats' Cheese (Unpasteurised)

~~~

Tea, Coffee & Petits Fours [N]

[A] *contains alcohol*
[N] *contains nuts*
Please note, the dishes on our menus may contain traces of nuts.
Please notify staff if you have a severe allergy to any food.
Some cheeses are made with unpasteurised milk which can be harmful to pregnant women and the elderly.

PROTECTING THE MENU

At the heart of every menu there is a paradox. Well, two in fact.

The first, and perhaps the more sensitive, is that the culinary individuality that is so attractive to many customers – and what at first sight appears to be based on the most creative and original recipes – is almost impossible to protect under the increasingly growing legal framework known as intellectual property, or IP, rights.

The second is that the only effective way for any chef to protect his recipes and his style of cooking – everything that makes what emerges from his kitchen so special – goes against the very spirit of the restaurant profession, the ethos of generosity that makes it so admirable.

The restaurant business is almost certainly the most open of all the professions. Prices are out there for all to see via the menu and the wine list. The rents at which deals are done are bandied about openly, often with great pride by the agents who have just concluded them. The costs of operating a restaurant fall into specific, oft-repeated bands, and everyone is soon aware of one universal financial principle of this business – that the profit generated by any restaurant is in inverse proportion to the quality of the food it serves.

Also, almost everyone who works in the restaurant business is open with their information and their advice. During my 35 years in and around restaurants,

the reasons for this openness have certainly changed. In the early 1980s this was a profession that attracted so few that those in it were only too happy to talk to anyone who showed the slightest interest in it, while today the subject seems to attract so many that avoiding talking about it is virtually impossible. But the spirit of openness is there and easily available for everyone to benefit from.

Over this same period, the global interest in the restaurant business has attracted many who never expected it to provide them with such interesting and intellectually challenging work. One such person is Joel Vertes who, as a partner in the eminent London firm of Olswang, has had his formidable intellect stretched on various aspects of the menu and its consequences: possible protection under IP; the consequences of trademarking and the benefits of franchising, as a result of London's success in exporting so many restaurant brands; and what chefs can do to protect their most creative and successful dishes.

PROTECTING AN INDIVIDUAL DISH

As we began to talk it became clear that Vertes may be even more aware, and appreciative, of a chef's talents than I am. He referred to the magic and creativity that these chefs can engender and that keeps customers coming back. But while companies – and here he quoted Coca-Cola's successful long-term protection of its secret recipe – can hold on to a single fundamental recipe over many years, this may not be possible to do so for chefs.

There are several reasons why a single dish cannot gain the intellectual security of a literary or artistic work, but the most fundamental has to do with the composition of a recipe. However exciting any finished dish may appear, the ingredients will generally be described on the menu – the only 'secrets' are precisely how the chef has combined them, how long he has cooked each, and so on. And that element is, from a legal perspective, almost impossible to protect.

Consequently, it is quite possible – and indeed common – for admiring chefs to seek to 'reverse engineer' a great dish to create the same effect.

Vertes describes this as being akin to fashion industry trends. Clothing designers will believe their creations to be innovative, protectable, even unique. And in many cases they are protectable and enforceable. But the reality is that the fashion industry lives off trends. Far-fetched and outlandish concepts strut the catwalks, and while the average high street fashion designs may seem quite far removed, fashion trends exist because people seek to emulate what they see on the runway, on TV and in magazines. Those in the know will be able to predict this season's colours and patterns. There is, consequently, a fine line between copying and emulating, between rip-offs and simply following a trend.

The same pattern is true in food – save that dishes are even less protectable because the creative output is in the taste rather than the appearance. While clothing can be protected by a host of design rights in different countries, it is hard to see how corresponding rights can protect a dish.

Then, because of various converging factors, there is the question of proving that a dish originated definitively in one place. The internet and social media, along with a plethora of recipe books and the popularity of cooking programmes, have given the public unprecedented access to a panoply of inventive dishes. Along with the cultural diversification of restaurant menus, this has given rise to plenty of experimental chefs, both at home and in restaurant kitchens, seeking to please a far more sophisticated diner. In reality, while the particular twist placed on a dish may be the signature of an individual chef, the creation of a dish will have taken place over a much longer period and will have been inspired by sources of all kinds.

I asked Vertes bluntly, putting all legal costs to one side for a moment, how and whether it would be possible to safeguard the genesis and genius of really creative cooking, and his response was a rather bleak, 'It is very, very difficult.'

Vertes was slightly more upbeat about the possibility of protecting certain 'signature dishes', those dishes that are now becoming increasingly popular items on the menus of those restaurants in which the public may first have become aware of them and obviously constitute a draw for their customers. He ran through a list of dishes that had been described in the press as being the signature dishes of a particular restaurant. Examples included the squid and mackerel burger from chef Anthony Demetre at Arbutus (*page 188*), now sadly closed, or Jacob Kenedy's shaved celeriac and radish salad at the nearby Bocca di Lupo (*page 189*). As a mere combination of ingredients, it is hard to see how, in principle, these chefs could not stop from being copied by other chefs elsewhere.

But then his eyes lit upon a photo of the meat fruit dish, the chicken liver parfait inside an orange casing in the form of a mandarin, that chef Heston Blumenthal created when he opened Dinner restaurant in the Mandarin Oriental Hotel in London (*pages 190–191*). While Vertes believes that Blumenthal's dish could almost be protected by requesting 'design rights' in the finished dish (in the same way as fashion designs), Blumenthal's interests were also more readily protected by the fact that anyone copying the dish could be accused of 'passing

off', which can be brought into effect to protect 'the goodwill' the original chef has created. 'It's as though you are saying Heston Blumenthal is in your kitchen creating his original dish, which is not, of course, the case.'

Vertes's conclusion is that, on a case-by-case basis, protecting individual dishes is almost impossible. However, he was at pains to stress that this is not the end of the story. When someone starts copying more than one dish, or a particular dish in combination with other aspects of a restaurant's style, more can be said. Let us turn to that.

Tuesday 19th March, 2013

Sparking Wine – Limney Blanc de Blancs, Davenport Vineyard, Sussex 2007 £11.00

Salad of new season broad beans, Moroccan lemon, goats cheese, wild garlic. £6.95
Scottish scallops, green vegetable tartare, potato mousse. £10.50
Slow cooked hare 'bolognese', pappardelle, Parmesan. £7.00
Dorset crab, avocado guacamole, peanut and mango. £10.50
Warm crisp pig's head, potato purée, pickled turnips. £8.00
Squid and mackerel 'burger', Cornish razor clams. £11.50

Slow cooked shoulder of venison 'cottage pie', winter greens (for two persons). £14.50 per person
With a carafe of Tempranillo, Artero, La Mancha. £17.50 per person

Welsh Elwy Valley lamb breast, sweet potato, Madeira braised celery, golden sultanas. £18.00
Scottish salmon, broccoli, colza oil, Swiss chard, hazelnuts. £18.00
Saddle of rabbit, roast onions, heritage carrots, freekeh, slow cooked shoulder cottage pie. £18.95
Cod fillet, roast cevenne onions, endive marmalade, pancetta. £19.00
Grilled piece of beef, wild garlic, pickled shallots, bone marrow gratin. £19.50
Pieds et paquets – lambs' tripe, shoulder, trotters. £19.00

Kirkham's Lancashire, Gubbeen, Lincolnshire Poacher, Roquefort, Ash Log. £3.25 each
Warre's, Quinta Da Cavadinha, 1996. £10.50

Desserts.
Classic English custard tart. £6.00
Dulce de Leche – milk jam ice cream. £4.95
Bitter chocolate mousse, mandarin sorbet. £6.00
Yorkshire rhubarb trifle £6.00
Pear clafoutis, vanilla ice cream,(to share). £5.95 per person

Pre Theatre

Chicken and eel terrine, fruit rlish, pickled turnip.
Minestrone of late winter vegetables, Parmesan, olive oil, basil.

Confit duck leg, pancetta, potted cabbage.
Fresh sheep's ricotta gnudi, spinach and preserved lemon.

Vanilla cheesecake scented with rosewater, pineapple.
Today's cheese.

£18.95 2 courses - £20.95 3 courses

Plat Du Jour
Lamb shoulder kofte, spinach, chickpeas and yougurt. £10
Including a 250ml carafe of red or white wine.

all prices include VAT, an optional service charge of 12.5% will be added to your bill

II MAY 2016
IF YOU HAVE ANY ALLERGIES , PLEASE SPEAK TO A MEMBER OF STAFF

CRUDI E SALUMI • RAW & CURED

		£/small	£/large
Rosamarina - shredded red mullet fermented with chilli	Calabria	£5	£10
Sea bream carpaccio with orange & rosemary	Veneto	£9	£18
Raw greens & young cheeses - fennel, peas & broad beans in their pods, broad bean puree, *caprino* & smoked ricotta	Primavera	£9	(£/person)
Home-made *soppressata* & *buristo* with *crescentine* & *squaaquerone*	Toscana	£9	£18
Parma ham & melon	Parma	£9	£18
Manzo di Pozza: home-cured beef, pecorino & rocket	Toscana	£10	£20
Buffalo mozzarella, tomatoes, rocket & basil	Campania	£10	£20

FRITTI • FRIED

		£/small	£/large
Fritti Romani:	Roma		
Sage leaves filled with anchovy		£1.5	each
Buffalo mozzarella bocconcini		£2.5	each
Olive stuffed with minced pork & veal		£2.5	each
Saffron, bone marrow & *gremolata* mini *arancino*		£3	each
Artichoke alla giudia		£4	each
Baccalà - home salted cod		£4.5	each
Lamb sweetbreads, artichokes & sage	Lazio	£7	£14
Squid & lemon slices	Veneto	£8	per 100g

PASTE E RISOTTI • PASTAS & 'RISOTTI'

		£/small	£/large
Fazzoletti with broad beans, their puree & pecorino	Liguria	£7	£14
Orecchiette with *'nduja*, red onion & tomato	Calabria	£7	£14
Spaghetti with anchovy, saffron, raisins, pine nuts & wild fennel	Sicilia	£8	£16
Orzotto - pearl barley 'risotto' with braised rabbit, broad beans & wild garlic	BDL	£8	£16
Rigatoni con la pajata - milk fed calf's intestines with the mother's milk inside, with tomato & pecorino	Lazio	£8.5	£17
Risotto of Italian prawns (red prawns & *mazzancolle*)	Campania	£9.5	£19
Nettle pappardelle with kid goat ragú	Trentino	£11	£22

FORNO E GRIGLIA • ROAST & GRILLED

		£/small	£/large
Grilled Sicilian prawns with *gremolata*	Sicilia	£5	each
Grilled mussels with chilli oil	Liguria	£6	£12
Galletto in spring *panzanella* - grilled, with wild garlic, peas, broad beans & rocket	Toscana	£9	£18
Fossil fish - sea bream charred in a crust of flour & salt	BDL	-	£18
Roast suckling pig with grapes, white wine & bay leaves	Emilia	-	£26
Tagliata - grilled bone-in sirloin, for 2-10 to share served with rosemary, balsamic vinegar, rocket & Parmesan	Toscana	-	£26.5 (£/person)

IN PENTOLA O PADELLA • FROM THE STEWING POT OR THE FRYING PAN

		£/small	£/large
U Morzeddhu - a stew of cow innards braised with tomato, oregano & copious chilli	Calabria	£8	£16
Chicken *scallopine* with artichokes & marsala	Roma	£9	£18
Ossobuco alla Milanese - veal shin braised 'in bianco' with white wine & bay, saffron risotto & *gremolata*	Milano	for two to share	£56
Langoustines, peas & tropea onions	Veneto	£15	£30

CONTORNI • SIDES

		£/small	£/large
Whole round lettuce & lemon dressing	Sperlonga	£5	-
Courgettes *trifolate* - sauteed with garlic & chilli	Lazio	£6	-
Braised chickpeas with tomato, chilli & mint	BDL	£6.5	-
Merinda tomatoes with *tropea* onion, salt & olive oil	Sicilia	£7	-
Braised peas, *tropea* onions & basil	Calabria	£7	-
Caponata - aubergines, celery & tomato *in agrodolce* served chilled or warm. To add anchovies	Sicilia	£7 +£2	£14 +£4
Agretti (monksbeard) with butter & lemon	Veneto	£7.5	-
Grilled asparagus & lemon	Lazio	£12	-

BOCCA DI LUPO • 12 ARCHER STREET, W1D 7BB • O2O 7734 2223 • PAINTINGS BY HAIDEE BECKER

CHEF: JACOB KENEDY / C. DE CUISINE: JAKE SIMPSON / SOUS-C: DEL GIUDICE & BALBINO

DINNER

SET LUNCH MENU

Grilled Hay Smoked Mackerel (c.1730)
Lemon salad, cucumber, dill & broad beans
2014 Acústic Blanc, Bodegas Acústic, Montsant, Spain £11.50

Dressed Snails (c.1880)
Grilled lettuce, parsley, anchovy, garlic & rock samphire
2014 'Les Argiles' Chenin Blanc, Francois Chidaine, Loire Valley,France £13.50

Cured Salmon (c.1660)
Roast beetroot, sea beet & parsley
Bacchus, London Cru, England £11.50

Slow Cooked Pork Belly (c.1920)
Pease pudding, bacon & mint oil
2013 Lagrein Riserva, Klause Lentsch, Alto Adige, Italy £13.50

Bohemian Cake (c.1890)
Chocolate & yuzu mousse with honey ice cream
Banyuls 'Reserva', Domaine la Tour Vieille, Roussillon, France £12.50

Strawberry Crust (c.1820)
Toasted vanilla cake, compressed strawberries, basil, puffed spelt & goats milk ice cream
2014 Moscato d'Asti Bricco Quaglia, La Spinetta, Piedmont, Italy £8.50

British Cheese
Cider apple, Yorkshire chutney, oat cakes & seeded crackers
(£7 supplement)
2011 Niepoort Late Bottled Vintage Port, Douro, Portugal £11.50

3 Course Menu £40.00

Please inform us of any allergies
& ask for further details of dishes that contain allergens

Please note all prices include VAT at the current rate.
A discretionary service charge of 13.5% will be added to your bill.

STARTER

Meat Fruit (c.1500)
Mandarin, chicken liver parfait & grilled bread
£17.50

Roast Marrowbone (c.1720)
Snails, parsley, anchovy, mace & pickled vegetables
£17.00

Rice & Flesh (c.1390)
Saffron, calf tail & red wine
£17.50

Salamagundy (c.1720)
Chicken oysters, salsify, marrowbone & horseradish cream
& pickled walnuts
£17.50

Savoury Porridge (c.1660)
Frog's legs, girolles, garlic, parsley & fennel
£17.50

Earl Grey Tea cured Salmon (c.1730)
Lemon salad, gentleman's relish, wood sorrel & Exmoor caviar
£17.50

Frumenty (c.1390)
Grilled octopus, spelt, smoked sea broth, pickled dulse & lovage
£18.50

Lobster & Cucumber Soup (c.1730)
Lobster salad, smoked onion, rock samphire & sorrel
£25.00

D I N N E R
ʙʏ heston blumenthal

STARTER

Meat Fruit (c.1500)
Mandarin, chicken liver parfait & grilled bread
£17.50

Roast Marrowbone (c.1720)
Snails, parsley, anchovy, mace & pickled vegetables
£17.00

Rice & Flesh (c.1390)
Saffron, calf tail & red wine
£17.50

Salamagundy (c.1720)
*Chicken oysters, salsify, marrowbone & horseradish cream
& pickled walnuts*
£17.50

Savoury Porridge (c.1660)
Frog's legs, girolles, garlic, parsley & fennel
£17.50

Earl Grey Tea cured Salmon (c.1730)
Lemon salad, gentleman's relish, wood sorrel & Exmoor caviar
£17.50

Frumenty (c.1390)
Grilled octopus, spelt, smoked sea broth, pickled dulse & lovage
£18.50

Lobster & Cucumber Soup (c.1730)
Lobster salad, smoked onion, rock samphire & sorrel
£25.00

MAIN

Powdered Duck Breast (c.1670)
Smoked confit fennel, smoked beetroot & umbles
£36.00

Roast Halibut (c.1830)
Mussel & seaweed ketchup, salmon roe & sea rosemary
£40.00

Lamb & Cucumber (c.1830)
*Short saddle of lamb with cucumber heart, sweetbread,
borage & mint*
£40.00

Roast Iberico Pork Chop (c.1820)
Pointy cabbage, onions & Robert sauce
£38.00

Braised Celery (c.1730)
Parmesan, morels, cider apple & smoked walnuts
£28.00

Cod in Cider (c.1940)
Chard, onions & smoked artichokes
£34.00

Chicken cooked with Lettuces (c.1670)
Grilled onion emulsion, spiced celeriac sauce & oyster leaf
£36.00

Hereford Ribeye (c.1830)
Mushroom ketchup & triple cooked chips
£38.00

Fillet of Aberdeen Angus (c.1830)
Mushroom ketchup & triple cooked chips
£42.00

Bone in Rib of Hereford Prime for 2 (c.1830)
Mushroom ketchup & triple cooked chips
£85.00

*(Our cuts of beef are dry aged for a minimum of 21 days and cooked over
wood and charcoal embers)*

Sides
*Mashed potatoes, Fries, Hispi cabbage & onions
Green beans, Carrots & caraway,
Mixed leaf salad. All at £4.75
Triple cooked chips £6.00*

DESSERT

Tipsy Cake (c.1810)
Spit roast pineapple
£14.50

Spring Tart (c.1720)
*Gariguette strawberries, rose, lovage & basil yogurt
& goats milk ice cream*
£13.50

Brown Bread Ice Cream (c.1830)
Salted butter caramel, pear & malted yeast syrup
£13.50

Sambocade (c.1390)
*Goats milk cheesecake, elderflower & apple, perry poached
pear & smoked candied walnuts*
£13.00

Chocolate Bar (c.1730)
Passion fruit jam & ginger ice cream
£13.50

Taffety Tart (c.1660)
Apple, rose, fennel & vanilla ice cream
£13.50

British Cheese
Cider apple, Yorkshire chutney, oat cakes & seeded crackers
£16.00

Please inform us of any allergies &
ask for further details of dishes that contain allergens

Please note all prices include VAT at the current rate. A discretionary
service charge of 13.5% will be added to your bill.

Sources of origin

Starter

Meat Fruit
c.13th–15th century

Roast Marrowbone
1720 The Cook's and Confectioner's Dictionary by John Nott

Rice & Flesh
1390 The Forme of Cury The Master Cooks of King Richard II

Salamagundy
1720 The Cook's and Confectioner's Dictionary by John Nott

Savoury Porridge
1660 The Whole Body of Cookery Dissected
by William Rabisha

Earl Grey Tea cured Salmon
1730 The Complete Practical Cook by Charles Carter

Frumenty
1390 The Forme of Cury The Master Cooks of King Richard II

Lobster & Cucumber Soup
1730 The Complete Practical Cook by Charles Carter

Main

Powdered Duck
1670 The Queen Like Closet or Rich Cabinet
by Hannah Woolley

Roast Turbot with Mussel & Seaweed Ketchup
1830 The Cook and Housewife's Manual
by Mistress Meg Dodds

Lamb & Cucumber
1830 The Cook and Housewife's Manual
by Mistress Meg Dodds

Roast Iberico Pork Chop
1820 based on Carême's residency in London

Braised Celery
1730 The Complete Practical Cook by Charles Carter

Cod in Cider
1940 Good Fish Dishes by Ambrose Heath

Chicken cooked with Lettuces
1670 The Queen Like Closet or Rich Cabinet
by Hannah Woolley

Fillet, Ribeye and Rib for 2 with Mushroom Ketchup
1830 The Cook and Housewife's Manual
by Mistress Meg Dodds

Dessert

Tipsy Cake
1810 The English cookery book by J.H. Walsh

Spring Tart
1720 The Cook and Confectioners Dictionary by John Nott's

Brown Bread Ice Cream
1830 A New System of Domestic Cookery
by Maria Eliza Rundell

Sambocade
1390 The Forme of Cury The Master Cooks of King Richard II

Chocolate Bar
1730 The Complete Practical Cook by Charles Carter

Taffety Tart
1660 W.M, The Queen's Closet Opened

PROTECTING THE OTHER INGREDIENTS OF A SUCCESSFUL RESTAURANT

Customers are drawn to restaurants because of a host of factors: the selection and quality of the food are obviously key – but also the style, the brand, the reputation of the chef and the 'X factor' (i.e. is this the place to be seen?). All of these will influence the clientele. And to some degree, many of these can be protected.

While dishes themselves cannot easily be protected, a menu as a whole can be. Taken as an entire work, it will automatically attract copyright protection as a 'literary work', much like any book, and even as an 'artistic work' if it has graphic elements. Under English law, it is possible that a particular dish description can attract copyright if it 'constitutes the author's own creation'. Certainly, there is a skill to crafting menu language to make each dish sound as attractive as possible to customers.

Similarly, Vertes counselled against lifting the accompanying notes from what others had written and posted on the internet when composing a wine list, however tempting this option may appear to busy sommeliers and restaurateurs.

Vertes did caution that the current trend of chefs stripping descriptions of their dishes of any adjectives and adverbs, and writing them in a very basic conjunction of ingredients – 'venison, potato, sour cream', for instance – makes them even harder to claim as original because they lack the same creativity.

Overall, however, a restaurateur could prevent a competitor copying a whole menu – or even substantial portions of it.

In an increasingly competitive world, Vertes counselled that of all the IP rights, 'passing off' is likely to be the most powerful tool against the copying of a restaurateur's style. A claim of 'passing off' protects against a competitor trading off your 'goodwill': the reputation you have acquired trading under certain brand names or get-up, i.e. those recognisable features that a consumer sees and recognises as yours. That might be a restaurant name; it might be a logo or even a

mere particular colour pattern that you use consistently throughout your branding.

If the public associates that with you, and would be confused if a third party started using it, that may be enough to give you a basis to object to its use. It is something that a restaurateur could be guilty of even without intentionally meaning to, by replicating too closely either dishes on the menu or the layout and design of the menu. Vertes cited the 2012 example of a restaurant opened in Harrogate, Yorkshire, by racing driver Jenson Button that was accused of borrowing too closely from the Leon menu pioneered by Henry Dimbleby. This became a news item that generated publicity for both sides; no legal action ensued but Button's restaurant subsequently closed.

This situation is evolving as the number of celebrity chefs proliferates alongside the growing number of companies seeking to franchise their names and protect not just their reputations but also their entire restaurant concepts, combining all of the elements described above, including those signature dishes for which they have best become known.

In such instances, the dish becomes more than just food on a plate, and these dishes and their names can be protected via a broader range of legal applications. This enables popular restaurants in the UK to create mirror-image franchisees in foreign countries, teaching them how to operate to the same standards, so that the customer has an identical experience wherever he is in the world – a business model Vertes specialises in and says is growing exponentially in popularity.

In terms of protecting the restaurant name (which might also be the chef's name) or a logo, Vertes strongly advocates applying to register a trademark. A trademark, once applied for and registered, will act effectively as an insurance policy against a competitor using an identical or even similar brand name (or logo) for a similar venture. It is possible to protect a brand without filing a trademark, but it is far harder and far more expensive to do so.

This will not be of interest to most chefs in whose kitchens there is today such a confluence of creative ideas and young cooks keen to climb the greasy pole to the pinnacle of their chosen profession. Vertes advocates that one

inexpensive method of protecting 'the magic in the kitchen' is to try and protect this knowledge as confidential information within an employment contract so that anybody who thinks about taking recipes with them at the end of their employment would be in breach of such a contract. Vertes quickly agreed with me that such an approach would be challenging to enforce and that such an approach would, in turn, lead to such dull menus – because it flies in the face of the industry traditions of sharing cooking styles, knowledge and expertise.

After Vertes and I parted, I thought of how two exceptional chefs had written their menus by borrowing information in very different styles.

The first is the London-based chef Marco Pierre White, who in the 1990s allegedly wrote his menus of classic French dishes without, he proudly claimed, having spent more than 24 hours in France. Instead, as cooks from leading restaurants in France had applied to him for a job, he had put them through their paces by getting them to execute a signature dish that he then replicated as effectively – and slightly less expensively – as the original.

Then there is the example of Michelle Garnaut, the Australian-born chef who made her name with her restaurants M on the Bund in Shanghai (*opposite*) and Capital M in Beijing. Her guiding principle for the dishes she put on her menus was that she had to have eaten each in its country of origin: an *ajo blanco* from her travels in southern Spain or a tagine from her holiday in Morocco.

But in each instance, the success of the dish on the menu depended on the chef's ability to transmit his or her interpretation of the dish to a brigade that had to absorb the information, make it themselves and serve it in precisely the same fashion time and time again.

Today, the internet cuts out the travel that was in the past the spur and inspiration to so many great menus. But chefs have always relied on the free passage of information, and the odd secret ingredient, to ensure that their recipes successfully see the light of day. It would be a great shame if the law were ever to interfere with this magical process.

M

ON THE BUND

SHANGHAI

米氏西餐厅

M's own Afternoon Blend	自制米氏混合茶—午间
M's own Evening Blend	自制米氏混合茶—晚间

The Classics ~   经典茶 ~
English Breakfast   英式早餐茶
Earl Grey   伯爵茶
Darjeeling   大吉岭茶

Song Fang, Maison de Thé ~   宋芳茶馆 ~

Chinese ~   中国茶 ~
Lapsang Souchong   正山小种
Pu'er Tuocha   沱茶

Blends ~   混合茶 ~
Carthage (black tea, mint, orange blossom, rose petals)
迦太基（红茶, 薄荷, 橙花, 玫瑰花瓣）
Pomme D'Amour (black tea, apple, caramel)
苹果之爱（红茶, 苹果, 焦糖）
Shanghai Dream (black tea, cherry, rhubarb, flowers)
上海之梦（红茶, 樱桃, 大黄, 干花）

Herbal ~   花茶 ~
Rooibo Reunion   留尼旺
Mint   薄荷
Chrysanthemum   菊花
Chamomile   洋甘菊

Fresh Teas ~   新鲜茶叶 ~
Fresh Mint   薄荷叶
Lemon & Ginger   柠檬生姜

Afternoon Tea at M

We carry a large selection of teas,
from our own blends
to the classics, from fine Chinese teas
to herbal, fresh and those modern ones too.
Please turn over to see our full list

M on the Bund's High Tea
138.00 per person
Go the whole hog, with scones, pastries, tarts
both sweet and savory, sandwiches and
sweet treats too, served with a pot of any tea
or a plunger of coffee
套餐含松饼, 甜品及三明治, 可选配咖啡或茶

M's lovely tea cups are for sale now ~
米氏精美骨瓷茶杯现已对外销售 ~

10% service charge applies 另加收10%服务费

Just Desserts

Choux Pastry Puffs filled with pastry cream
and drizzled with chocolate sauce 78.00
奶油泡芙配巧克力沙司

Clafoutis with poached pear and Chantilly cream 78.00
生梨烘饼配香草奶油

Rhubarb Crumble served with ginger ice cream 78.00
大黄坚果面包碎配生姜味冰淇淋

M's very famous Pavlova 98.00
米氏名点 ~ 蛋白饼
激情果冰淇淋, 奶油, 新鲜水果丁及激情果沙司

Ice creams and sorbets ~
our own ice creams and sorbets
made with the best seasonal produce
~ you pick and choose 96.00
自制冰淇淋及雪芭拼盘

Turkish coffee with Turkish delight and baklava 78.00
土耳其咖啡配土耳其糖果和核桃酥

THE WINE LIST

The menu is, of course, only one of a restaurant's many attractions. There is the warmth of the hospitality that emanates from the waiting staff. There is the pleasure of sitting in an attractive and comfortable room often surrounded by striking art on the walls. There is the theatre on show, provided not just by the interaction of the chefs and the staff but also by the chance to see the other customers. In fact, it was this final element that provided such a strong attraction for visitors to Paris in the early 19th century because in those days the city's emerging restaurants provided a rare opportunity to watch the fashionable French at play.

There are also the special attractions of a carefully chosen and fairly priced wine list, an attraction that fulfils several diverse criteria. Although I do not believe that the pairing of food and wine can be raised to the scientific levels many claim, nothing improves – or lifts, as the chef Daniel Boulud so eloquently puts it – a good plate of food as much as a good glass of wine alongside it. The choice of wines is also a very strong expression of the restaurateur's aims and ambitions, of how assiduously he takes his role and of how up-to-date he wants to appear in the rapidly changing wine world. Finally, nothing else can contribute to a restaurant's financial well-being as much as a wine list that induces its customers to spend slightly more than they had originally anticipated.

This is because any restaurant has only two major sources of income: the profit it generates from its menu and that from its wine list. By and large, the income from the service charge goes entirely to covering the cost of employing the staff.

In both instances, restaurateurs aim for the same gross margin on food and drink sales: costs must be kept under 30 per cent to allow a gross profit of at least 10 per cent. This is a general rule that can be achieved by various different methods, making more, for example, on certain dishes and wines than others, or by applying only a fixed cash margin to more expensive ingredients and bottles. This is a trusted, well-worn, universal and reliable formula.

Equally important – and here the wine list really does come into its own – is optimising the sales mix for the restaurant, ensuring that it does not become too overdependent on its labour-intensive menu. For any restaurant that is only open for lunch and dinner, it is difficult to achieve a sales mix better than 70 per cent of the total from the food and 30 per cent from the wine. However, that is becoming more difficult to maintain as customers drink less at lunchtime, particularly in the US, and water is given away. For those café/restaurants that now stay open throughout the day, this split is easier and, as I was to discover, can be improved to 50/50 in the right setting and with the right approach.

To learn how this can be done, I gathered five very successful practitioners of the art of selling and serving wine across Europe around the private dining room in Portland restaurant, London. They were: Charlotte Sager-Wilde, co-founder of the highly popular Sager + Wilde Wine Bar and Sager + Wilde Restaurant, two wine-led establishments that specialise in wines from the US and fine wine, and are based in London's increasingly fashionable East End; Charlie Young, who migrated from a career in the wine trade to open the ever-expanding Vinoteca group; Xavier Rousset, who came to the UK initially to work as a sommelier at Le Manoir aux Quat'Saisons before becoming a founding partner in the 28°–50° group, and has now gone on to open Blandford Comptoir and Cabotte, a Burgundy-themed restaurant in the City of London; Ferran Centelles, who for

11 years worked as the sommelier at the world-famous El Bulli restaurant in Spain; and, last but not least, Enrico Bernardo, the founder of the renowned Parisian restaurants Goust and Il Vino – where the customer chooses the wine before the food – and who in 2004 won the Best Sommelier of the World competition.

I asked them to put their minds to one question: how must, can and should a wine list support the menu? I was encouraged by Sager-Wilde's immediate response, 'I very rarely think of anything else anyway.'

Our conversation began with a synthesis of their accumulated experiences. 'The problem is,' Centelles opined, 'that these are lists and therefore not easy for the guests to get their heads round. If you use the phrase "game sauce" alongside a dish, then most customers can imagine not only what this will look like on a plate but also what it will taste like. If you describe a wine as Hermitage, only a very few will understand what this will taste like. We all need far more tools to describe wine.'

Everyone around the table agreed that they were part of a process that was at last leading to a breakdown in the snobbery that has long surrounded wine, but that although the public's knowledge of wine was increasing, it was not doing so as swiftly as their knowledge of food. Thick, heavy, leather-bound wine lists would remain a reason for a visit to some of the longest established restaurants but they did not provide a viable model for the future – all agreed because the cellar ties up so much stock and this particular medium seems today to be so old-fashioned.

These heavy wine lists also smack of a sense of arrogance that has also to be a thing of the past. Young summed this up by saying that his attitude was to not take himself too seriously but to approach what he and his partner do – putting together a list of over 300 exciting wines, of which at least 70 are changed every six months – extremely seriously. A wine list, and its contents, can provoke more confrontation than a menu, all agreed. There was more opportunity via the wine list to make the customer feel stupid, which, Sager-Wilde added, was a situation that had to be avoided at all costs.

Bernardo explained that it was his years carrying a big wine list round the

tables of the George V Hotel in Paris that convinced him that this medium was flawed. 'Most of the guests don't understand wine and just as relevantly they don't want their conversation interrupted. The key,' Bernardo emphasised, 'is to win your guests' trust within minutes of them sitting down and then using a combination of wines by the glass and by the bottle to steer them through what they have chosen to eat from the menu.'

Bernardo has made a success of this in his restaurants, initially by setting an example and then by training his staff to follow his example. But before we moved on to how best to effect this, Rousset concurred and then added a caveat: 'I am sure that shorter, more personal wine lists represent the future, particularly as most customers today seem to be in a rush, to have less time to choose what they want to drink. In my opinion, it becomes then a question of signposting, how best to steer your customer to something that you are excited about.'

The key, in his opinion – and Rousset described himself as someone who enjoys drinking from wine lists others have assembled as much as assembling his own – is navigation. 'Chablis will always sell, no matter where it appears on the list, but the excitement today lies elsewhere,' even this Frenchman admitted.

This comment provided nods of agreement. Shorter, well-balanced lists are the future – especially now that modern printing technology provides contrasting colour, typography and forms of layout. The advice of designer Mary Lewis in Chapter Five applies equally forcefully to the wine list as it does to the menu. Take every opportunity to link the wine list to the menu, to make it fun and different. Rousset added that they had considerable success when they changed the headings of their wines from geographical to more sensory, such as aromatic, light and fresh, or fruity (a layout I also introduced in my restaurant in 1981).

Young concurred, at least in part. 'We used to rely heavily on geography but we came to realise that this approach was asking too much of the customer. And we would write three or four lines describing each wine but now we have simplified that to one line. Yet writing that one line does not have to follow any particular script.' Young explained that they had had particular success with a

The Ambassador Hotel, Los Angeles

A wine list with visual style and humour. Where are they today? Courtesy of The Culinary Institute of America Menu Collection.

WE SERVE ONLY 17 AND 18-YEAR OLD BOURBON AND RYE WHISKIES,
AND THE FINEST IMPORTED GINS IN ALL MIXED DRINKS
FROM 40 CENTS AND UP.

CUSTOMS

DON'T

Don't shake any wine.

Don't put ice in the glass.

Don't serve white wine at room temperature.

Don't serve a sweet wine before a dry one.

Don't ice or heat red wines.

Don't serve in too small a glass.

Don't fill the glass—should be a little over half full.

Don't tilt bottle backward after beginning to serve.

Don't place more than three glasses on table at one time,
if more than two wines are served, the glasses are
placed on table just before wine is served.

Don't serve a dry wine after a sweet dish.

DO

Do serve white wine chilled.

Do serve a dry wine before a sweet one.

Do serve white wines with fish.

Do serve white wines before reds.

Do pour into the host's glass first, then serve to right.

SERVE

Lighter wines before wines of heavier texture and fullness.

Young wines before old wines.

If only one wine at luncheon, it should be light, such as
Rhine, Sauterne, light Burgundy or light Claret.

In choosing wine select the one that will blend harmoni-
ously with the food to be served, and one that is
appropriate to the dish.

Place three glasses on table slightly to the right, water
glass in line with knife. The glass of wine to be
served first, to right of water glass.

WE SERVE ONLY 17 AND 18-YEAR OLD BOURBON AND RYE WHISKIES,
AND THE FINEST IMPORTED GINS IN ALL MIXED DRINKS
FROM 40 CENTS AND UP.

PORTS, SHERRIES, ANGELICAS, DUBONNET AND VERMOUTH

American		Per Glass	Per Bottle
30	Muscat, Napa and Sonoma	.25	1.50
31	Madeira, Napa and Sonoma or S. & J.	.25	1.50
33	Angelica, Napa and Sonoma or S. & J.	.25	1.50
167	Tokay, S. & J.	.25	1.50
38	Sherry, Beringer	.25	1.50
41	Port, Beringer	.25	1.50
229	Vodka, Smirnoff	.35	2.50
231	Vodka, Zubrovka, Smirnoff	.35	2.50

Imported		Per Glass	Per Bottle
43	Port, Commodore	.35	2.50
413	Port, Warre's Invalid Fine Old Tawny	.40	3.00
208	Port, Sandeman, Five Star, Tawny	.50	3.25
423	Port, Warre's White Heart—Old White	.50	3.50
211	Port, Sandeman, V. C. O.	.55	3.75
412	Port, Warre's Old Vintage Ruby	.60	4.00
149	Sherry, "Diamond Jubilee"	.35	2.50
190	Sherry, Ideal Pale, Pedro Domecq	.40	2.75
34	Sherry, Sandeman Five Star	.45	3.50
196	Sherry "Delicia" Pedro Domecq	.45	3.50
32	Sherry, Sandeman Brown Bang	.50	3.75
206	Sherry, Victoria (1900) Manuel Fernandez	.50	3.50
151	Sherry, "Dry Sack," Williams & Humbert	.60	3.50
158	Sherry, East India (1834)	.50	4.00
124	Sherry, "Amontillado" Sandeman	.65	4.25
68	Sherry, "Amontillado Selecto" Pedro Domecq	.65	5.50
126	Sherry, Gloriosa, Manuel Fernandez	.60	4.25
36	Sherry, Sandeman Royal	.65	5.00
35	Sherry, "British Cream" (1840) Santiago & Gross	.75	6.00
44	Sherry, Harvey's Bristol Cream	1.00	7.00
427	Marsala, Florio & Co. (1925)	.40	3.00
37	Madeira, Leacock's (99)	.40	3.00
45	Madeira, Leacock's Fine Old Sercial	.50	4.00
42	Tokay, Royal Gold, Five Puttonos Aszu	.40	3.00
53	Vermouth, Noilly-Prat	.35	2.25
57	Vermouth, Martini and Rossi	.35	2.25
123	Vermouth, Cinzano	.35	2.25
61	Dubonnet	35	2.50
428	Vodka, Carl Keller	.45	3.50

ALL COCKTAILS 40 CENTS AND UP ARE THREE OUNCES

(N. B.—Prices subject to change without notice)

Ports
Sherries
Vermouths
— Customs —

Imported
Sweet Wines
Spanish

California
White and
Red Wines

Imported
White Wines
French

Imported
Red Wines
French and
Italian

Imported
White Wines
German and
Italian

Classifications
of Wines

Champagnes

Imported
Liqueurs
Cordials
Wine Cups
Cognacs

Cocktails

Whiskies
Bourbons
Rye
— Apple Jack —

Whiskies
Scotch
Rums

Soft Drinks

Cocktails
and Hi-Balls
on Last Page

WE SERVE ONLY 17 AND 18-YEAR OLD BOURBON AND RYE WHISKIES,
AND THE FINEST IMPORTED GINS IN ALL MIXED DRINKS
FROM 40 CENTS AND UP.

CLASSIFICATION OF WINES
ACCORDING TO TYPE

Chablis: Natural or Blended (from Burgundy).
White, dry, full. **France.**

Sauternes: Natural or Blended (from Bordeaux).
White. **France.**

Burgundy: Natural or Blended (from Province of Burgundy).
Red and White. **France.**

Claret: Natural or Blended—Red (Bordeaux wines from the district of
Medoc, Graves, St. Emilion). **France.**

Rhine Wines: Natural. **Germany.**

Tokay: Natural or Blended. **Hungary.**

Chianti: Natural or Blended. **Italy.**

Muscatel: Natural. **Italy.**

Sherry: Fortified. **Spain.**

Port: Fortified. **Portugal.**

Madeira: Fortified. **Portugal.**

Champagne: Fortified—sparkling. **France.**

Champagne: Champagne is an artifical, fortified, blended wine. The
sparkle is a result of sealing the wine against oxygen during
fermentation, and thus imprisoning the gases which rise in bubbles
as soon as the wine is uncorked. Blending is a complicated art and
every great champagne house has its own formula. You are
guaranteed uniformity and quality. Blended Champagnes are
called Monopoles.

Vintage Champagne is the wine made in a good year, when the
quality is so fine that there is no need to blend any other wine with
it. Champagne can be doux (sweet) demi-doux, demi-sec (dry) or
brut. This is controlled by the addition of sugar during the manu-
facture or through ageing.

Resume: Fortified—A wine to which liqueur distilled from fresh wine has
been added to raise the alcoholic strength.

Blended—A mixture of wines from several vineyards, or vintages,
nursed along to give a particular taste.

ALL COCKTAILS 40 CENTS AND UP ARE THREE OUNCES

WE SERVE ONLY 17 AND 18-YEAR OLD BOURBON AND RYE WHISKIES,
AND THE FINEST IMPORTED GINS IN ALL MIXED DRINKS
FROM 40 CENTS AND UP.

Courtesy Chas. A. Faissole

Classifications
of Wines

Champagnes

Imported
Liqueurs
Cordials
Wine Cups
Cognacs

Cocktails

Whiskies
Bourbons
Rye
———
Apple Jack

Whiskies
Scotch
Rums

Soft Drinks
———
Cocktails
and Hi-Balls
on Last Page

THE TEMPERATURES AT WHICH WINE
SHOULD BE SERVED

Old Vintage Champagnes	45°
While young vintages showing more life	38°
Non Vintage Champagnes	32°
Red Burgundy	65°
White Burgundy	50°
Clarets	65°
Sauterne	42°
Rhine and Moselle Wines	45°
Port, Sherry, etc. (sweet wines)	70°

ALL COCKTAILS 40 CENTS AND UP ARE THREE OUNCES

Gavi di Gavi 2014 from Picollo Ernesto in Piedmont, at £32.50, described as 'an unusually tangy Gavi which will wake you up and take you on a day trip with Mr Peach and Mrs Apricot'.

In the right hands, and eloquently described, wine has an immediate attraction thanks to its natural, almost bucolic image. Although the alcohol does help, of course. But it was these very charms that the introduction of the iPad as a wine list failed to get across and explains why they came and went. 'They conveyed the information all right, perhaps too much,' Centelles explained, 'but customers now spend too much of their time surrounded by technology and this innovation seemed to go against the natural image of wine. They seemed to stand in the way, to be like an ATM machine. Choosing wine does allow for human interaction.'

But all agreed how useful it is to upload the restaurant's full wine list on to the website, particularly to excite the bigger spenders who will come in having already decided which of the more expensive bottles to enjoy. But here too Sager-Wilde added a very relevant piece of advice: 'I use social media to make customers aware of some special bottles we have available in limited quantity, but I never put them all out there. It is important to have a few bottles available for an occasion or for a customer you may not have expected.'

Now the conversation turned to that particular aspect of wine that had made all those round the table so successful in their restaurants – actually selling it – perhaps because they were all determined to shatter several illusions about the wine service that are shared not just by the general public but also by many chefs.

This illusion centres around the fact that while the menu is the careful, time-consuming and labour-intensive transformation of raw ingredients into finished dishes, a successful wine list seems merely to involve the pulling of a cork, the washing of a few glasses and, to make life increasingly easy, the turning of a growing number of screw caps.

Putting aside the considerable time spent at wine tastings (invariably held in the morning, not many hours after the restaurant has closed after the dinner service), assembling and looking after a wine list involves physical activity

that makes gym membership superfluous. Cellars are inevitably down one or more flights of stairs below the restaurant. A bottle of wine is heavier than most ingredients in a kitchen; a case weighs an unwieldy 18 kilos, with cases of champagne and Bordeaux in a wooden box even more. Nothing matches a bottle of wine for fragility or the sense of loss when a damaged case is discovered. And, of course, the more successful the wine list, the more frequently the process of restocking the cellar has to be repeated.

And then, in our increasingly crowded cities with temperatures higher and seemingly 'more sticky' than in the past, serving the wine at the correct temperature provides new and growing challenges. Red wine must not be allowed to get too warm because that can damage its flavour profile and, although this can be resolved by putting the bottle in an ice bucket for a few minutes, this never looks too professional. By contrast, although refrigeration will keep white and rosé wines at the most suitable temperature, these machines struggle in the warmer months to draw in sufficient cool air to keep their motors turning smoothly.

All this before the wine waiter confronts the customer, a meeting that the chefs may choose to do – although this is not a requirement – and one that Sager-Wilde described as similar to that of a swan on a pond. 'Visually we have to appear calm and in control but really we are pedalling like hell underneath.' A busy service may involve a wine waiter looking after five or six tables at least, which is extremely demanding and can lead to equal amounts of frustration and pleasure.

Centelles ran through these emotions that quite quickly can change from *I want to spend time with you*, to a brief chat, to the feeling of *why can't you see other tables want me so let's stop the chat*, to finally – with the bottle served to the customer – *why don't you stop talking and taste?* Sager-Wilde recalled the service the previous Saturday when she went to her cellar and discovered all four of her other sommeliers were already down there, all looking for bottles, and no one was actually upstairs on the floor looking after her customers. All present were in agreement that no matter what the style of food the restaurant serves, its location or its décor, the prerequisite for a successful wine waiter is patience.

For those like the five round the table, patience brings its own rewards, as all of them resoundingly expressed 'no regrets' for the career path they have followed.

'Absolutely not,' said Young who had started at catering college at the age of 16, 'except of course for the lack of sleep, although I find that customers give you the adrenalin to carry on.' Centelles, after 11 years on the floor at El Bulli, no longer misses it, while Bernardo, after 26 years, cannot stop looking after customers and revealed a distinctively Italian way of looking at the tables in his restaurant. 'I look at my customers in my restaurants as though they are sitting in a piazza. That is how they live, enjoy themselves and how, in my view, the world goes by.'

And what all agreed upon was that the passion for wine that initially set them on this career has only increased as more and more ways of sharing the pleasures it evokes have become available: wines by the glass, with the 175ml option particularly attractive to female customers after work; flights of wine, that can involve the same grape variety from producers in different regions; corkage-free Mondays to boost the quietest night of the week; wine pairings chosen to accompany a set menu; the greater flexibility of the headings that can be used, which only 20 years ago were invariably limited to Europe vs The New World and Oaky or Fresh; a party to celebrate the grape harvest; the fact that many customers today are less loyal to the big brands than they once were; the willingness of winemakers from around the world to travel and to take part in winemakers' dinners; and the opportunity today to make the dinner a multi-savoury experience by offering wine alongside beer and sake with various courses of the meal. 'Always be provocative,' was the collective advice.

Alongside these changes, the arrival of websites – such as wine-searcher.com, Vivino and others – that offer customers information on the retail prices of wines, and therefore the mark-ups that restaurateurs are adding, is also interpreted optimistically. 'I believe that this is forcing restaurateurs to be more transparent about their margins, and that is a very good thing,' Rousset explained. 'I would obviously like to see wines priced as inexpensively as possible, but I know that

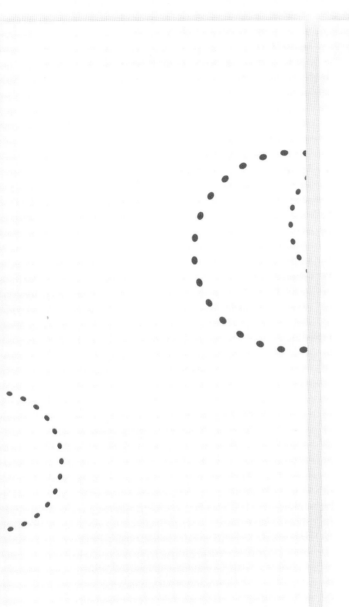

SIX COURSE TASTING MENU

DUCK TERRINE WITH MARCONA ALMOND
Honeycrisp Apple Confit, Sauternes Glazed Date
Mâche Salad, Hazelnut-Cider Vinaigrette
or
VENISON AND DAIKON RADISH MOSAÏC
Juniper Berries, Dinosaur Plum, Mustard Salad
Karthäuserhof Riesling Spätlese "Eitelsbacher", Ruwer, Germany 2004

· · · · · · ·

WASABI CURED FLUKE WITH SHISO BAVAROIS
Roasted Beets, Edamame Coulis, Seaweed Bread Tuile
or
TASTING OF YELLOWFIN TUNA
"En Tartare" with Northern Lights Caviar
Cured with Compressed Celery
Confit with Anchovy Dressing
Domaine Bailly Sancerre "Cuvée Chavignol", Loire Valley 2010

· · · · · · ·

CRISPY SCOTTISH LANGOUSTINES
Tandoori Hearts of Palm, Pickled Kumquat, Lemon Balm Salad
or
ARTICHOKE AND SQUID INK RAVIOLINI
Little Neck Clams, Ruby Red Shrimp, Razor Clams
Sea Beans, Saffron Cream, Opal Basil
Domaine Monpertuis Châteauneuf du Pape, Rhône 2008

· · · · · · ·

BACON WRAPPED SWORDFISH
Spaghetti and Butternut Squash, Confit Cipollini Onion
Pumpkin Seed Gremolata, Ommegang Beer Jus
or
ATLANTIC FLAKED COD WITH TARBAIS BEANS
Wild Lambsquarters, Chorizo, Parsley and Marcona Almond Emulsion
Domaine Faiveley Mercurey, Burgundy 2007

· · · · · · ·

ROASTED VEAL TENDERLOIN WITH CREAMY POLENTA
Poached Cheeks with Parsley Pasta
Crispy sweetbreads with Chanterelles and Crosnes
or
DUO OF BEEF
Black Angus Short Ribs with Cauliflower Mousseline
Seared Wagyu Tenderloin, Oyster Mushroom
Crispy Potato, Poached Bone Marrow
J. L. Chave Selection, Saint Joseph "Offérus", Rhône 2007

· · · · · · ·

LEMONGRASS POACHED PINEAPPLE
Coconut Meringue, Lime-Rum Gelée, Piña Colada Sorbet
Château Pajzos 5 Puttonyos Aszú, Tokaji 2000
or
WARM GUANAJA CHOCOLATE COULANT
Liquid Caramel, Fleur de Sel, Milk Sorbet
Domaine du Rancy Rivesaltes Ambré, Roussillon 1996

· · · · · · ·

Six Course Tasting $195   Paired with Wine $105
The Tasting Menu is available until 10:30PM, for the entire table

We kindly request that all guests refrain from cell phone use in the restaurant.

DANIEL

Daniel, New York

Dishes to lift whatever wines the sommelier or you, the customer, decide to choose. This is the six-course tasting menu from Daniel, Daniel Boulud's flagship restaurant in New York.

practically this is not always possible. But pricing fairly is an expression of showing your respect for the customer.'

Young added that, in their experience, buying direct from the producers and shipping 30 wines directly from Spain, Germany and France had saved considerable sums, savings that they could then pass on. But so did simply talking to the winemakers. 'We've found that if one wine is less price-sensitive than others, we can offer to pay slightly more for that wine so that they can charge us somewhat less on a wine that we can sell in volume.'

The results of such an approach are already obvious in Paris, Bernardo explained, where there has been a significant rise in the number of small, independent restaurants with 25–30 covers that prosper thanks to the combination of a short menu, an enticing wine list and reasonable prices. 'Seven years ago there were 30 restaurants with one Michelin star, today there are 64.'

Bernardo believes that this trend, which has already taken hold in London, will only continue.

Happily, my choice of a 2011 Pegasus Riesling made by Howard Booysen in Stellenbosch, South Africa, and a 2004 Quartz Reef Pinot Noir from Central Otago, New Zealand, had met with the unanimous approval of my guests, whom I asked to give their predictions of wine regions to watch out for. These ranged from Galicia, north-west Spain, to Serbia and Hungary, to the vineyards around Mt Etna in Sicily and those in the Swartland in South Africa, to the increasingly good wines from Paso Robles, San Luis Obispo and Santa Barbara in California.

Reflecting on this informative and optimistic discussion, I came away with three further reasons why the wine list has to support the menu. The first is that wine develops the contact between the customer and the restaurant in a way that successive plates of food cannot. A succession of different wines by the glass, or just one bottle that develops throughout the meal, provides opportunities for discussion and chat that plates of food, even those delivered by a chef/waiter invariably only too keen to return to the kitchen, cannot.

The second is that it broadens the restaurant's appeal, not just to customers but also to the increasing number of people who find restaurants fascinating. Those who took part in this discussion have been impressed by how, over the past few years, the availability of well-chosen wines by the glass has brought in new and engaged customers, such as younger women and visitors from Asia. A good wine list also gives the hard-pressed journalist, blogger or simply the enthusiast something extra to write about.

Finally, in an increasingly competitive world, it makes sense on so many different fronts. The restaurant will be more profitable. The customers will leave happier. And the dishes on the menu will taste even better.

BOTTLES

FRENCH REDS

BURGUNDY

BENJAMIN LEROUX
Bourgogne Rouge *2013* — 65

DOMAINE ROUMIER
Bourgogne Rouge *2007* — 185

GROS FRÈRE ET SŒUR
Hautes-Côtes-de-Nuits *2005* — 105

BACHELET
Côtes de Nuits-Villages *2005* — 135

CHANDON DE BRIAILLES
Savigny-lès-Beaune
1ER CRU FOURNEAUX 2005 — 160

DOMAINE MARQUIS D'ANGERVILLE
Volnay *1ER CRU CHAMPANS 2007* — 265

DOMAINE DE L'ARLOT
Nuits-St.-Georges
1ER CRU CLOS DE L'ARLOT 1999 — 275

RENE ENGEL
Vosne-Romanée *2004* — 220

MUGNERET-GIBOURG
Vosne-Romanée *2008* — 275

SYLVAIN CATHIARD
Vosne-Romanée *2010* — 230

DUJAC FILS ET PÈRE
Chambolle-Musigny *2012* — 160

L & A LIGNIER
Chambolle-Musigny *BUSSIÈRES 2005* — 165

DOMAINE FOURRIER
Gevrey-Chambertin *V.V. 2007* — 275

BEAUJOLAIS + JURA

JEAN-PAUL THÉVENET
Morgon *2013* — 75

DOMAINE DU PÉLICAN
Arbois *TROIS CÉPAGES 2013* — 90

JEAN-FRANÇOIS GANEVAT
Côtes du Jura *CUVÉE JULIEN 2011* — 125

RHÔNE

ALAIN GRAILLOT
Crozes Hermitage *2013* — 70

DOMAINE FAURY
St. Joseph *2012* — 65

JEAN LOUIS CHAVE SELECTIONS
St. Joseph *OFFERUS 2012* — 70

MONIER-PERRÉOL
St. Joseph *CHÂTELET 2013* — 85

FRANCK BALTHAZAR
Cornas *SANS SOUFRE 2013* — 120

MARCEL JUGE
Cornas *2011* — 125

AUGUSTE CLAPE
Cornas *2004* — 295

THIERRY ALLEMAND
Cornas *CHAILLOT 2009* — 275

MARIE ET PIERRE BÉNÉTIÈRE
Côte-Rôtie *CORDELOUX 2011* — 155

JAMET
Côte-Rôtie *2004* — 295

BETTS & SCHOLL
Hermitage *2001* — 160

DOMAINE GRAMENON
Côtes du Rhône *SAGESSE 2013* — 75

CHÂTEAU DES TOURS
Côtes du Rhône *2011* — 80

DOMAINE CHARVIN
Châteauneuf-du-Pape *2009* — 170

SOUTHERN FRANCE + CORSICA

MATASSA
Roussillon *COUME DE L'OLLA 2013* — 45

LA TOUR VIEILLE
Collioure *PINÈDE 2013* — 50

DOMAINE COMTE ABBATUCCI
Ajaccio *CUVÉE FAUSTINE 2012* — 90

DOMAINE TEMPIER
Bandol *CABASSAOU 1991* — 295

"ALL WINES ARE AVAILABLE AS A HALF BOTTLE" *JOHN Z. SLOVER*

Charlie Bird, New York

ITALIAN REDS

TUSCANY

ISOLE E OLENA
Chianti Classico *2012* — 60

FONTODI
Chianti Classico *2010* — 75

CASTELLO DI AMA
Chianti Classico *SAN LORENZO 1990* — 195

IL COLLE
Rosso di Montalcino *2013* — 55

IL POGGIONE
Brunello di Montalcino *2010* — 160

CERBAIONA
Brunello di Montalcino *2008* — 290

CONTI COSTANTI
Brunello di Montalcino *1997* — 225

MONTEVERTINE
IL SODACCIO 1998 — 180

FONTODI
FLACCIANELLO 1997 — 295

FELSINA
FONTALLORO 1993 — 165

CERBAIONA
ROSSO 2010 — 100

CASTELLO DI RAMPOLLA
VIGNA D'ALCEO 1998 — 290

SOUTHERN ITALY

TAMI
Nero d'Avola *2013 (SICILY)* — 45

MONTEVETRANO
Aglianico *CORE 2013 (CAMPANIA)* — 50

OGNOSTRO
Aglianico *MONTEMARANO 2010 (CAMPANIA)* — 80

LA DISTESA
Montepulciano *NOCENZIO 2012 (MARCHE)* — 85

ANGELO ROCCA
Primitivo *MILLENIUM 1985 (PUGLIA)* — 125

PIEDMONT

PROPRIETÀ SPERINO
Nebbiolo *UVAGGIO 2011* — 75

PETTERINO
Gattinara *2004* — 75

SERAFINO RIVELLA
Barbaresco *MONTESTEFANO 2010* — 120

PRODUTTORI DEL BARBARESCO
Barbaresco Riserva *RIO SORDO 2004* — 210

G.D. VAJRA
Barolo *ALBE 2011* — 80

BARTOLO MASCARELLO
Barolo *2008* — 275

FRANCESCO RINALDI
Barolo *1988* — 295

VIETTI
Barolo *LAZZARITO 2006* — 250

ELIO GRASSO
Barolo *CHINIERA 1990* — 275

GIUSEPPE RINALDI
Barolo *CANNUBI-SAN LORENZO 2008* — 295

CASCINA FONTANA
Dolcetto d'Alba *2013* — 45

CASCINA DELLE ROSE
Barbera d'Alba *2012* — 50

GIACOMO CONTERNO
Barbera d'Alba *CERRETTA 2012* — 110

GIUSEPPE RINALDI
Barbera d'Alba *2012* — 130

G.B. BURLOTTO
Verduno Pelaverga *2014* — 50

TRENTINO + FRIULI

FORADORI
Teroldego *2012* — 60

VIGNAI DA DULINE
Merlot *2011 MAGNUM* — 280

GRAVNER
ROSSO 1995 — 275

BORGO DEL TIGLIO
ROSSO RISERVA 1997 — 250

SPARKLING + CHAMPAGNE

NINO FRANCO
Prosecco *RUSTICO NV* — 50

BÉRÊCHE
BRUT RÉSERVE NV — 85

CHARTOGNE-TAILLET
CUVÉE SAINTE ANNE NV — 90

KRUG
GRANDE CUVÉE NV (DISGORGED 2006) — 295

AGRAPART
Blanc de Blancs *7 CRUS NV* — 115

PIERRE PETERS
Blanc de Blancs *L'ESPRIT 2008* — 180

CÉDRIC BOUCHARD
Blanc de Noirs *CÔTE DE VAL VILAINE (2011)* — 150

BÉRÊCHE
Meunier *RIVE GAUCHE (2011)* — 155

DOM PÉRIGNON
VINTAGE 2005 — 295

KRUG
Rosé *NV (375 ML)* — 250

SAVART
Rosé *BULLE DE ROSÉ NV* — 160

VOUETTE ET SORBÉE
Rosé *SAIGNÉE DE SORBÉE NV* — 200

FRENCH WHITES

LOIRE + JURA

THOMAS-LABAILLE
Sancerre *LES MONTS DAMNÉS 2014* — 65

DIDIER DAGUENEAU
Pouilly-Fumé *BUISSON-RENARDES 2004* — 275

THIBAUD BOUDIGNON
Anjou Blanc *2012* — 80

DOMAINE DU PÉLICAN
Savagnin *2013* — 90

JEAN-FRANÇOIS GANEVAT
CUVÉE DE GARDE (SOUS-VOILE) 2007 — 140

BURGUNDY

DOMAINE LAFARGE
Aligoté *2011* — 50

DOMAINE LAVANTUREUX
Chablis *VIEILLES VIGNES 2013* — 60

FRANCINE + OLIVIER SAVARY
Chablis *1ER CRU FOURCHAUME 2014* — 75

RENÉ + VINCENT DAUVISSAT
Chablis *1ER CRU FOREST 2007* — 225

DOMAINE DE LA CADETTE
Bourgogne Vézelay *LA CHÂTELAINE 2012* — 45

DOMAINE A. + P. DE VILLAINE
Bourgogne Blanc *CLOUS 2013* — 70

DOMINIQUE LAFON
Bourgogne Blanc *2013* — 80

FRANTZ CHAGNOLEAU
Saint-Veran *A LA CÔTE 2013* — 75

BENJAMIN LEROUX
Auxey-Duresses *2013* — 85

PAUL PILLOT
Chassagne-Montrachet *2013* — 110

BERNARD MOREAU
Chassagne-Montrachet
1ER CRU VERGERS 2012 — 225

LOUIS CARILLON
Puligny-Montrachet *2008* — 180

ETIENNE SAUZET
Puligny-Montrachet *2013* — 150

DOMAINE ROULOT
Meursault *MEIX CHAVAUX 2007* — 290

CHANDON DE BRIAILLES
Corton-Charlemagne *2004* — 295

SOUTHERN FRANCE + CORSICA

YVES LECCIA
CUVÉE YL 2014 (CORSICA) — 55

DOMAINE U STILICCIONU
Vermentinu *2014 (CORSICA)* — 90

DOMAINE DE TRÉVALLON
BLANC 2001 (PROVENCE) — 150

BOTTLES

ITALIAN WHITES

BRUNA
Pigato *LE RUSSEGHINE 2014 (LIGURA)* 45

LAMBRUSCHI
Vermentino *COSTA MARINA 2013 (LIGURIA)* 95

VENICA & VENICA
Sauvignon *RONCO DEL CERÒ 2014 (FRIULI)* 55

BORGO DEL TIGLIO
Friulano *RONCO DELLA CHIESA 2012 (FRIULI)* 150

KUENHOF
Riesling *KAITON 2005 (ALTO ADIGE)* 85

FIORANO
Sémillon *1992 (LAZIO)* 170

I VIGNERI
Carricante *VIGNA DI MILO 2013 (SICILY)* 90

BENANTI
Carricante *PIETRAMARINA 2010 (SICILY)* 95

CIRO PICARIELLO
Fiano di Avellino *2013 (CAMPANIA)* 55

SPANISH + PORTUGUESE WHITES

DO FERREIRO
Albariño *2013 (GALICIA)* 60

CAVES SÃO JOÃO
Arinto *1995 (BEIRAS)* 65

LÓPEZ DE HEREDIA
Rioja Gran Reserva *VIÑA TONDONIA 1994* 175

AMERICAN WHITES

MASSICAN
ANNIA 2014 (NAPA) 65

PEIRSON MEYER
Chardonnay *RUSSIAN RIVER 2012 (SONOMA)* 95

KALIN CELLARS
Chardonnay *CUVEE W 1995 (LIVERMORE)* 95

PETER MICHAEL
Sauvignon Blanc *L'APRÈS-MIDI (SONOMA)* 150

GERMANY + AUSTRIA

KELLER
Riesling Trocken *2014 (RHEINHESSEN)* 50

JOH. JOS. PRÜM
Riesling Kabinett
WEHLENER SONNENUHR 2007 (MOSEL) 100

MAXIMIN GRÜNHAUS
Riesling Auslese *ABTSBERG 1983 (RUWER)* 295

MORIC
Grüner Veltliner
SANKT GEORGEN 2013 (BURGENLAND) 120

F.X. PICHLER
Grüner Veltliner
KELLERBERG 2001 (WACHAU) 190

SPANISH REDS

CRATER
Listan Negro *2012 (CANARY ISLANDS)* 65

TERROIR AL LÍMIT
Priorat *TORROJA 2012* 90

ALGUEIRA
Brancellao *2013 (GALICIA)* 95

LA RIOJA ALTA
Rioja Gran Reserva *904 2004* 100

LÓPEZ DE HEREDIA
Rioja Gran Reserva *VIÑA TONDONIA 1987* 290

NEW WORLD REDS

WENZLAU VINEYARD
Pinot Noir *2012 (STA. RITA HILLS)* 110

LITTORAI
Pinot Noir *HIRSCH 2012 (SONOMA COAST)* 150

COPAIN
Pinot Noir *CLOS PEPE 2007 (STA. RITA HILLS)* 160

SANDLANDS
Trousseau *2013 (SONOMA COAST)* 65

ARNOT-ROBERTS
Syrah *2013 (CLEAR LAKE)* 85

CHACRA
Merlot *MAINQUÉ 2011 (PATAGONIA)* 65

MOUNT EDEN
Cabernet Sauvignon *2010 (STA. CRUZ MTS)* 120

WINES BY THE GLASS

SPARKLING + WHITES

NINO FRANCO
Prosecco *RUSTICO (VENETO)* 13

BÉRÊCHE & FILS
BRUT RÉSERVE NV (CHAMPAGNE) 28

KELLER
Riesling Trocken *2014 (RHEINHESSEN)* 13

BRUNA
Pigato *LE RUSSEGHINE 2014 (LIGURA)* 15

VENICA & VENICA
Sauvignon *RONCO DEL CERÒ 2014 (FRIULI)* 15

BORGO DEL TIGLIO
COLLIO 2013 (FRIULI) 19

ROSÉ + REDS

COPAIN
Rosé of Pinot Noir *2014 (NORTH COAST)* 14

BENJAMIN LEROUX
Bourgogne Rouge *2013 (BURGUNDY)* 16

TAMI
Nero d'Avola *2013 (SICILY)* 12

IL COLLE
Rosso di Montalcino *2013 (TUSCANY)* 15

G.B. BURLOTTO
Verduno Pelaverga *2014 (PIEDMONT)* 14

DOMAINE FAURY
St. Joseph *2012 (NORTHERN RHONE)* 18

SHAMELESS PLUG

(FOR OUR SOMMELIER FRIENDS WHO MAKE WINE)

THOMAS PASTUSZAK (THE NOMAD, NYC)
Terrassen Dry Riesling
2013 (FINGER LAKES) 50

ALDO SOHM (LE BERNARDIN, NYC)
Sohm & Kracher Grüner Veltliner
2012 (AUSTRIA) 90

ERIC RAILSBACK
(MATTEI'S TAVERN, STA. BARBARA)
Lieu-Dit Chenin Blanc *2013 (STA. YNEZ)* 60

FRANCESCO GROSSO (MAREA, NYC)
Altamarea Chardonnay
2013 (STA. BARBARA CTY) 60

BOBBY STUCKEY (FRASCA, BOULDER)
Scarpetta *TIMIDO SPARKLING ROSÉ*
Blaufränkisch/Pinot Noir *NV (FRIULI)* 45

RAJAT PARR (RN74, SAN FRANCISCO)
RPM Gamay *2013 (EL DORADO)* 75

JORDAN SALCITO
(MOMOFUKU, NYC)
Bellus Frappato *2013 (SICILY)* 45

JOE CAMPANALE
(EPICUREAN GROUP, NYC)
Annona Montepulciano *2012 (ABRUZZO)* 65

BEERS

KÖLSCH
REISDORFF (GERMANY) 9

WHEAT
OMMEGANG (COOPERSTOWN, NY) 6

'PEEPER' ALE
MAINE BEER COMPANY 16 OZ 14

TRAPPIST ALE
ORVAL (BELGIUM) 12

COCKTAILS

MIMOSA
FRESH ORANGE, PROSECCO 14

STREET COOLER
VODKA, DRY VERMOUTH, CITRUS 14

BLOODY MARY
CUCUMBER, PICKLED TOMATOES 14

MAI TAI
DARK RUM, ORGEAT, COINTREAU 14

WHISKEY SMASH
BOURBON, MINT, LEMON 14

TAILLEVENT

Crème de Lentilles en Cappuccino 140
Asperges vertes poêlées au Jus de Truffes 220
Escargots braisés au Curry 160
Ballottine de Foie gras de Canard 230
Oeufs brouillés au Risotto truffé 230
Huîtres tièdes au Fenouil 190
Paupiettes de Thon et d'Aubergines aux Herbes 170
Mousse d'Oursins à la Crème d'Escabèche 210
Salade de Coquilles Saint Jacques à la Maraîchère 220
Cannellonis de Tourteau, Sauce Ravigote 170
Boudin de Homard à la Nage 240

Daurade au gros Sel et à la Tapenade 220
Coquilles Saint Jacques poêlées au Jus de Truffes 230
Sole en Filets aux Pâtes fraîches et au Basilic 240
Bar de Ligne au Cresson 260
Darne de Turbot rôtie au Beurre fumé 260
Cassolette de Langoustines Bretonnes 260
Fricassée de Homard aux Châtaignes 350

Pigeon rôti en Bécasse 250
Poulette de Bresse en Cocotte lutée (2 personnes) 560
Canard sauvage aux Poivres doux 240
Tourte de Gibier à l'Armagnac 230
Noisettes de Chevreuil, Sauce Poivrade 270
Andouillette de Pied de Porc aux Truffes 230
Foie de Canard au Pain d'Épices et au Gingembre 260
Carré d'Agneau rôti, Sauce aux Herbes 260
Côte de Veau fermier au petit Lait 260
Fricassée de Rognon et de Ris de Veau au Verjus 250
Pot au Feu aux trois Viandes 230
Côte de Bœuf Grillée aux trois Sauces (2 personnes) 560

Taillevent, Paris

A classic from my collection, the four-page menu from Taillevent that begins with first and main courses on the front, lists the desserts on the back and contains the wine list inside.

LA CAVE DE

BORDEAUX BLANCS

1996	Château Turcaud	Entre deux Mers	120
1996	Château Charron, Cuvée Acacia	Premières Côtes de Blaye	140
1996	Château Brown	Pessac Léognan	230
1995	Château d'Ardennes	Graves	160
1995	Château de France	Pessac Léognan	230
1995	Château Laville Haut Brion	Pessac Léognan	840
1993	M. de Malle	Graves	200
1993	Château de Sainte Hélène	Sauternes	340
1988	Château Climens	Barsac	480
1988	Château Rieussec	Sauternes	520
1986	Château du Cros	Loupiac	180
1986	Château Suduiraut	Sauternes	480
1985	Château Fayau	Cadillac	170
1985	Château de Cérons	Cérons	190
1985	Château Suduiraut	Sauternes	600
1983	Château Lousteau Vieil	Sainte Croix du Mont	230
1983	Château d'Yquem	Sauternes	2300
1981	Château Piada	Barsac	360
1979	Château d'Yquem	Sauternes	2400
1976	Château Haut Mayne	Sauternes	440
1971	Château Doisy Védrines	Barsac	800
1970	Château Filhot	Sauternes	1000
1970	Château Climens	Barsac	1100
1967	Château Suduiraut	Sauternes	2100
1964	Château Rayne Vigneau	Sauternes	1400
1961	Château d'Yquem	Sauternes	4800
1937	Château Gilette	Sauternes	3800

BORDEAUX ROUGES

1996	Château Maine Gazin	Premières Côtes de Blaye		130
1996	Château Peychaud	Côtes de Bourg		140
1994	Château d'Ardennes	Graves		160
1994	Château Ponteilh Monplaisir	Pessac Léognan		220
1994	Château de Viaud	Lalande de Pomerol		240
1994	Château Chasse Spleen	Moulis		270
1994	Château Grand Pontet	Saint Émilion	M D	300
1994	Château Monbrison	Margaux		360
1994	Château Clos René	Pomerol	D	390
1994	Château Lagrange	Saint Julien	M D	440
1994	Château Grand Puy Lacoste	Pauillac	M D	480
1994	Château La Dominique	Saint Émilion	D	500
1994	Château Montrose	Saint Estèphe	M D	560
1994	Château Pavie	Saint Émilion	M D	600
1994	Château Lynch Bages	Pauillac	M D	680
1994	Vieux Château Certan	Pomerol	M D	680
1993	Château de Francs	Côtes de Francs		160
1993	Château Roudier	Montagne Saint Émilion		200
1993	Château de Cardaillan	Graves		260
1993	Château Moulin Riche	Saint Julien		280
1993	Château Bellegrave	Pomerol		350
1992	Château la Haye	Saint Estèphe		270
1992	Château Bonalgue	Pomerol		260
1991	Château Haut Brion	Pessac Léognan		980
1990	Château d'Aiguilhe	Côtes de Castillon		200
1990	Château Lestage Simon	Haut Médoc		380
1990	Château Potensac	Médoc		380
1990	Château Olivier	Pessac Léognan		480
1990	Château Les Ormes Sorbet	Médoc	D	480
1989	Château Fieuzal	Pessac Léognan		580
1989	Château Canon	Saint Émilion		820
1989	Château La Violette	Pomerol	M D	980
1989	Château Léoville las Cases	Saint Julien		1200
1989	Château Latour	Pauillac		1900
1989	Château Margaux	Margaux		1900
1989	Château Mouton Rothschild	Pauillac		1900
1988	Château Ducluzeau	Listrac		320
1988	Château Croque Michotte	Saint Émilion		420
1988	Château Sociando Mallet	Haut Médoc	M	640
1988	Château Calon Ségur	Saint Estèphe		680
1988	Château Pape Clément	Pessac Léognan		780
1988	Château Ducru Beaucaillou	Saint Julien		860
1988	Château Magdelaine	Saint Émilion	M	940
1988	Château La Conseillante	Pomerol		940
1988	Château Pichon Lalande	Pauillac		1200
1988	Vieux Château Certan	Pomerol	M	1200
1988	Château La Mission Haut Brion	Pessac Léognan		1600
1988	Château Latour	Pauillac		1900
1988	Château Margaux	Margaux	M	1900
1988	Château Mouton Rothschild	Pauillac		1900
1986	Château Rolland Maillet	Saint Émilion		460
1986	Château Bonalgue	Pomerol		520
1986	Château Figeac	Saint Émilion		1100
1986	Château Ducru Beaucaillou	Saint Julien	M	1100
1986	Château Pichon Lalande	Pauillac		1400
1986	Château La Mission Haut Brion	Pessac Léognan		2000

BORDEAUX ROUGES (suite)

1985	Château Magdelaine	Saint Émilion	D	1100
1985	Château La Lagune	Haut Médoc		1100
1985	Château Ducru Beaucaillou	Saint Julien		1100
1985	Château Trotanoy	Pomerol	D	1100
1985	Château Cos d'Estournel	Saint Estèphe		1300
1985	Château Léoville las Cases	Saint Julien		1300
1985	Château La Mission Haut Brion	Pessac Léognan		2000
1985	Château Ausone	Saint Émilion		2000
1985	Château Mouton Rothschild	Pauillac		2900
1982	Château Bertineau Saint Vincent	Lalande de Pomerol		480
1982	Château Belair	Saint Émilion		720
1982	Château Petit Village	Pomerol		1200
1982	Vieux Château Certan	Pomerol	D	1500
1982	Château Léoville las Cases	Saint Julien	D	2200
1982	Château La Mission Haut Brion	Pessac Léognan		3300
1982	Château Haut Brion	Pessac Léognan		4600
1981	Château Petrus	Pomerol		4600
1978	Château Ausone	Saint Émilion		2800
1978	Château Petrus	Pomerol		4600
1975	Château Figeac	Saint Émilion		1600
1975	Château Ducru Beaucaillou	Saint Julien		1600
1975	Château Cos d'Estournel	Saint Estèphe		1700
1975	Château Lafite Rothschild	Pauillac		3500
1975	Château Latour	Pauillac	M	3500
1971	Château La Lagune	Haut Médoc		1400
1971	Château Mouton Rothschild	Pauillac		3700
1971	Château Haut Brion	Pessac Léognan		3700
1971	Château Latour	Pauillac		3700
1970	Château Prieuré Lichine	Margaux		840
1970	Château Léoville Poyferré	Saint Julien		960
1970	Château Montrose	Saint Estèphe		1800
1970	Château La Lagune	Haut Médoc		1800
1970	Château Beychevelle	Saint Julien		1800
1970	Domaine de Chevalier	Pessac Léognan		1800
1970	Vieux Château Certan	Pomerol		2000
1970	Château Figeac	Saint Émilion		2000
1966	Château Pichon Lalande	Pauillac		2400
1961	Château Calon Ségur	Saint Estèphe		2700
1961	Château Léoville las Cases	Saint Julien		4800
1959	Château Pichon Longueville	Pauillac		3000
1955	Château Calon Ségur	Saint Estèphe		3100
1955	Château Pichon Longueville	Pauillac		4200
1937	Château Nenin	Pomerol		5800

CHAMPAGNE

Coteaux Champenois

S.A.	Blanc de Blancs de Chardonnay	Vve Laurent-Perrier		290
S.A.	Cumières Rouge	R. Geoffroy		330
S.A.	Brut, Grande Sélection	Champagne Taillevent	M D	420
1993	Brut, Rosé	Champagne Taillevent		440
1989	Blanc de Blancs	Champagne Taillevent		520

Une Carte Spéciale présente d'autres grands Noms de la Champagne et les Eaux de Vie de Taillevent.

DE VIGNOBLES EN VIGNOBLES

1997	Domaine d'Aupilhac	VDP Mont Baudile	V	140
1996	Domaine des Chênes, Les Magdaléniens	VDP Vals d'Agly		150
1996	Domaine de Souch	Jurançon		170
1996	Château Bouscassé	Pacherenc du Vic Bihl		200
1996	Domaine de l'Hortus, Gde Cuvée	VDP Val de Montferrand		220
1996	Domaine de la Capelle	Muscat de Mireval	V	220
1996	Clos Nicrosi	Coteaux du Cap Corse		280
1994	Château Les Crostes	Côtes de Provence	V	180
S.A.	Domaine Vial Magnères, R. Ambré	Banyuls	V	340
1986	Domaine J. Puffeney	Arbois		180
1982	Domaine Ch. Clavelin	Château Chalon		760
1981	Domaine des Tres Cantous, Vin de Voile	Gaillac		660
1979	Domaine L. Florin	Côtes du Jura		250
1961	Domaine M. Bouilleret	Arbois		1200
1997	Domaine H. Lapierre, V. Vignes	Moulin à Vent		190
1996	Domaine de la Coste, C. Sélection	Coteaux du Languedoc	V	130
1996	Domaine J.-M. Alquier, Les Bastides	Faugères		240
1996	Domaine de l'Aiguelière, Tradition	Coteaux du Languedoc		250
1996	Domaine Ilarria, C. Bixintxo	Irouléguy		300
1996	Domaine de la Rectorie, C. Léon Parcé	Banyuls	V	320
1995	Domaine des Chênes, Les Alzines	Côtes du Roussillon Villages		190
1995	Domaine Vial Magnères	Collioure	V	200
1995	Domaine de la Grange des Pères	VDP Hérault		380
1994	Mas Champart	Saint Chinian		130

TAILLEVENT

BOURGOGNES BLANCS

1996	Saint Véran, Les Chailloux	Dom. des deux Roches	160
1996	Saint Romain	Domaine A. Gras	230
1996	Pernand Vergelesses	M. Muskovac	260
1996	Ladoix	Domaine Ravaut	280
1996	Saint Aubin, Les Dents de Chien	Domaine Larue	300
1995	Petit Chablis	R. Lavantureux	180
1995	Auxey Duresses	Comte Armand	290
1995	Santenay Beauregard	V. Girardin	340
1995	Meursault Narvaux	B. Michelot · D	460
1995	Corton Charlemagne	Dom. Bonneau du Martray	960
1994	Chablis, Montmains	Domaine Race	260
1994	Hautes Côtes de Nuits	Domaine Jayer-Gilles	290
1994	Chassagne Montrachet	Dom. Blain-Gagnard	390
1994	Puligny Montrachet, Champ Canet	Domaine Sauzet · D	700
1994	Criots Batard Montrachet	Dom. Fontaine-Gagnard	860
1993	Meursault Narvaux	B. Michelot	490
1993	Nuits Saint Georges, La Perrière	Domaine H. Gouges	620
1993	Puligny Montrachet, Caillerets	H. de Montille	680
1993	Corton	Dom. Chandon de Briailles	980
1992	Chablis, Les Clos	J.-M. Raveneau	520
1992	Chassagne Montrachet, Les Caillerets	Dom. Blain-Gagnard · D	540
1992	Puligny Montrachet, Clavoillons	Domaine Leflaive · D	720
1992	Meursault Perrières	J.-L. Fichet	740
1992	Morey Saint Denis, Les Monts Luisants	Domaine Ponsot	760
1992	Batard Montrachet	Dom. Fontaine-Gagnard	820
1992	Chevalier Montrachet	Domaine Leflaive · D	980
1991	Meursault, Clos de la Barre	Dom. des Comtes Lafon	800
1991	Bienvenues Batard Montrachet	Domaine Leflaive	840
1991	Montrachet	E. Delagrange-Bachelet	2000
1990	Meursault Poruzot	F. Jobard	720
1990	Puligny Montrachet, Champ Canet	Domaine Sauzet · D	820
1989	Chassagne Montrachet, Caillerets	B. Morey	680
1989	Criots Batard Montrachet	Dom. Fontaine-Gagnard	980
1989	Montrachet	E. Delagrange-Bachelet	2200
1988	Meursault Poruzot	F. Jobard	720
1988	Chassagne Montrachet, Caillerets	M. Colin	740
1988	Chevalier Montrachet	Domaine Leflaive · D	1300
1986	Corton Charlemagne	M. Juillot	1300
1985	Chassagne Montrachet, Morgeot	B. Morey	820
1983	Meursault Perrières	Dom. des Comtes Lafon	1100

*Pour votre cave personnelle,
pour un conseil amical,
rendez-nous visite aux :*

Caves Taillevent
199, rue du Faubourg Saint-Honoré - 75008 Paris
Tel. : 01-45-61-14-09

BOURGOGNES ROUGES

1996	Bourgogne, Les Perrières	Domaine P. Bize	220
1996	Côtes de Nuits	Domaine Ravaut	240
1996	Santenay, La Comme	Domaine Belland	300
1996	Auxey Duresses	Domaine A. Gras	340
1995	Rully, La Chatalienne	Dom. Laborde-Juillot	260
1995	Givry	J.-M. Joblot	280
1995	Chassagne Montrachet	Dom. Fontaine-Gagnard	340
1995	Fixin	Dom. L. Boillot	360
1994	Hautes Côtes de Nuits	Domaine Jayer-Gilles	280
1994	Nuits Saint Georges, Forêts St Georges	Domaine de l'Arlot	380
1993	Santenay, Clos de la Confrérie	V. Girardin	310
1993	Savigny lès Beaune, La Dominode	B. Clair	330
1993	Ladoix, Les Corvées	Domaine Ravaut	360
1993	Meursault, Les Durots	P. Morey	360
1993	Pernand Vergelesses	Dom. Chandon de Briailles · D	400
1993	Gevrey Chambertin	D. Mortet	460
1993	Vosne Romanée, Les Suchots	J. Confuron-Cotetidot · D	580
1993	Chambolle Musigny, Les Beaux Bruns	Domaine G. Barthod · D	620
1993	Pommard Epeneaux	Comte Armand · D	660
1992	Volnay Taillepieds	Marquis d'Angerville	440
1992	Chambolle Musigny, Les Veroilles	Domaine G. Barthod	480
1992	Vosne Romanée, La Grande Rue	Domaine Lamarche	740
1992	Chambertin, Clos de Bèze	P. Damoy	780
1991	Hautes Côtes de Beaune	Domaine Jayer-Gilles	280
1991	Volnay, Caillerets	Marquis d'Angerville	440
1991	Clos Vougeot	Domaine Méo-Camuzet · D	780
1990	Blagny, La Pièce sous le Bois	F. Jobard	300
1990	Santenay, La Comme	Domaine Belland	380
1990	Beaune, Clos des Mouches	A. Leroyer-Girardin	460
1990	Nuits Saint Georges, Les Pruliers	L. Boillot	540
1990	Corton Perrières	Domaine Belland	580

BOURGOGNES ROUGES (suite)

1989	Gevrey Chambertin, Les Cherbaudes	L. Boillot	560
1989	Vosne Romanée, Les Suchots	J. Confuron-Cotetidot	600
1989	Corton Perrières	Domaine Belland	660
1989	Pommard Rugiens	J. Arbon	720
1989	Bonnes Mares	G. Roumier	820
1989	Echezeaux	Domaine Jayer-Gilles	880
1988	Rully, Les Clouds	P. et H. Jacqueson	420
1988	Morey Saint Denis, Monts Luisants	Domaine Pernin-Rossin	620
1988	Volnay Champans	Marquis d'Angerville · D	680
1988	Chambolle Musigny	G. Roumier	780
1988	Corton Renardes	M. Gaunoux	820
1988	Clos Vougeot	Domaine Méo-Camuzet	980
1988	Echezeaux	E. Rouget	980
1985	Pernand Vergelesses	R. Rapet	470
1985	Santenay, La Comme	A. Belland	490
1985	Volnay, Champans	H. de Montille	820
1985	Corton Renardes	M. Gaunoux	920
1985	Pommard Rugiens	J. Arbon	920
1985	Bonnes Mares	G. Roumier	980
1983	Nuits Saint Georges, Aux Boudots	Domaine Méo-Camuzet	860
1983	Clos Vougeot	G. Mugneret	860
1983	Corton Renardes	M. Gaunoux	860
1983	Echezeaux	Domaine Jayer-Gilles	980
1978	Gevrey Chambertin, Pte Chapelle	Domaine L. Trapet	1100
1976	Savigny, Lavières	Domaine Tollot-Beaut	680
1976	Corton Perrières	R. Rapet	1300
1976	Pommard Epenots	M. Gaunoux	1500
1972	Morey Saint Denis	Domaine Dujac	1100
1972	Corton Renardes	M. Gaunoux	1800
1972	Latricières Chambertin	Domaine L. Trapet	1800
1972	Bonnes Mares	G. Roumier	1800
1972	Chapelle Chambertin	Domaine L. Trapet	2000
1971	Beaune, Les Teurons	Domaine J. Germain	1400
1969	Gevrey Chambertin	Domaine L. Trapet	1400
1969	Beaune, Cent Vignes	Domaine Duchet	1600
1966	Beaune	M. Gaunoux	1000
1961	Beaune, Cent Vignes	Domaine Duchet	1800
1961	Pommard Epenots	M. Gaunoux	2600

CÔTES DU RHÔNE BLANCS

1996	Coteaux du Tricastin	L. Cornillon	180
1996	Muscat, Beaumes de Venise	Domaine Castaud-Maurin	240
1995	Châteauneuf du Pape	Domaine de Marcoux	260
1994	Condrieu, Château du Rozay	J.-Y. Multier	460
1993	Saint Joseph, Clos de l'Arbalestrier	E. Florentin	220
1991	Condrieu	G. Vernay	490
1991	Châteauneuf du Pape	Château Rayas	700
1987	Châteauneuf du Pape, V. Vignes	Château de Beaucastel	960
1986	Château Grillet	Domaine Neyret-Gachet	720

CÔTES DU RHÔNE ROUGES

1995	Crozes Hermitage	A. Graillot	190
1994	Châteauneuf du Pape	Domaine de Marcoux	240
1993	Gigondas, Cuvée Florence	J.-P. Cartier	340
1989	Saint Joseph	B. Gripa	280
1989	Châteauneuf du Pape	Château de Beaucastel	900
1988	Hermitage	J.-L. Chave	900
1987	Côte Rôtie	R. Jasmin · M	700
1985	Hermitage	J.-L. Chave	960
1984	Côte Rôtie, La Landonne	E. Guigal	1500
1983	Hermitage, La Chapelle	J. Jaboulet	1200
1970	Châteauneuf du Pape, Château Fortia	P. Le Roy de Boiseaumarié	1100

ALSACE

1995	Gewürztraminer	P. Hager	190
1994	Pinot Noir	Cave Vin. de Turckheim	200
1994	Tokay, Pinot Gris	M. Kreidenweiss	220
1993	Riesling, Clos Sainte Hune	F.-E. Trimbach	700
1992	Muscat, Steiner	Domaine P. Frick	190
1990	Riesling, Sélection Grains Nobles	R. Mure	900
1989	Tokay Pinot Gris, Vendange Tardive	Domaine Hugel	820
1983	Gewürztraminer, Cuvée Christine	Domaine Schlumberger	460

LOIRE

1997	Sancerre, Les Baronnes	H. Bourgeois	240
1996	Savennières, Clos de Coulaine	C. Papin-Chevalier	240
1995	Chinon, Les Picasses	J.-M. Raffault	260
1995	Pouilly Fumé, Fines Caillottes	J. Pabiot	260

LES ENTREMETS DE DOUCEUR

Farandole de Desserts 120

Crème brûlée à la Bergamote 110
Griottes de Fougerolles en Chaud-Froid 110
Terrine de Fruits au Miel safrané 110

Sorbets aux trois Parfums 110
Nougatine glacée aux Poires Williams 110
Fondant lacté au Thé fumé 110
Crème glacée au Caramel salé 110
Parfait glacé aux deux Marrons 110

Dacquoise au Café 110
Moelleux au Chocolat et au Thym 110
Pomme en Surprise 110
Mille-Feuille tiède à la Vanille 110
Marquise au Chocolat et à la Pistache 110

Soufflé chaud au Pain d'Épices et à l'Orange amère 120
Crêpes soufflées au Citron vert 120

Prix Taxes et Service 15 % compris

*

Lorsqu'il commença sa carrière d'Enfant de Cuisine de Jeanne d'Evreux,
Guillaume Tirel reçut le nom de Taillevent,
avant de devenir, successivement, Maître Queux de Philippe de Valois, du Duc de Normandie, de Charles V et de Charles VI.

Taillevent, dont le blason était « à trois marmites bordé de six roses » et dont « Le Viandier », commandé par Charles V le Sage, en 1379,
est le Premier Livre de Cuisine en Français, inspira à François Villon, dans son « Grand Testament », un texte prophétique :
« Si allé veoir en Taillevent ou Chapitre de Fricassure... »

Untitled

Autumn Wine

The sweltering days and hot nights of summer are definitely behind us. We are now awaiting the colorful turning of the leaves, enjoying the cool breeze of Fall and relishing the first opportunities to don a sweater and our favorite scarf. We also switch gears with regards to what we pour in our glasses. Autumn is a perfect time to sip more restrained and elegant red wines, wines that evoke the season and pair beautifully with what our kitchen has to offer.

See below for outstanding examples of one of the more perfect grapes for the season: Gamay. Be it in the form of a terrific Cru Beaujolais or in a blend from Burgundy, this little grape is the foundation for some of the more pleasurable wines to drink today.

Gamay

Julie Balagny, 'Chavot' Fleurie '14	76
Marcel Lapierre, Morgon '14	59
Jean Foillard, 'Côte du Py' Morgon '13	78
Jean-Paul Thevenet, Morgon '13 (Magnum)	129
Joseph Chamonard, 'Le Clos de Lys' Morgon '10 (Magnum)	117
Château Cambon '13	44
Jean-Claude Lapalu, 'Cuvée des Fous' Brouilly '13	75
Pierre-Marie Chermette, 'Pierreux' Brouilly '13	49
Laurence & Rémi Dufaitre, Brouilly '13	44
Dupeuble, Beaujolais '13	36
Bruno Debize, 'Apinost' '13	60
Domaine Fontaine-Gagnard, Bourgogne Passetoutgrain '13	48

Untitled, New York

Sparkling

SPARKLING

Belluard, 'Mt. Blanc' Savoie '11	74
Pierre Richard, Crémant de Jura '10	55
Heymann-Löwenstein, Riesling Sekt, Mosel '08	69
Peter Lauer, 'Réserve' Riesling Sekt, Saar '91	95
De Bartoli, 'Terzavia' Brut Nature, Sicily '11	79
Mata i Coloma, 'Cupada No. 15' Cava Brut Nature '11	48

SPARKLING ROSÉ

Cruse Wine Co., Valdiguié Pétillant, Napa '14	66

CHAMPAGNE

Christophe Mignon, 'Pur Meunier' Brut Nature	69
Diebolt-Vallois, 'Tradition'	76
Leclerc Briant, Brut Réserve	72
Bérêche & Fils, Brut Réserve	84
Guy Larmandier	75
Agrapart, '7 Crus'	88
R. Pouillon, Blanc de Blancs	96
Larmandier-Bernier, 'VV' Blanc de Blancs Grand Cru '06	177
Ulysse Collin, 'Les Pierrières' Blanc de Blancs	155
David Léclapart, 'L'Amateur' Blanc de Blancs '10	185
Jacques Lassaigne, 'La Colline Inspirée' Blanc de Blancs	151
Hubert Soreau, 'Le Clos l'Abbé' Blanc de Blancs '07	139
Emmanuel Brochet, 'Le Mont Benoit'	120
H. Billiot, 'Brut Réserve' Grand Cru	112
Jacquesson, 'Cuvée 737' Extra Brut	142
Gatinois, Grand Cru '08	126
Egly-Ouriet, 'Brut Tradition' Grand Cru	131
Dom Pérignon '02	220
Nathalie Falmet, 'Le Val Cornet' '09	135
Cédric Bouchard, 'Les Ursules' Blanc de Noirs '10	208
Goutorbe, 'Collection René' '99	236
Krug '00	497

ROSÉ CHAMPAGNE

Savart, 'Bulle de Rosé'	119
La Caravelle	73
Vilmart & Cie, 'Cuvée Rubis'	157
Ruinart	149
Henriet-Bazin, Grand Cru	99

White

UNITED STATES

Keuka Lake, 'Estate' Dry Riesling, Finger Lakes '12	45
Wiemer, 'Magdalena' Riesling, Finger Lakes '13	78
Silas, 'Enna Hay' Pinot Blanc, Willamette '14	52
Tatomer, Gruner Veltliner, Santa Barbara '14	57
Lieu-Dit, Sauvignon Blanc, Santa Barbara '14	60
Kalin Cellars, Sauvignon Blanc, Livermore '01	89
Tyler, Chardonnay, Santa Barbara County '13	76
Lioco, 'Estero' Chardonnay, Russian River '13	80
Calera, Chardonnay, Central Coast '13	56
Ceritas, 'Peter Martin Ray' Chardonnay, Santa Cruz '13	129
Hanzell, Chardonnay, Sonoma '12	139

LOIRE

Luneau-Papin, 'Clos des Allées' Muscadet VV '13	36
Haut Bourg, 'Origine' Muscadet Côtes de Grandlieu '05	45
Eric Morgat, 'L'Enclos' Savennières '10	70
Château Yvonne, Saumur '13	75
Domaine Huet, 'Le Mont' Vouvray Sec '14	68
Lemaire Fournier, Vouvray Sec '04	48
Philippe Foreau, 'Clos Naudin' Vouvray Sec '99	66
Cailbourdin, 'Les Cris' Pouilly-Fumé '14	60

RHÔNE & LANGUEDOC

Hervé Souhaut, Blanc '12	55
Jean-Louis Chave, Hermitage '07	244
Maxime Magnon, 'La Bégou' Corbières '12 (Magnum)	147

GERMANY

Hild, Elbling, Mosel '13	37
Weiser-Künstler, Mosel '14	48
Immich-Batterieberg, 'Zeppwingert' Mosel '11	89
Clemens Busch, 'Marienburg Rothenpfad' Mosel '11	77
Bischofliches, 'Ürziger Würzgarten' Spätlese, Mosel '83	98
Egon Müller, 'Scharzhofberger' Kabinett, Saar '13	132
Karthäuserhof, Kabinett, Ruwer '13	69
Emrich-Schönleber, 'Monzinger Halenberg' Nahe '12	73
Seehof, Feinherb, Rheinhessen '14	44
Keller, 'Hipping R' Rheinhessen '13	99

ETC.

Bechtold, 'Engelberg' Gewürztraminer, Alsace '10	58
Quinta da Muradella, 'Alanda' Monterrei, Spain '11	67
Ferrando, 'La Torrazza' Erbaluce, Piedmont, Italy '12	44
Samuel Tinon, 'Birtok' Furmint, Hungary '13	59
Knoll, 'Schütt' Riesling Smaragd, Wachau '10	98

White

CHABLIS

Savary, 'Vieilles Vignes' '13	62
Samuel Billaud, 'Mont de Milieu' 1er '13	74
Pattes Loup, 'Butteaux' 1er '13	100
Boudin, 'Fourchaume' 1er '10	72
Olivier Morin, 'Constance' Chitry '14	44

CÔTE D'OR

Claire Naudin, 'Le Clou 34' Aligoté '13	68
Marc Roy, 'Champs Perdrix' Marsannay '13	74
Alain Gras, Saint-Romain '12	76
J. P. Fichet, Auxey-Duresses '13	89
François Mikulski, 'Poruzots' Meursault 1er '13	178
Domaine Roulot, Meursault '12	199
Bitouzet-Prieur, 'Les Corbins' Meursault '11	120
Jacques Carillon, Puligny '13	153
Bouzereau-Gruère, Puligny '12	145
Bernard de Chérisey, 'Chalumeaux' Puligny 1er '10	182
Paul Pillot, 'Les Charmois' Saint-Aubin 1er '13	90
Prudhon, 'Les Castets' Saint-Aubin 1er '12	78
V & F Jouard, 'Vieilles Vignes' Chassagne '13	104
J-M Morey, 'Les Champs-Gains' Chassagne 1er '09	137

MÂCONNAIS

Frantz Chagnoleau, 'La Roche' Saint-Véran '13	70
Guillot-Broux, 'Les Combettes' '13	56
Domaine de Roally, Viré-Clessé '13	63

JURA

Les Dolomies, 'En Novelin' Chardonnay '13	57
Stéphane Tissot, 'La Mailloche' Chardonnay '12	78
Ganevat, 'Cuvée Marguerite' '12 (Magnum)	249
Macle, 'Ouillé' '10	83
Montbourgeau, L'Étoile '11	47
Puffeney, Savagnin '11	79

Rosé

Château Maupague, Sainte-Victoire, Provence '14	52
Jolie-Laide, Trousseau Gris, Russian River Valley '14	58
Château Simone, Palette, Provence '13	94

Red

CÔTE DE NUITS

Geantet-Pansiot, 'Pinot Fin' Bourgogne '11	69
Sylvain Pataille, Marsannay '12	64
Jean-Yves Bizot, 'Clos du Roy' Marsannay '12	192
Harmand-Geoffroy, 'Bossière' Gevrey 1er '08	138
Fourrier, 'Clos St.-Jacques' Gevrey 1er '09	459
Ponsot, 'Cuvée Alouettes' Morey-St.-Denis 1er '12	316
Léchenaut, Morey-St.-Denis '10	144
Collotte, 'Vieilles Vignes' Chambolle '12	96
Burguet, 'Rouges Dessus' Vosne-Romanée 1er '07	214
J. Chauvenet, 'Argillas' Nuits-St.-Georges 1er '10	186
David Duband, Côte de Nuits-Villages '12	59
Petitot, Côte de Nuits-Villages '12	76
Gachot-Monot, Côte de Nuits-Villages '12	68

CÔTE DE BEAUNE

Fontaine-Gagnard, Bourgogne Passetoutgrain '13	48
Simon Bize, 'Les Perrières' Bourgogne '12	72
Rollin, 'Les Fichots' Pernand-Vergelesses 1er '08	74
Michel Gaunoux, Beaune '01	112
R. Dubois, Volnay '10	68
Marquis d'Angerville, 'Champans' Volnay 1er '09	199

YONNE & CÔTE CHALONNAISE

Bersan, 'Cuvée Louis Bersan' Irancy '13	65
David Renaud, 'Vaupessiot' Irancy '10	69
Michel Juillot, 'Vignes de Maillonge' Mercurey '12	56
Meix Foulot, 'Clos du Château' Mercurey 1er '10	74
Clos Salomon, 'Clos Salomon' Givry 1er '12	77

BEAUJOLAIS

Balagny, 'Chavot' Fleurie '14	76
Lapierre, Morgon '14	59
Foillard, 'Côte du Py' Morgon '13	78
Thevenet, Morgon '13 (Magnum)	129
Chamonard, 'Le Clos de Lys' Morgon '10 (Magnum)	117
Château Cambon '13	44
Lapalu, 'Cuvée des Fous' Brouilly '13	75
Chermette, 'Pierreux' Brouilly '13	49
Debize, 'Apinost' '13	60

JURA

Bornard, 'La Chamade' Ploussard, Arbois Pupillin '11	69
Les Chais de Vieux Bourg, Pinot Noir '10	65

ROSSO

TRENTINO - ALTO ADIGE

PINOT NERO • Abbazia di Novacella '12	60
LAGREIN • 'Berger Gei' Ignaz Niedrist '11	59
TEROLDEGO • Rotaliano, Foradori '12	44
CABERNET SAUVIGNON • Tenuta San Leonardo '07	98

FRIULI

SCHIOPPETTINO • Colli Orientali, Ronchi di Cialla '04	98
MERLOT • Colli Orientali, Miani '10	189

LOMBARDIA

OLTREPO PAVESE • 'Cavariola' Bruno Verdi '08	48
OLTREPO PAVESE • 'Giorgio Odero' Frecciarossa '08	76
VALTELLINA SUPERIORE • Grumello, Prevostini '10	48
VALTELLINA SUPERIORE • Sassella 'Stella Retica' Ar.Pe.Pe. '06	79

PIEMONTE

RUCHÈ • di Castagnole Monferrato, Crivelli '11	37
BRACHETTO • 'Mate' Sottimano '13	48
FREISA • 'La Villarina Secca' Brovia '13	52
DOLCETTO • d'Alba - 'Dabbene' Gianfranco Bovio '12	40
DOLCETTO • Dogliani Superiore 'Bricco Botti' Pecchenino '11	52
BARBERA • d'Asti 'Montebruna' Braida di Giacomo Bologna '11	52
BARBERA • d'Asti 'Vigna del Noce' Trinchero '04	72
BARBERA • d'Alba 'Sori del Drago' Brovia '12	39
BARBERA • d'Alba 'Falletto' Bruno Giacosa '08	82
SPANNA • 'Cuvée Bernardo' Vallana '10	38
GATTINARA • Petterino '01	58
GATTINARA • Vallana '97	72
'BRICCO MANZONI' • Rocche dei Manzoni '05	84

BARBARESCO

CASTELLO di NIEVE • Riserva 'Santo Stefano' '06	94
PRODUTTORI del BARBARESCO • Riserva 'Montefico' '08	108
ROAGNA • 'Paje' '05	144
PRODUTTORI del BARBARESCO • '78	298

BAROLO

ERALDO VIBERTI • '01	76
ROCCHE dei MANZONI • 'Big d' Big' '00	96
PIANPOLVERE SOPRANO • Riserva '00	144
BARTOLO MASCARELLO • '00	198
GUISEPPE RINALDI • 'Brunate-Le Coste' '00	278
GUISEPPE RINALDI • 'Brunate-Le Coste' '98	298

VENETO

TEROLDEGO • Marion '10	68
VALPOLICELLA • Brigaldara, Veneto '12	32
VALPOLICELLA • Classico Superiore 'TB' Tomasso Bussola '09	68
VALPOLICELLA • Classico Superiore, Giuseppe Quintarelli '99	95
VALPOLICELLA • Superiore, Romano Dal Forno '07	144
AMARONE • della Valplicella 'Saint Urbano' Speri '09	128
AMARONE • della Valplicella, Giuseppe Quintarelli '98	348
'ALZERO' • Giuseppe Quintarelli '98	398

TOSCANA

VINO NOBILE • di Montepulciano, Il Macchione '09	58
ROSSO di MONTALCINO • Casanuova delle Cerbaie '09	48
ROSSO di MONTALCINO • Casa Raia '09	78
'MONTEVERTINE' • Agricola Montevertine '11	88
'CEPPARELLO' • Isole e Olena '10	118
'SAMMARCO' • Castello dei Rampolla '09	145
'GRATTAMACCO' • Podere Grattammacco '11	198
'FLACCIANELLO' • della Pieve, Fontodi '95	275
'SASSICAIA' • Tenuta San Guido '05	398

ROSSO

Marta, New York

BIANCO

VALLE d'AOSTA
BLANC de MORGEX • 'Cuvée Nathan' Ermes Pavese '06	44
PINOT GRIS • Valle d'Aosta 'Vigne Creton' Grosjean Freres '11	35

PIEMONTE
ARNEIS • Roero 'Vigne Sparse' Giovanni Almondo '12	42
ARNEIS • Roero, Matteo Correggia '13	48
GAVI • Franco Martinetti '13	37
RIESLING • 'Herzu' Ettore Germano '12	42

LIGURIA
VERMENTINO • Portofino 'Vigna In Trigoso' Bisson '12	44
VERMENTINO • Colli di Luni 'Corsano' Terenzuola '13	65

TRENTINO-ALTO ADIGE
KERNER • Manni Nössing '13	44
NOSIOLA • 'Fontanasanta' Foradori '12	78
PINOT GRIGIO • Elena Walch '13	44
PINOT BIANCO • 'Vorburg' Terlano '11	54
RIESLING • Pacherhof '12	52
SAUVIGNON BLANC • 'Karneid' Franz Gojer '12	52
SYLVANER • 'Praepositus' Abbazia di Novacella '12	56

FRIULI
COLLIO • Borgo del Tiglio '11	58
SAUVIGNON BLANC • Collio 'Ronco delle Mele' Venica & Venica '13	84
CHARDONNAY • Colli Orientali, Meroi '12	98
RIBOLLA GIALLA • Ronchi di Cialla '13	36
RIBOLLA GIALLA • 'Anfora' Venezie Giulia, Gravner '04	145
FRIULANO • Colli Orientali, Villa Russiz '13	54
FRIULANO • Colli Orientali, Ronco del Gnemiz '12	59
FRIULANO • Colli Orientali, Miani '12	138
'FLORS di UIS' • Isonzo, Vie di Romans '11	68

VENETO
SOAVE • Classico 'Monte Alto' Ca' Rugate '12	56
SOAVE • Classico 'Calvarino' Pieropan '11	54

TOSCANA
VERNACCIA • di San Gimignano 'Fiore' Montenidoli '12	44
CHARDONNAY • Isole e Olena '12	76

MARCHE
VERDICCHIO • dei Castelli di Jesi, Sartarelli, Marche '13	32
VERDICCHIO • dei Castelli di Jesi, Villa Bucci, Marche '01	98

UMBRIA
'CERVARO' • Castello della Salla '11	86

LAZIO
FRASCATI • Superiore 'Poggio Verde' Principe Pallavicini '13	36
'COENOBIUM' • Monastero Suore Cistercensi '12	46

ABRUZZI
TREBBIANO • d'Abruzzo, Edoardo Valentini '09	178

CAMPANIA
GRECO di TUFO • Cantine di Marzo '13	38
FIANO DI AVELLINO • Ciro Picariello '12	39
FALANGHINA • 'Via del Campo' Quintodecimo '12	75

CALABRIA
GRECO • Ciró 'Res Dei' Ippolito '13	44

ISOLE
ETNA BIANCO • Tenuta delle Terre Nere '13	34
ETNA BIANCO • 'A Puddara' Tenuta di Fessina '12	72
ETNA BIANCO • 'Pietramarina' Benanti '08	84
CHARDONNAY • Sicilia 'Guardiola' Passopisciaro '11	88
ZIBIBBO • Sicilia 'Pietra Nera' Marco de Bartoli '11	56
ALBANELLO/ZIBIBBO • Terre Siciliane 'SP68' Arianna Occhipinti '13	60

BIANCO

THE MENU BRIEFING AT BABBO, NEW YORK

I t was just before 4pm on a clear, sunny Monday afternoon when I walked into Babbo, the Italian restaurant that restaurateur Joe Bastianich and chef Mario Batali have made so famous since they inspired its change from the Coach House, as it was known, in 1998.

My meeting was with neither of them, however, but rather with Frank Langello, the restaurant's Head Chef, with whom I had come to share their 'family meal' or staff meal – fuel that would see the waiting staff through until they closed up at half past midnight. And at 4.30pm sharp I was to attend their staff meeting, their equivalent of the menu briefing. These now take place on a daily basis in most serious restaurants. They have had a huge impact not just on how customers are treated but on relations between the kitchen and the waiting staff. And they are rarely talked about.

This is not just my viewpoint but, more perceptively, that of Michael Romano, currently Director of Culinary Development at the Union Square Hospitality Group, responsible for the supply, delivery and execution of approximately 2 million meals a year. Having begun his professional career in the kitchens of restaurants in France and Switzerland, Romano returned to New York where he was the Executive Chef of Union Square Café for 18 years. For him these

meetings are the key to 'the most significant improvement in how customers are treated in the dining room'.

I found Langello taking his seat alongside his sous chef and one other chef, right by the vast autumnal leaf display that is one of this brownstone's visual attractions. Others include a well-worn wooden bar by the entrance, at which several bar staff were setting up; a vast array of wines in different formats, quite a lot of which I could not help but notice had been opened and the cork replaced; and a layout spread over two floors, with the top floor acting as the service station for the chafing dishes that held the ground beef, rice and guacamole that, along with bread, constituted that evening's staff meal.

Langello spoke, ate and made decisions all at the same time, and, like most chefs, he ate quickly. He spoke first of all about the run-through of the staff meeting that would start promptly at 4.30pm. Then he stopped talking as his cell phone rang. A few hurried words followed but I could make out the gist of his conversation: the first white truffles had clearly arrived in New York earlier that week. He put the phone down after agreeing with Paolo, his supplier, that at $2,300 a pound he had the right to pick through them at 1.30pm the following afternoon.

There then ensued a happy five minutes as the three chefs chomped and talked about their favourite staff meals. Lunch meat, waffles and fries was one call; meatloaf another; sandwich day, when the kitchen prepared whole chickens and top sirloin was Langello's choice. He added that these meals were far better today than those he had been served at Le Cirque 20 years ago and that they were inviolate. 'This one hour is crucial for staff morale, knowledge and communication,' he added, before hurrying off to the kitchen, warning me that he would be back to collect me at 4.29pm.

In the nine minutes that followed, a hush fell over the entire room as though a witch had waved her magic wand. Staff finished off their jobs, several eating at the bar polished off their plates, while others donned their ties. Then, right on cue, Langello reappeared clutching three main course plates and everybody headed upstairs.

This was the sight I had been anticipating, one that must take place at many restaurants the world over. And I barely had time to put my jacket down and get my pen and notebook out before this particular menu briefing got under way.

There were about 40–50 people waiting to hear what Langello had to say, mostly waiters with the occasional manager around the room. Most were sitting on the far side of a large white table with the serving dishes for the staff meal on the sideboard behind, to which Joe Bastianich helped himself as he walked through while Langello was speaking.

Langello had three dishes he wanted to talk about. The first, which he picked up, was a first course, their grilled octopus with borlotti beans. He described the cooking process: the cephalopod (90 per cent water, he pointed out) is braised in olive oil and chilli before being cut into 4oz pieces and then grilled and served with the borlotti beans that have been simmered in chicken stock with pancetta.

He then pointed to the Babbo beef cheek ravioli, filled with braised beef and pureed Parmesan. 'At the end the piece of meat is browned in a sauté pan with truffles and anchovies to give it that briny flavour.' Finally, he pointed to a fillet of wild striped bass that they were serving with porcini, a variation that Langello wanted the staff to fully appreciate. 'Go on, eat it and see for yourselves,' he urged as several volunteers happily dug in. Although there was, as usual, just one plate of the dish, everyone had a go.

While they were doing so, Langello ended with a note of caution. 'White truffles will be on the menu, but only from tomorrow, and there are only four of our deconstructed osso bucco for two, and one for one, left. See me as you sell them, would you please.' Langello wrapped it up and sat down.

As the Head Pastry Chef acknowledged that there was nothing much for him to add during that particular menu briefing, he left a vacancy for Bastianich, back to his owner's role and having polished off a plate of the spicy guacamole.

He had a bottle of the latest release of the Ursini olive oil from Abruzzo straight in from JFK airport, which he wanted all the staff to taste with several

baskets of bread, cut into small chunks for dunking. Appreciative comments ensued. This stuff was on the trees only two weeks ago, Bastianich explained, before handing back to Langello.

Langello, in turn, handed over to the maître d'. 'There are 171 booked for this evening, a Monday night, with the restaurant seating 90 at any one time. It's pretty solid for the first hour or so,' he added, 'with some holes at 7.15pm and 8.45pm. And we have two tables in later who are friends of Mario's,' whom he mentioned by name. (His words were obviously well meant but I heard subsequently from Langello that they served 250 that night.)

Then came a bit more fun as Juan Pablo Escobar, currently the head of the wine department, stepped in. Asked to talk about a wine that is a particular favourite, he had chosen a new Barbera 2010 from Enzo Boglietti in La Morra. He described its production as 'nine months in stainless steel and barriques' before adding its price: $24 by the quartino (a carafe that holds a quarter of a litre) or $75 by the bottle.

He then handed small tastes of the wine round for the staff to enjoy, adding that it would provide 'a nice spiel for the customers'. He concluded this section by saying that anyone interested should come along to the next day's 1:30pm tasting of Brunello di Montalcino, which he described as 'very elegant wine'.

His final words were directed at all the waiting staff. 'Let me know as soon as possible, please, the tables that order the tasting menus (there are three with 19 different wine combinations) or those where the customer has allergies.'

Those words were particularly welcome to Nico Satryan and Meghan Loghan, who were that night's floor managers and needed to liaise closely with the receptionists. 'Tasting menus can be 7–10 courses and take longer to serve so we don't get the tables back as swiftly,' Loghan explained. 'It is important to know this from the outset.'

The meeting started to break down into smaller groups, but before everyone left for their particular area, Tom Stelle, the manager responsible for the overall maintenance of the building, spoke up. He had a few words to say about the

maintenance of the glassware and silverware in particular and had quite a strong word to say exhorting all the staff to remember that they must clock in and out 'most diligently'.

By 4.50pm the staff meeting drew to a close. It had been beneficial for me, and for Langello, I believe, that this 'professional invasion' took place on a Monday when there were fewer questions to be asked. The bar was polished. The bottles of wines to be served by the glass went out on to the large table in the centre of the room as the volume of the music was turned up. The cutlery was set out on the bar tables as the receptionists looked at the list of the bookings on their screens.

As the first customer walked in, 30 minutes early but more than happy to wait, I took my leave.

ANTIPASTI

Marinated Fresh Sardines with Caramelized Fennel and Lobster Oil 13

Grilled Octopus with "Borlotti Marinati" and Spicy Limoncello Vinaigrette 19

Steamed Cockles with Red Chilies and Basil 16

Mussels "alla Tarantina" 16

"Carciofi alla Romana" 16

Asparagus "Milanese" with Duck Egg and Parmigiano 16

Roasted Beet Tartare with Chianti Vinegar and Ricotta Salata 15

Baby Wild Arugula with Parmigiano and Aceto Manodori 17

Warm Tripe "alla Parmigiana" 14

Warm Lamb's Tongue Vinaigrette with Brown Beech Mushrooms and a 3-Minute Egg 17

Pig Foot "Milanese" with Rice Beans and Arugula 16

Testa with Pickled Pearls and Thyme Vinaigrette 11

Prosciutto San Daniele "Riserva" with Black Pepper "Fett'unta" 15

Armandino's Salumi - Culatello and Hot Sopressata 17

Babbo Salumi with Baby Fennel 18

PRIMI

Goat Cheese Tortelloni with Dried Orange and Wild Fennel Pollen 21

Spaghettini with Spicy Budding Chives and a One Pound Lobster 29

Maccheroni alla Chitarra with Oven Dried Tomatoes, Red Chilies and Bottarga di Muggine 20

Bucatini all'Amatriciana with Guanciale, Hot Pepper and Pecorino 21

Garganelli with "Funghi Trifolati" 24

Sweet Potato "Lune" with Sage and Amaretti 22

Mint Love Letters with Spicy Lamb Sausage 21

Lamb "Testa" Ravioli with Lemon and Sage 19

Goose Liver Ravioli with Balsamic Vinegar and Brown Butter 25

Chianti Stained Pappardelle with Wild Boar Ragu 24

Pappardelle Bolognese 26

Gnocchi with Braised Oxtail 22

Homemade Orecchiette with Sweet Sausage and Rapini 22

Beef Cheek Ravioli with Crushed Squab Liver and Black Truffles 25

Stinging Nettle Fettuccine with House-Made Pancetta and Asparagus 24

Linguine with Clams, Pancetta and Hot Chilies 25

Black Spaghetti with Rock Shrimp, Spicy Salami Calabrese and Green Chilies 29

SECONDI

Spicy Two Minute Calamari Sicilian Lifeguard Style 28

Whole Grilled Branzino with Spring Radishes, Olives and Lemon Oregano Jam 37

Monkfish Piccata with Caperberries and Preserved Lemons 32

Barbecued Squab with Roasted Beet "Farrotto" and Porcini Mustard 34

Grilled Quail with "Scorzonera alla Romana" and Saba 29

Duck with Sunchokes, Fiddleheads and Chianti Agrodolce 32

Rabbit with Honey-Glazed Baby Carrots, Peas and Pink Peppercorn Honey 32

Grilled Lamb Chops "Scottadita" with Broccoli Rabe Pesto, Grilled Onions and Lemon Yogurt 38

Fennel Dusted Sweetbreads with Sweet and Sour Onions, Duck Bacon and Membrillo Vinaigrette 29

Grilled Pork Chop with Cherry Peppers, Cipolline and Aceto Manodori 33

"Brasato al Barolo" Braised Beef with Porcini Mushrooms 30

Barbecued Skirt Steak with Asparagus "alla Piastra" and Salsa Verde 32

Charred Beef Tongue with Green Market "Krauti" and Grain Mustard 29

Grilled Ribeye for Two with Charred Ramps and Aceto Manodori 120

CONTORNI

Roasted Beet "Farrotto" 11   **Rapini** with Roasted Garlic 11   **Roasted Potatoes** with Rosemary 11

Sweet Peas with Pancetta 11   **Babbo Greens** with Roasted Shallots 11

SPECIALS

Mozzarella di Bufala with Ramps and Capezzana Oil 19

Primavera ed Alici - Spring Vegetable Salad with Bagna Cauda and Boquerones 17

Bavette with Ramps, Breadcrumbs and Pecorino 23

Asparagus Ravioli with Ricotta and Spring Onion Butter 24

Crispy Soft Shell Crabs with Cavolo Nero and Spicy Pepper Jelly 35

Applewood-Smoked Sea Scallops with Snap Peas, Baby Carrots and Horseradish 36

Grilled Guinea Hen with Asparagus, Morels and Black Garlic Zabaglione 29

PASTA TASTING MENU

Black Tagliatelle with Peas and Castelmagno
Casebianche "Il Fric" 2014

"Casunzei" with Poppy Seeds
Bastianich "Adriatico" Friulano 2013

Garganelli with "Funghi Trifolati"
Gulfi, Cerasuolo di Vittoria 2014

"Agnolotti al Pomodoro"
Selvapiana, Chianti Rufina 2014

Pappardelle Bolognese
La Mozza "Aragone" 2009

Vanilla Panna Cotta with Raspberry Vincotto
Cascina Ca' Rossa "Birbét" Brachetto del Roero NV

Olive Oil Cake and Gelato – Capezzana Olive Oil, Two Ways + NaCl
Cardamaro, Amaro al Cardo e Carciofo NV

95 per person *

(Accompanying wines 75 per person – As listed above)

(*"The Riserva Selection"* of wines 115 per person – For details ask our Sommeliers)

*Our Pasta Tasting requires the participation of the entire table.

TRADITIONAL TASTING MENU

Babbo Coppa with Favas, Mint and Kinderhook Pecorino
Venica & Venica "Ronco delle Mele" 2014

Pappardelle with Morels and Thyme
Bastianich "Vespa Bianco" 2013

Duck Tortelli with "Sugo Finto"
Brandini "Filari Lunghi" Dolcetto d'Alba 2014

Hanger Steak with Fregula Verde and Black Truffle Vinaigrette
Tenuta Sette Ponti "Poggio al Lupo" 2005

Sottocenere with Whipped Honey
Cantina Terlano, Gewürztraminer 2012

"Piccolo Cannolo" with Espresso and Candied Cashews
Ancarani "Uvappesa" 2011

"Torta Caprese" with "Fior di Latte" and Vincotto
Caravaglio, Malvasia della Lipari 2013

99 per person *

(Accompanying Wines 75 per person – As listed above)

("*The Riserva Selection*" of wines 115 per person – For details ask our Sommeliers)

*Our Traditional Tasting requires the participation of the entire table.

DOLCI E FORMAGGI

Chocolate Hazelnut Cake
Orange Sauce and Hazelnut Citrus Sorbetto 15

Poppy Seed Meringue
Fresh Grapefruit and Lime Cream 15

White Chocolate Cheesecake
Rhubarb Composta, Caramel and Crème Fraîche 15

Saffron Panna Cotta
Apricot Agrumata, Saffron Shortbread and Coconut Sorbetto 15

Lemon Crostata
Toasted Meringue and Graham Cracker Gelato 15

Buttermilk Budino
Red Velvet Apricot and Sesame Gelato 15

Pistachio and Chocolate Semifreddo 15

Olive Oil Cake and Gelato
Capezzana Olive Oil + NaCl 17

Biscotti and Cookies 15

Assortment of Gelati and Sorbetti 15

One Cheese 9
Selection of Three Cheeses 15
of Five Cheeses 18
Pecorino Oro Antico with Orange Blossom Honey
Capra Sarda with Spicy Honey
Quadrello di Bufala with Butterscotch
Robiola Bosina with Meyer Lemon Marmellata
Gorgonzola DOP with Duck Bacon
Parmigiano Reggiano

THE MENU AS MEMENTO

Anyone at all interested in food tends to have a personal collection of menus. Perhaps not many but a few stashed away that mean something to them. Menus that mark a proposal of marriage, an engagement, a wedding, a special birthday, an anniversary or a particular chapter in their lives, either personal or professional.

Then there are those menus that recall travel. Menus stuffed in your suitcase from trips abroad, menus from planes, menus from cruise liners, and in certain instances, even menus from train journeys.

Most of this book has been written in an office in which menus abound. Boxes of them collected principally in the pre-internet days. Menus that range from my 40th birthday dinner, held at my sister's house in north-west London, to my 60th, held at Almadraba Park Hotel outside Roses, on the Costa Brava, north-east Spain.

On each occasion that I have looked through these menus, a slight shiver has run through me. They immediately bring back floods of memories: of the restaurant itself; of the people we were eating with; of the trip we were on at the time; of the wines we drank with the food; ultimately, for me at least, the most gratifying recollection of times well spent.

These menus generate such feelings because the pieces of paper that they are printed on often convey the dates on which the meals took place as well as

the names of the restaurants and the lists of the dishes we chose from. For me, a physical copy of a menu still means something. I don't bother looking at a menu on a restaurant's website (it will ruin the surprise) and menus downloaded and printed at home do not carry the same weight as the restaurant's own.

Menus could, I realise, become less important in a restaurant's way of life. In-house printing facilities now mean that those working in leading restaurants can quite easily print out the list of dishes you ate while you were in their care – meaning that what you take home with you is far from being the restaurant's menu but rather a list of the dishes that your table enjoyed. The increasing popularity of set menus and tasting menus, often paired with a sommelier's choice of wines by the glass, means that the actual menu – what the customer could have experienced – is being prescribed by the chef and the restaurateur.

In the instances I refer to, however, menus perform a very personal function. They may be cumbersome, often awkward, and occasionally they will fade, but they survive to bring back the happiest of memories. Because mine are so personal, they do not really provide enough 'weight' for a more serious consideration of the menu as memento. For this, I am indebted to two professional collectors of menus, Eugen Beer, an Englishman now residing in New York who runs www.lovemenuart.com, and Henry Voigt, retired from DuPont and who runs www.theamericanmenu.com.

It was over a coffee in the W Hotel, Union Square, New York that Voigt explained to me how the menu has become the momentum of social change across the US and how, thanks to the emergence of eBay, his own collection has emerged along with several others – most notably those of Johnson & Wales University in Providence, Rhode Island; City College of San Francisco; the Los Angeles Public Library; Cornell University; and, last but not least, those housed within the New York Public Library's collection.

It was President Thomas Jefferson who kick-started the whole process. As a constant traveller, he was reluctant to be beholden to private individuals in whose houses he was normally offered an overnight stay. Hotels began to be built that

housed places in which food was served. From the late 1830s, customers were offered choice and the American menu was born.

The subsequent almost 200 years of economic prosperity have been a huge boon to the US's growing number of chefs and restaurateurs, their graphic artists, their growing number of mouths to feed and the increase in their ability to get in their cars and to travel. The menus that emanate from Chicago, San Francisco, Los Angeles and New York at certain periods – the 1890s, the 1920s, 1945–1965 and the 1980s – certainly reflect this economic confidence.

These thoughts have guided my selection of menus for this chapter.

LEDOYEN, 200 ANS DE VIE PARISIENNE

Sous Louis XV, la partie des Champs-Elysées comprise entre la Place Royale et le Rond-Point devient la promenade la plus fréquentée d'Europe, tant par les piétons que les cavaliers et les carrosses.

L'ensemble des pelouses, bosquets et bassins s'anime de guinguettes, glaciers, limonadiers, cabarets et "baraques d'amusements" de toutes sortes.

En 1791, Pierre-Michel Doyen, cadet d'une famille de traiteurs réputés, loue l'une de ces guinguettes qu'il transforme en restaurant de qualité ; il invente même le service à la carte. Robespierre, Danton, Marat sont clients assidus du restaurant de DOYEN, que Barras décrit comme *une maisonnette blanche, aux volets verts, entourée d'un treillage et, dans le jardin, un manège de chevaux de bois et un jeu de tonneau*.

Sous le Directoire, Madame Tallien, Madame Hamelin, Juliette Récamier donnent, à la belle saison, déjeuners et dîners chez DOYEN où Joséphine de Beauharnais aurait rencontré Bonaparte pour la première fois.

En 1814, le restaurant devenu "LEDOYEN", a les honneurs du Guide des Dîneurs, qui note *"l'élégance des salons, l'heureuse disposition des cabinets particuliers et la promptitude dans le service"*.

Mais, la même année, le campement des cosaques ravage les jardins des Champs-Elysées et ruine tous les établissements abrités par les frondaisons.

Il faudra attendre la Monarchie de Juillet pour que le talentueux architecte Jacques-Ignace Hittorff dessine le nouveau PAVILLON LEDOYEN, au cœur du Carré Marigny, dans un cadre de marronniers, saules pleureurs, pelouses et fontaines.

En 1842, lors de l'inauguration, tout ce que Paris compte de beaux esprits et de jolies femmes se presse dans le cadre champêtre de LEDOYEN.

La proximité du Palais de l'Industrie et le tourbillon fastueux du Second Empire vont contribuer à la notoriété du restaurant qui, dans ce quartier de musique et de fêtes, conserve un charme bon enfant. Au point que les duellistes s'y donnent rituellement rendez-vous pour déjeuner avec leurs témoins, au retour d'une "rencontre" au Bois de Boulogne !

Gloires du "Salon des Refusés", Degas, Manet, Cézanne, Pissaro, Monet prennent également leurs quartiers chez LEDOYEN. Les jours de vernissage, la fréquentation est à son comble, ainsi que l'évoque le fameux tableau de James Tissot, daté de 1885, Les Femmes d'Artistes.

Le PAVILLON LEDOYEN, agrandi en 1898, est rénové à nouveau en 1909. Dès lors, le monde de l'édition - de Maupassant, Zola, Flaubert aux Goncourt - en fait son quartier général. C'est au cours d'un dîner que Gide et Copeau y fondent la NRF.

" Le restaurant avait l'air d'une ruche trop pleine et vibrante, un bourdonnement confus d'appels, de cliquetis de verres, d'assiettes, voltigeait autour, en sortant par toutes les fenêtres et les portes grandes ouvertes ; les tables étaient répandues en longues files dans les chemins voisins, à droite et à gauche du passage étroit où les garçons couraient, assourdis, affolés, tenant à bout de bras des plateaux chargés de viandes et de fruits". (Guy de Maupassant).

Les Années Folles vont, une fois de plus, placer LEDOYEN au cœur des modes, accueillant mondains, excentriques et célébrités. Giraudoux, Claudel côtoient les actrices du Français, les couturiers Poiret et Madeleine Vionnet. Mais après la guerre, il subit une longue mise en sommeil et la ville de Paris le met à disposition du Quai d'Orsay pour ses réceptions.

Réouvert en 1962, le PAVILLON LEDOYEN n'a cessé d'être depuis lors le rendez-vous du monde politique et de la grande bourgeoisie parisienne.

LEDOYEN

CARRÉ DES CHAMPS-ELYSÉES - 75008 PARIS · TÉLÉPHONE 01 53 05 10 01 · FAX 01 47 42 55 01

The front and back of the menu from Pavillon Ledoyen, Paris

Under the heading '200 Years of Parisian Life', the history of this extraordinary building – which takes its name from Pierre-Michel Doyen, scion of a family of *traiteurs* who first practised here as its chef in 1791 (it is now home to three-star Michelin chef, Yannick Alléno) – describes how it has witnessed many of the city's important social events: it was here that Joséphine de Beauharnais first met Napoleon; it was home to Degas, Manet, Cézanne and Pissarro; and it was here that Gide and Copeau founded the *Nouvelle Revue Française*. This is a historical document few restaurants, if any, can match.

CHOISI POUR VOUS

- Fine gelée d'un jambon Ibérique
  mousse fermentée de pain de seigle aux éclats d'olives Kalamata

- Dans une coque de pamplemousse brulée,
  une soupe d'oursin servie chaude
  Peau de canard croquante au foie gras de canard en amertume et granité iodé

- Noix de coquilles Saint-Jacques en soupe « vrai » Viroflay
  à la truffe noire

- Filet de rouget à la « royale »
  Boudins à la chair et encre de seiche croustillants

- Bœuf wagyu Gunma « grade 4 » en aiguillettes
  « Onigiris» iodés, langues d'oursin et anguille fumée glacée
  céleri rave en croûte d'argile à la cuillère

- Meringue de mangue rôtie
  vinaigre de mangue et poivre

- Mousse aérée de cacao fleurée de sel
  mucilage de fèves fermentées

295 €

MENU TRUFFE NOIRE

- Vapeur d'artichaut à la truffe noire, feuilles à croquer en vinaigrette
  le fond à déguster avec un soufflé à la pistache verte

- Œuf en raviole aux épinards à la truffe noire

- Sole contisée et soufflée à la truffe noire
  laitue fondue au jus végétal

- Agneau de lait d'Aveyron bien rôti, pâtes maison aux truffes et à la crème muscadée
  Petite pomme Elstar acidulée en salade d'épaule confite

- Caillé de lait cru au sel de citron confit, neige de truffe et mimolette
  Bành chuoï trung croustillant

- Fuseau croustillant au chocolat et caramel, truffe noire à la fleur de sel

520 €

Selon les dispositions régies par le décret n° 2002-1465 en date du 17 décembre 2002.
Alléno Paris ainsi que ses fournisseurs garantissent l'origine des viandes bovines de France et du Japon
Les plats « faits maison » sont élaborés sur place à partir de produits bruts. Toutes nos truffes sont des Tuber Melanosporum
Prix nets, service compris · La liste des allergènes est disponible sur simple demande

The interior of the menu from Pavillon Ledoyen, Paris

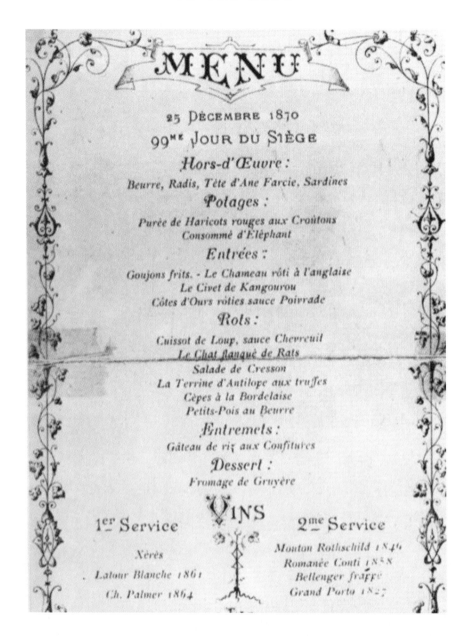

The menu from Christmas Day 1870, the 99th day of the Siege of Paris

Under siege from the Prussians, the Parisians proved highly resourceful until their final surrender on January 28th 1871. This menu reveals how one practical restaurateur managed to get enough protein to satisfy his customers by raiding the local zoo.

The menu begins in undramatic fashion with an hors d'œuvre that involves the stuffed head of a donkey, then progresses to an elephant consommé before a series of entrées and roast dishes that incorporate camel, kangaroo, wolf, cat and antelope. Happily, at least, the wines seem highly drinkable.

The menu as postcard: America from the 1930s to the 1960s

This was a period in American history when excellent graphic design met a growing number of restaurateurs who were keen to reach an ever-growing number of interested customers. The menu became a postcard, available at the reception desk as a giveaway, the easiest and cheapest form of publicity for the restaurateur.

These four are from the Hotel New Yorker in 1942 and reveal the more propaganda-like uses a menu can be put to. Courtesy of LoveMenuArt.com.

The menu and photo (opposite) from the 20th anniversary dinner of Camille and Eugenie Mailhebuau

Dated February 9th 1920, this photograph shows all those who were at this dinner, given by Camille Mailhebuau, the French-born restaurateur who had made such a success of the Old Poodle Dog, then one of the most successful restaurants in San Francisco.

But why do most of those in the photo look so glum? It was because the Eighteenth Amendment, known commonly as Prohibition, had been passed the year before and was to become law within weeks. Four years later this long-established restaurant was forced to close. Images courtesy of the Henry Voigt Collection of American Menus.

The House of Lords, May 2nd 1972

A menu whose cover recalls the setting of yore, with the Court respectfully in awe of
Queen Elizabeth I, while the inner two pages (*opposite*) convey the style of cooking which
was then prevalent across the UK – with prices to match.

HOUSE OF LORDS

A la Carte

TABLE MONEY—Visitors 12p   Peers 6p

FRUIT JUICES
Pineapple, Orange, Tomato or Grapefruit Juice 11p
Shrimp Cocktail 35p   Paté 40p   (half) Fresh Grapefruit 14p
Smoked Salmon 57p   Melon 28p   Smoked Cods Roe 40p

SOUP
Green Pea 14p

FISH
Fried or Grilled Dover Sole £1.05   Grilled or Fried Fillets of Plaice 48p
Grilled Cod Steak Maitre d'Hotel 48p

OMELETTES
Chicken 32p   Mushroom 32p   Tomato 28p   Cheese 28p

ENTREES
Cottage Pie 48p   Lambs Kidneys Bourgignone 48p
Roast Veal 49p   Roast Chicken Wing 48p, Leg 42p

GRILLS (20 minutes)
Fillet Steak and Mushrooms £1.05   Grilled Lamb Cutlets and Tomato 48p

VEGETABLES
Brussels Sprouts 15p   Sliced French Beans 12p
Mashed, Roast or French Fried Potatoes 12p

COLD
Beef 48p   Ham 48p

SALADS
Mixed 12p   Tomato 10p   Beetroot 6p   Potato 6p

SWEETS
Baked Coffee Sponge 15p   Tapioca Pudding 12p
Compôte of Apples 15p   Honey and Brandy Ice Cream 16p
Ginger and Cream 30p   Meringue Glacé 20p
Yoghurt 12p
Vanilla, Chocolate, Coffee or Strawberry Ice Cream 10p

CHEESES
Selection of Cheese 18p   Stilton 23p   Blue Wensleydale 23p
or
FRUIT BASKET
Coffee per cup – 7p

LUNCHEON
2nd MAY 1972

Table d'Hôte
£1.07

Pineapple, Orange, Tomato or Grapefruit Juice
or
Fresh Grapefruit
or
Green Pea Soup
———
Grilled or Fried Fillets of Plaice
or
Grilled Cod Steak Maitre d'Hotel
or
Lambs Kidneys Bourgignone
or
Roast Veal

Brussels Sprouts
Mashed, Roast or French Fried Potatoes
———
Baked Coffee Sponge
or
Vanilla, Chocolate, Coffee or Strawberry Ice Cream
or
Cheese

COVER ILLUSTRATIONS
Front Cover
From Sir Simonds D'Ewes' Journal, published 1682.

"QUEEN ELIZABETH IN PARLIAMENT
A. Ld Chancellor B. Marquises Earls & C. Barons D. Byshops E. Judges F. Masters of Chancery G. Clerks H. Speaker of y^e Co^{m̄}ens I. Black Rod K. Sergeant at Armes L. Members of the Co^{m̄}ens hou^s N. Sr Francis Walsingham Secretary of State.

Back Cover
Queen Elizabeth II in Parliament, 28th October, 1958

THE CLOVE CLUB

A selection of snacks to start

....

Slow Poached Oyster, Beef Jelly & Grilled Cream

Raw Orkney Scallop, Hazelnut, Brown Butter & Perigord Truffle

Warm Chestnut & Oyster Broth

Charcoal Grilled Pollock, Carrot & Calamansi

Little Pancake of Devilled Chicken

Pheasant Consommé & Hundred Year Old Madeira

Roast Hebridean Lamb, Mint, Seaweed & January King Cabbage

Yorkshire Rhubarb & Grapefruit Jelly

Burnt Clementine & Buttermilk Mousse

£95

Wine Pairing £65

Please notify your waiter if you have any allergies
Please be aware we serve wild game that may contain traces of shot
A discretionary 12.5% service charge will be added to your bill
Shoreditch Town Hall, 380 Old Street, London, EC1V 9LT. Telephone: + 44 (0) 20 7729 6496
hello@thecloveclub.com www.thecloveclub.com

THE CLOVE CLUB

A selection of snacks to start

....

Fennel, Bay & Montgomery Cheddar

Dried Salsify, Trompette, Buckwheat & Perigord Truffle

Wild Seaweed Broth & Miyagawa Satsuma

Steamed Enoki, Sesame & Tangerine

New Season's Parsley Root, Savory & Hazelnut

Mushroom Consommé & Hundred Year Old Madeira

Risotto of Kale, Pecorino & Oat Groats

Yorkshire Rhubarb & Grapefruit

Burnt Clementine & Buttermilk Mousse

£95

Wine Pairing £65

Please notify your waiter if you have any allergies
A discretionary 12.5% service charge will be added to your bill
Shoreditch Town Hall, 380 Old Street, London, EC1V 9LT. Telephone: + 44 (0) 20 7729 6496
hello@thecloveclub.com www.thecloveclub.com

The Clove Club, Shoreditch Town Hall

Exemplary menus from the far more confident London chefs of 2016.

Restaurant de la Pyramide

FERNAND POINT
VIENNE (ISÈRE)

17 Février 1969

Brioche de Foie gras
Mousse de Brochet Périgueux

Truite Saumonée farcie braisée au Porto
ou Filet de Barbue aux amandes

Caneton Nantais grillé Béarnaise
ou Rumpsteak poêlé au poivre vert
Gratin Dauphinois

Carte
Caviar Extra
Saumon fumé   Fromages
Huîtres pleine mer
Terrine de Foie gras
Terrine de grives   Glace ou Sorbet
Jambon de Parme   Gâteau Marjolaine
Jambon cuit maison   Friandises
Rosette de campagne   Corbeille de fruits

Omble-Chevalier
Gratin de queues d'Écrevisses
Saumon frais   60 Francs sans vin
Pièce de Chevreuil grand-veneur
Volaille de Bresse
Carré et Selle d'agneau

Restaurant de la Pyramide, Vienne, France

The restaurant where so many future three-star Michelin chefs began their careers, chez Fernand Point in Vienne. Note the relatively straightforward nature of the dishes and the low price by today's standards.

Lista del Bar

Vini in caraffa selezionati per questo mese

Soave Classico Doc 2000
Bardolino Classico Doc 2000

Caraffa grande	€	19,55
Caraffa media	€	12,85
Caraffa piccola	€	10,06

Cipriani, i vini preferiti

Cancello della Luna 2000	€	20,66
Cancello del Sole 1998	€	26,81
Recioto di Soave DOC 99	€	44,12
Prosecco Cipriani DOC	€	19,55

Per altre scelte consigliamo di consultare la carta dei vini

Acqua minerale 75 cl.	€	9,39
Acqua minerale 25 cl.	€	3,35
Birra Moretti Sans Souci	€	10,61

SERVIZIO IN AGGIUNTA 15%

Americano	€	10,06
Bitter Campari	€	10,06
Aperitivo Doge	€	10,06
Martini Cocktail	€	10,06
Cocktail Cipriani	€	10,06
Negroni	€	10,06
Manhattan	€	12,00
Daiquiri	€	12,00
Bellini	€	12,85
Bloody Mary	€	12,00
Roger's	€	12,85
Whisky Sour	€	12,00
Screwdriver	€	12,85
Coppa di Prosecco	€	5,58
Coppa di Champagne Brut	€	18,43

Champagnes

Krug Brut	€	170,36
Mumm Cordon Rouge Brut	€	110,60
Louis Roederer Cristal 95	€	175,39
Louis Roederer Premier	€	110,60
Veuve Clicquot Ponsardin Brut	€	110,60
Moët & Chandon Reserve Impèriale	€	110,60
Moët & Chandon Brut Rosé 93	€	135,73
Moët & Chandon Döm Perignon 93	€	170,36
Pommery Vintage 87	€	148,02
Pommery Brut	€	110,60
Bollinger Brut	€	118,41
Taittinger Brut Reserve	€	118,41
Taittinger Comtes de Champagne 93	€	160,30

SERVIZIO IN AGGIUNTA 15%

Harry's Bar, Venice

Memorable for the fact that our dinner was for my 50th birthday. Memorable also for the words of restaurateur Arrigo Cipriani to our then 17-year-old son, encouraging him to eat: 'We must look after our future customers.'

Venezia, Lunedì 8 Aprile 2002

LA DIETA DEL LUNEDI' SERA

Tartare di vero tonno
€ 47,48

Pollo di Verona arrosto
con
legumi misti
€ 55,86

TRE MENU'

1
Salmone fresco marinato in casa
Pollo di Verona arrosto legumi misti
Crespelle alla crema pasticcera
€ 92,17

2
Tagliolini alle seppie
Salmone alla salamandra
Scelta di dolci dell'Harry's Dolci
€ 92,17

3
Brodetto di pesce
Sampietro al curry con riso pilaf
Scelta di sorbetti e gelati
€ 92,17

SERVIZIO 15%

GRILL

Pollo di Verona
€ 55,86

Fegato di vitello
€ 55,86

Pesce del giorno
€ 61,44

I piatti sono serviti
con legumi o insalata

COPERTO € 5,16
SERVIZIO 15%

American Express
é la nostra
Carta preferita

PIATTI CLASSICI

BRODETTO DI PESCE	€ 33,52
PASTA E FAGIOLI	€ 25,14
TAGLIOLINI GRATINATI	€ 39,09
RISO PILAF ALLA VALENZIANA	€ 41,88
RISOTTO ALLA PRIMAVERA	€ 41,88
SCAMPI ALLA THERMIDOR*	€ 61,44
SOGLIOLA ALLA CASANOVA	€ 61,44
POLLO AL CURRY	€ 55,86
FEGATO ALLA VENEZIANA	€ 55,86
CARPACCIO ALLA CIPRIANI	€ 55,86
MOUSSE AL CACAO FREDDA	€ 16,77
CRÊPES ALLA CREMA	€ 25,14

COPERTO € 5,16
SERVIZIO 15%

I CAMBI DELL'EURO

1 $ Usa	€ 1,13
1 Sterlina Inglese	€ 1,63
1 Franco Svizzero	€ 0,68
1000 Yen Giapponese	€ 8,60

LA BIBLIOTECA:

Arrigo Cipriani **"ANCH'IO TI AMO"** Ed. Baldini & Castoldi € 10,33	Arrigo Cipriani **"ELOISA E IL BELLINI"** Ed. Longanesi € 9,81
Arrigo Cipriani **"IL MIO HARRY'S BAR"** Ed. Sperling & Kupfer € 36,15	Arrigo Cipriani **"HARRY'S BAR"** The Life and Times Ed. Arcade New York € 18,07
Carmela e Arrigo Cipriani **"PAPPE DA FAVOLA"** Ed. Spelling & Kupfer € 12,91	Arrigo Cipriani **"HARRY'S BAR"** La storia Ed. Sperling & Kupfer € 13,89

LA CARTA DI QUESTA SERA

ANTIPASTI

Salmone fresco marinato in casa	€ 36,31
Scampi* e fagioli di Lamon	€ 47,48
Tartare di tonno	€ 47,48
Gamberetti all'olio con carciofini novelli	€ 47,48
Prosciutto dolce di Parma	€ 47,48
Pomodoro e mozzarella	€ 27,92
Asparagi con salsa olandese	€ 27,92

ZUPPE

Consommè della casa	€ 19,55
Minestrone di verdura	€ 25,14
Crema di asparagi	€ 25,14
Zuppa di trippe	€ 25,14
Passato di carciofi	€ 25,14
Brodetto di pesce	€ 33,52

PASTA E RISO

Tagliarelle verdi all'Amatriciana	€ 39,09
Tagliarelle con sarde in saor	€ 39,09
Tagliardi verdi al ragù di vitello	€ 39,09
Cannelloni alla Piemontese	€ 39,09
Tagliarelle alla Bolognese	€ 39,09
Ravioli gratinati al prosciutto	€ 39,09
Farfalle con scampi* all'Armoricaine	€ 41,88
Tagliolini alle seppie	€ 41,88
Risotto alla Cipriani	€ 41,88
Risotto di scampi* e asparagi	€ 41,88

PESCE, CARNE E VOLATILI

Scampi* all'Armoricaine con riso pilaf	€ 61,44
Scampi* fritti con salsa tartara	€ 61,44
Salmone alla salamandra	€ 61,44
Filetto di sogliola con carciofi	€ 61,44
Sampietro alla Carlina con riso pilaf	€ 61,44
Rombo alla salamandra	€ 61,44
Seppie di Aprile in tecia con polenta	€ 55,86
Trippa alla Parmigiana con riso pilaf	€ 55,86
Pollo di Verona alla Cacciatora	€ 55,86
Rognoncini di vitello con risotto	€ 55,86
Piccate di vitello al limone	€ 55,86
Entrecôte di Chianina alla griglia	€ 64,24
Tournedos mignon cinque stelle	€ 64,24

DOLCI E GELATI

Sorbetti e gelati fatti in casa	€ 16,75
Mousse al cacao freddo	€ 16,75
Scelta di dolci fatti in casa	€ 25,14

COPERTO € 5,16 SERVIZIO 15%

AMBIENTE E NOTIZIE

L'uso dei telefoni cellulari nel Ristorante compromette seriamente la preparazione del risotto.

Fumare il sigaro od usare profumi sexy molto violenti può essere un piacere più per sé stessi che per gli altri.

AVVISO DI GARANZIA PER IL CLIENTE

I piatti contrassegnati con questo segno sono conservati con il sistema della congelazione.

CHAPTER
11

THE MENU AS EDIBLE ART

This chapter encompasses menus from many different countries and for many different occasions.

The majority originated in the US in the heyday of menu design from the late 19th century to the outbreak of the Second World War, and they range from New York down to Texas. The design and contents of the menu for dinner on New Year's Eve 1935–36 at the Cumberland Hotel reveal that menus inspired artists and chefs on both sides of the Atlantic. The Oyster Loaf menu originates from a San Francisco restaurant of the same name and was created by artist and author Andrew Loomis.

Menus from Arnaud Lallement's three-star Michelin restaurant in Reims, France; the Cantonese dim sum menu from the Luk Yu Tea House in Hong Kong; Eleven Madison Park in New York; Thitid Tassanakajohn's Le Du in Bangkok; Hoppers' Sri Lankan menu in Soho, London; and John Broadley's stunning drawings for the Quo Vadis restaurant complete this section, which ends with an old Fergus Henderson menu when he was cooking at The French Dining House in the early 1990's – a style of menu-writing that has influenced so many other chefs.

Private dinner given by Louis Sherry, New York

The wall on which Humpty Dumpty sits, with his right arm stretching out to Alice, provides a colourful backdrop to what must have been a glorious dinner put on by New York restaurateur Louis Sherry, whose chocolate business thrives to this day. Courtesy of the Henry Voigt Collection.

Alamo Plaza Chicken Shack, Chattanooga, Tennessee

There is no doubt what is on the menu at the Alamo Plaza Chicken Shack: chicken, including gizzards and livers, unusual items on menus in America today. Courtesy of LoveMenuArt.com.

SOUTHERN
FRIED CHICKEN

AT ITS BEST

NO. 1 . . . . 95¢

REGULAR ORDER OF FRIED CHICKEN
FRENCH FRIED POTATOES
HONEY AND HOT ROLLS

NO. 4 . . . . 95¢

SIX LIVERS
FRENCH FRIED POTATOES
HONEY AND HOT ROLLS

NO. 2 . . . . 60¢

ONE HALF REGULAR ORDER
FRENCH FRIED POTATOES
HONEY AND HOT ROLLS

NO. 5 . . . . 75¢

SIX GIZZARDS
FRENCH FRIED POTATOES
HONEY AND HOT ROLLS

NO. 3 . . . . $1.40

ALL WHITE MEAT
FRENCH FRIED POTATOES
HONEY AND HOT ROLLS

NO. 6 . . . . 85¢

THREE LIVERS AND THREE GIZZARDS
FRENCH FRIED POTATOES
HONEY AND HOT ROLLS

All prices charged are at OPS ceiling or lower. A list showin

— 254 —

STEAKS

K. C. TOP SIRLOIN STEAK, FRENCH FRIED
    POTATOES, SALAD AND HOT ROLLS...............$2.50
HAMBURGER STEAK................................$1.00
SMALL CLUB STEAK, FRENCH FRIED
    POTATOES AND SPICED PEACH...................$1.35
SMALL T-BONE STEAK, FRENCH FRIED
    POTATOES AND SPICED PEACH...................$1.85

SALADS

DELUXE SALAD.........................45¢
LETTUCE AND TOMATO...................30¢
SLICED TOMATO........................35¢
HEAD OF LETTUCE......................40¢
POTATO SALAD.........................30¢
COTTAGE CHEESE.......................30¢
PEACH, PEAR OR PINEAPPLE
    AND COTTAGE CHEESE...............35¢
FROZEN FRUIT SALAD...................45¢

CHOICE OF CANNED SOUP................30¢

BEVERAGES

COFFEE................................10¢
TEA...................................10¢
MILK..................................12¢
BUTTERMILK............................10¢
HOT CHOCOLATE.........................15¢
SOFT DRINKS...........................10¢

SANDWICHES

HAM (BAKED OR FRIED).................45¢
HAM AND EGG..........................55¢
HAM AND CHEESE.......................55¢
BACON AND TOMATO.....................45¢
AMERICAN CHEESE......................30¢
HAMBURGER............................30¢
CHEESEBURGER.........................35¢
EGG..................................30¢
PIMENTO CHEESE.......................30¢

SIDE ORDERS

FRENCH FRIED ONION RINGS.............30¢
FRENCH FRIED POTATOES................30¢

DESSERTS

HOME MADE PIE........................20¢
PIE A LA MODE........................30¢
ICE CREAM............................15¢

THREE HOT ROLLS, BUTTER AND HONEY 25¢

ing the ceiling price of each item is available for inspection.

New Year's Eve at the Cumberland Hotel, London

What a sophisticated start to 1936 this dinner menu must have heralded. Courtesy of LoveMenuArt.com.

MENU

Les Perlières de Whitstable et la Sauce 1936
Les Canapés fin d'Année

La Coupe de Tortue Verte au Vin des Iles
Les Profiteroles au Curry

Le Zéphyr de Sole Auréole

Le Suprème de jeune Poularde Nouvelle Mode
Les Pointes d'Amour fine bouche

La délicieuse Brioche Strasbourgeoise
La Salade aux Œufs d'Or

La Doyenne de Comice Récamier
Les Friandises mon régal

New Year's Eve 1935-36   Cumberland Hotel, London, W.1.

Delmonico's, New York

Mark Antony's famous speech from Shakespeare's *Julius Caesar* is used here to provide the elegant backdrop to a menu from Delmonico's, which opened in 1837 on its location in New York. Courtesy of the Henry Voigt Collection.

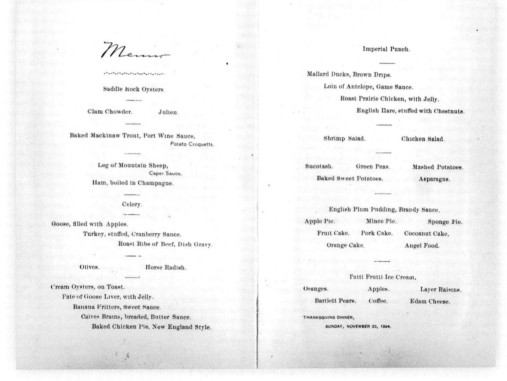

Menu

Saddle Rock Oysters.

Clam Chowder.   Julien.

Baked Mackinaw Trout, Port Wine Sauce,
Potato Croquetts.

Leg of Mountain Sheep,
Caper Sauce.
Ham, boiled in Champagne.

Celery.

Goose, filled with Apples.
Turkey, stuffed, Cranberry Sauce.
Roast Ribs of Beef, Dish Gravy.

Olives.   Horse Radish.

Cream Oysters, on Toast.
Pate of Goose Liver, with Jelly.
Banana Fritters, Sweet Sauce.
Calves Brains, breaded, Butter Sauce.
Baked Chicken Pie, New England Style.

Imperial Punch.

Mallard Ducks, Brown Drips.
Loin of Antelope, Game Sauce.
Roast Prairie Chicken, with Jelly.
English Hare, stuffed with Chestnuts.

Shrimp Salad.   Chicken Salad.

Sucotash.   Green Peas.   Mashed Potatoes.
Baked Sweet Potatoes.   Asparagus.

English Plum Pudding, Brandy Sauce.
Apple Pie.   Mince Pie.   Sponge Pie.
Fruit Cake.   Pork Cake.   Cocoanut Cake.
Orange Cake.   Angel Food.

Tutti Frutti Ice Cream.
Oranges.   Apples.   Layer Raisins.
Bartlett Pears.   Coffee.   Edam Cheese.

THANKSGIVING DINNER,
SUNDAY, NOVEMBER 30, 1884.

Thanksgiving at the Revere House Hotel, Clinton, Iowa

An extraordinary combination of a talented artist and an equally talented chef from a Thanksgiving dinner held in Iowa in 1884. The English presence is notable via the hares and the plum pudding, but what, I wonder, were the brown drips served with the mallard ducks? Courtesy of the University of Nevada, Las Vegas, Special Collections and LoveMenuArt.com.

PIC, Valence, France

Anne-Sophie Pic uses colour and the history behind her long-established family restaurant to demonstrate just what a menu can look like when expense is no object.

The Oyster Loaf, San Francisco

Artist Andrew Loomis's masterpiece for the San Francisco restaurant that took its name from the oyster loaf speciality it served – a thick chunk of crusty bread, hollowed out and filled with breaded and fried oysters. Courtesy of LoveMenuArt.com.

OYSTERS and CLAMS

Eastern Oysters in Half Shell	1.35
Eastern Oysters Fried	1.10
Eastern Oyster Milk Stew . . 1.15; Cream	1.50
Eastern Oysters, Hangtown Fry	1.75
Eastern Oysters, Kirkpatrick or Rockefeller	1.50
Olympia Oysters, Fried or Milk Stew	1.30
Fried Little Neck Clams	.90
Little Neck Clam Milk Stew .90; Cream	1.25
Little Neck Clams in Half Shell	.90
Steamed Clams, Drawn Butter	.90

CRABS

Cracked Half Crab, Mayonnaise	.90
Crab Meat in Casserole a la Newburg	1.25
Crab Meat, Creole with Rice	1.25
Deviled Crab Meat in Casserole	1.00
Crab Meat au Gratin	1.00

☆ Have you ever tried a bottle of Riesling with your Crab? ☆

Shrimps or Louisiana Prawns

Prawns or California Shrimps, Creole with Rice	1.25
Fried Prawns, Tartar Sauce	1.25
California Shrimps or Prawns, Newburg	1.25
Shelled Prawns, Chilled en Mayonnaise	1.25
Prawns en Shell, Cocktail Sauce	1.00
Prawn Saute Sec	1.50

ABALONE and SCALLOPS

Fried Abalone, Tartar Sauce	1.50
French Fried Abalone, Chili Sauce	1.50
Abalone, Supreme (dipped in egg yolk)	1.65
Fried Scallops, Tartar Sauce	1.35
Scallop Saute, Meuniere	1.35

We recommend a bottle of Chablis with Abalone or Scallops

Smoked and Salt Fish

Steamed Alaska Cod with Boiled Potato	1.10
Steamed Finnan Haddie with Boiled Potato	1.10
Salted Mackerel	1.10
Smoked Salmon with Potato Salad	1.00

Potatoes
Fresh Asparagus . . .50
Shoestring or Longbranch .20
Cottage Fried or O'Brien .30
Lyonnaise or Hash Brown .30
French Fries 20; American .30

Vegetables
Fresh Artichoke, Butter . . .40
Green Peas or Spinach . . .35
String or Lima Beans . . .35
Cut Corn Saute 40

☆ Bread and butter with soup only, 10 cents extra ☆
Not responsible for loss or exchange of personal property

Cocktails
Old Fashion	.50	Daiquiri	.65
Martini	.50	Mermaid	.60
Manhattan	.50	Whisky Sour	.50

Seafood Cocktails and Appetizers

Crab Meat Cocktail	.50	Chilled Tomato Juice	.25
Lobster Cocktail	.50	Celery en Branch	.35
Olympia Oyster Cocktail	.60	Ripe Olives	.35
Eastern Oyster Cocktail	.60	Green Olives	.35
Prawn Cocktail	.50	Fruit Cocktail	.35

Smoked Salmon (half portion) .60; (whole) . . . 1.00
Marinated Herring (half portion) .45; (whole) . . .80
Oyster Loaf Special Appetizer 40
Stuffed Celery with Roquefort Cheese 75

Soups

Boston Clam Chowder	(bowl) 30; (cup)	.20
Clam Broth	(bowl) 30; (cup)	.20
Coney Island Clam Chowder	(bowl) 30; (cup)	.20
Genuine Green Turtle Soup	(bowl)	.35

Fresh Fish in Season

Oyster Loaf Sea Food Combination a la Rod Pohl
Scallops, abalone, fried oysters, filet of sole and
prawns with tartar sauce) 1.75

Steamed Deep-sea Cod, Provencale	.95
Fried Filet of Sole, Tartar Sauce	.95
Grilled Fresh Mackerel	.90
Grilled Sea Bass, Parsley Butter	1.00
Rainbow Trout Saute, Meuniere	1.75
Fried Rex Sole	.95
Fried Sandabs	.95
Sandabs Saute	.95
Fried or Broiled Barracuda	.95
Fried Boned Smelts, Tartar Sauce	.95
Bouillabaisse (Fish Stew)	1.50
Broiled or Fried Halibut Steak	1.00
Fried or Broiled Salmon Steak	1.00
Sea Food Risotto a la Chef	.85
Fried or Broiled Individual Turbot	.95

☆ We suggest that you try one of our fine Sauternes ☆

Lobsters

Broiled Half Lobster, Drawn Butter	1.75
Lobster, Thermidor	1.85
Lobster a la Newburg en Casserole	1.85
Lobster a la King en Casserole	1.85
Lobster, Creole, Rice en Casserole	1.85

Personalized Service

THE OYSTER LOAF prepares its food especially for you
with the same chefs who have been serving you for years

We recommend Concannon Sauterne, Chablis or Moselle (split) .60

☆ OUR DAILY MEAT SPECIALS ☆

Monday	Shortribs of Beef with Browned Potato . 1.10	**Thursday**	Beef Stew 95
Tuesday	Corned Beef and Cabbage, Boiled Potato 1.35	**Friday**	Baked Sea Bass, Spanish . . . . . . 1.00 Bouillabaisse (Fish Stew) 1.50
Wednesday	Baked Breast of Lamb a la Archie . 1.10	**Saturday**	Prime Ribs of Beef au Jus, Baked Potato 2.25

Sunday
Roast Young Tom Turkey with Cranberry Sauce 1.75

Salads You Will Remember

Stuffed Avocado with Chicken Salad 1.10
Anchovy Salad, half .45; whole 85
Smoked Salmon with Potato Salad 1.00
Fresh California Crab Louie, half .85; whole 1.50
California Shrimp Louis, half .85; whole 1.50
California Lobster Louis 1.50
California Crab or California Shrimp Salad 90
Prawn "Louisiana Shrimp" Louis (half portion) .95; (whole) 1.60
De Luxe Marine Salad Bowl (Combination sea food and mixed green salad) . . 1.25
Combination Mixed Green and Vegetable Salad (half portion) .50; (whole) . . .90
Mixed Green Salad (Escarole, chicory, romaine and tomato) with French Dressing .85
Cottage Cheese Salad with Pineapple, Peach or Pear and French Dressing 85

Fruit Salad 85
Chicken Salad 90
Stuffed Tomato with Chicken Salad 1.00
Hearts of Lettuce with Anchovies 95
Stuffed Tomato with Crab Meat, Mayonnaise . . 1.00
Sliced Tomatoes with Green Peppers 50
California Lobster Salad, Mayonnaise . . . 1.20
One-half Avocado .75; stuffed with Crab Meat . . 1.30
Heart of Lettuce, French Dressing .35
Lettuce-Tomato, French Dressing .50
Sliced Cucumbers 40
Green Onions 35

Desserts

Ice Cream Sundaes 40
Rice Pudding 25
Ice Cream 25
Assorted Pies . .20   Assorted Cakes .20

Beverages

Coffee .10   Milk . .15
Tea 15
Postum 15
Chocolate 15

Cheese

Wisconsin Swiss Cheese 40
Roquefort Cheese 45
Camembert Cheese 40
American or Swiss Cheese 40

☆ For a mild appetizer or dessert, drink a glass of chilled Dubonnet, Sherry or Port ☆

OUR FAMOUS OYSTER LOAF
★ KNOWN THE WORLD OVER ★ $1.50
BABY OYSTER LOAF with COLE SLAW 75

Steaks and Chops
Charcoal Broiled

New York Cut Steak or Filet Mignon 3.00
Club Steak 2.25
French Lamb Chops 1.50
Breaded Veal Cutlets with Tomato Sauce 1.50
Ham and Eggs or Bacon and Eggs 1.35

Pork Chops 1.50
Hamburger Steak 1.00
Fried Half Spring Chicken 1.50
Half Spring Chicken Saute Sec 1.75
Veal Porterhouse 1.75

☆ Nothing tastes better than a bottle of Burgundy or Cabernet with a good Steak ☆

Sandwiches

Turkey or Chicken Sandwich 75
Oyster Loaf Sandwich on Bun with Cole Slaw 75
Lettuce and Tomato Sandwich 50
American Cheese Sandwich 60
Swiss Cheese Sandwich 60

Club House Sandwich 90
Monterey Cream Cheese Sandwich 60
Smoked Salmon Sandwich on Rye with Potato Salad .80
Hamburger Sandwich 50
Denver Sandwich 75

A FULL ASSORTMENT OF WINES AND LIQUORS ON BACK PAGE

Skillern's, Texas

From 1940 when the artist managed to create a 'wow' factor out of a traditional café menu. There were many branches of this café across Texas until the 1970s when they closed down. Courtesy of LoveMenuArt.com.

SUNDAES
Topped With Whipped Cream

Fresh Strawberry .... 15¢
Frosted Fudge .... 15¢
Crushed Pineapple .... 15¢
Butterscotch .... 15¢
Chocolate Nut .... 20¢
Marshmallow .... 15¢

DOUBLE DIP SODAS
In Frosted Glasses

Crushed Pineapple .... 10¢
Crushed Strawberry ...... 10¢
Chocolate Soda .... 10¢
Vanilla Soda .... 10¢
Cherry Soda .... 10¢
Root Beer Soda .... 10¢

WE SERVE ONLY OUR OWN DOUBL' RICH ICE
CREAM, TAKE HOME A HAND PACKED QUART — 45¢

From The Fountain
SKILLERN'S
— FRIENDLY —
FOUNTAINS

Fresh Orange Freeze, with
Diced Mixed Fruits and
Cooling Orange Sherbet.15¢

Fresh Fruit Salad
Banana Split With
Three Flavors of
Ice Cream Topped
With Whipped Cream
and Chopped Pecans
.... 20¢

Try a Nationally Famous
Doubl' Rich Malted Milk
Any Flavor, Served With
Wafers .... 15¢

A Slice of Brick Ice Cream
Topped with Your Choice of
Syrup or Fruits, Whipped
Cream and Nuts .... 20¢

Orange Melody
Pure Orange Juice Mixed
With Whole Milk, Fresh
Egg and Orange Ice, A
Real Treat ....15¢

MILK DRINKS

Doubl' Rich Malted Milk . 15¢
With Egg .... 20¢
Milk Shake .... 15¢
With Egg .... 20¢
Chocolate Milk .... 05¢
All Fresh Fruit Ades .. 10¢, with Sherbet .. 15¢

CHILLED JUICES

Fresh Orange Juice .... 10¢
V-8 Cocktail .... 10¢
Dole's Pineapple Juice ... 10¢
Texas Grapefruit Juice ... 10¢
Tomato Juice .... 10¢

Tasty Treats

Buttered Chip Steak on a Bun, with a Doubl'
Rich Chocolate Soda .... 25¢

Barbecued Beef with Potato Salad and a Strawberry
Milk Shake Made the Skillern Way .... 25¢

Freshly Made Chicken Salad Sandwich, Potato
Chips and a Fresh Limeade .... 30¢

GOOD QUALITY MEANS GOOD FOOD

Double Deckers
Served With Potato Salad

Sliced Breast of Chicken, Grilled Bacon, Lettuce
and Sliced Tomato on your choice of Toast .... 40¢

Baked Virginia Ham, Peanut Butter and Jelly,
Garnished with Sweet Pickle Chips and Olives .... 35¢

Roast Beef and American Cheese with Sweet Relish
and Mayonnaise .... 35¢

Sliced Egg, Lettuce and Ripe Tomato on Toast with
Pickles and Olives .... 30¢

Seasonable Suggestions

MADE FRESH
TO
ORDER

Home Baked Virginia Ham with Fresh Potato Salad on Crisp Lettuce, Tomato Slice, Pickle Chips, Toast .... 30¢

FRUIT PLATE
Bartlett Pear, Alberta Peach, Pineapple with Cottage Cheese, Banana Topped with Whipped Cream, Buttered Raisin Toast — ....25¢

Whole Ripe Tomato Filled with Freshly Made Potato Salad, Served with Toast or Saltines .... 25¢

Chef's Special Salad Garnished with Hard Egg, Pickle and Radishes, Served with Buttered Toast.. 25¢

Chilled Red Alaska Salmon and Hard Egg on Lettuce Bed, Lemon Slice, Potato Salad, Saltines .... 30¢

A Buttered Juicy Chip Steak on a Poppy Seed Bun ..... 15¢

Sandwiches
(On Your Choice of Toast)

Baked Virginia Ham	15¢	Chicken Salad	20¢
Grilled Bacon and Tomato	20¢	Cream Cheese	15¢
Tuna Fish Salad	15¢	Pimiento Cheese	15¢
Ham Salad	10¢	American Cheese	15¢
Deviled Egg Salad	15¢	Swiss Cheese	15¢
Liver Sausage	15¢	Roast Beef	15¢

Barbecue Beef on a Toasted Bun with Relish ... 10¢

PASTRY FRESH DAILY FROM OUR SANITARY BAKERY

Fresh Apple Pie	10¢	Assorted Cookies	05¢
Layer Cake	10¢	Doughnuts	05¢

LAYER CAKES BAKED FOR ANY OCCASION

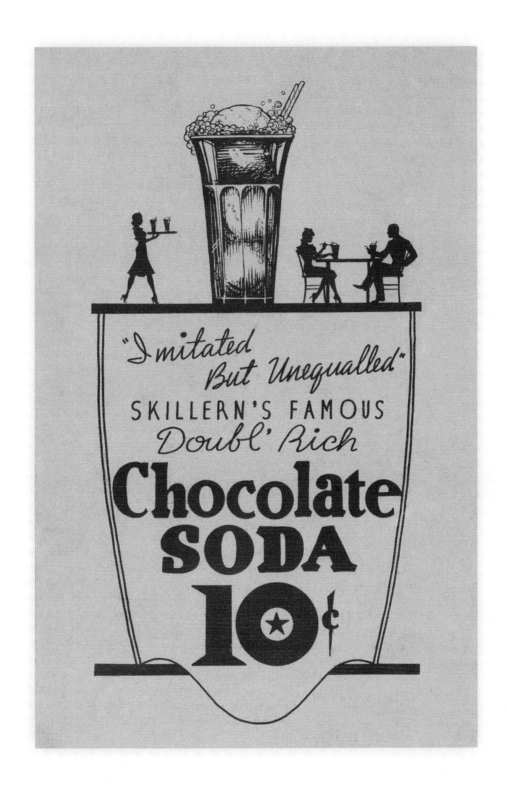

The Neil Tavern, Columbus, Ohio

A colourful map of the bountiful USA graces this menu. I love the pineapples sailing in from Hawaii. Courtesy of LoveMenuArt.com.

Year after year vineyards, growers, gatherers, fishermen, hunters all bring me their finest production. The fruits of their labours feed my culinary imagination and delight the traveler.
This is a passion my family has shared for four decades, and I proudly continue this tradition of serving only the best from the sea and the land.

Arnaud Lallement

L'Assiette Champenoise, Reims, France

Arnaud Lallement's terse but passionate explanation of what drives him to cook so well.

MENUS

HERITAGE

To recreate essential flavours, this is a menu which changes
with the season and my mood. It is a mix of classical
and innovative dishes. Quintessential cuisine which evokes
my childhood memories and pays homage to my Father.

Served with a Champagne Grande Cuvée
and a specially discovered Champagne winemaker

BLACK TRUFFLE

EMULSION / Black truffle

ROLLED PASTRY / Ham, black truffle

LOCALLY FISHED BRITTANY TURBOT / Vin jaune, black truffle

A. POLMARD'S BEFF / Potatoes, black truffle

CHEESE SELECTION / Philippe Olivier

DESSERT

SAVEUR

BRITTANY SCALLOPS / Celery, curry

POTATOE GNOCCHIS / Matcha tea

LINE CAUGHT SEA BASS / Cabbage

FARM REARED CHICKEN COUR D'ARMOISE / Albufera

CHEESE SELECTION / Philippe Olivier

DESSERT

Black truffle on a dish of the menu « Héritage » or « Saveur », in extra.

CARTE   INNOVATION

POTATOE GNOCCHIS / Black truffle

BRITTANY LANGOUSTINE ROYALE / « Nage », Caviar lemon

GOOSE FOIE GRAS / Preserved quail, chervil

BRITTANY SCALLOPS / Celery, curry

JOHN DORY / Shallot, parsley

LOCALLY FISHED BRITTANY TURBOT / Vin jaune, black truffle

LINE CAUGHT SEA BASS / Cabbage

FARM REARED CHICKEN COUR D'ARMOISE / Albufera

VEAL SWEET BREAD / Parsnip

DOE / Turnip, épine-vinette

TIMELESS

30g of « KAVIARI » / Cress, leek

BRITTANY BLUE LOBSTER / In homage to my father

A. POLMARD'S BEEF / Potatoes, black truffle

CHEESE SELECTION / Philippe Olivier

DESSERTS

CHOCOLATE / Mexican lemon

APPLE / Y. Colombie

PINA COLADA / A. Guindo

PEAR / Candied chestnut

HALIBUT
tea and seaweed lavash

FLUKE AND SCALLOP
basil and meyer lemon; tangerine

GOAT CHEESE
lollipop with beets; croquette with watercress and chive

SEA URCHIN
panna cotta with apple and celery

SMOKED STURGEON AND CAVIAR
sabayon with chive; fingerling potato and crème fraîche

MACKEREL
marinated with lemon, yogurt and sunflower seeds

CELERY ROOT
roasted with smoked puree and celery root bordelaise

CARROT
roasted with cumin, dates and wheat berries

CHICKEN
poached with black truffles, butternut squash and parsnip

JASMINE AND TANGERINE
jasmine sorbet, orange shortbread and cilantro

COCONUT
vacherin with passion fruit and mango

MIGNARDISES

MARCH 23, 2011

MACKEREL	SALSIFY	OYSTER	FOIE GRAS
CARROT	CELERY ROOT	HALIBUT	LOBSTER
CHICKEN	PORK	BEEF	SQUAB
CHEDDAR	COCONUT	LEMON	CHOCOLATE

FOUR COURSES: 125
TASTING MENU: 195
WINE PAIRINGS: 95 / 145

Eleven Madison Park, New York

The changing menu from William Guidara and Daniel Humm's Eleven Madison Park, New York.

The Shiori, London

This beautiful menu was written every day by Hitomi Takagi to accompany the food cooked by her husband, Takashi, at their former jewel-like restaurant, The Shiori, in west London. Plus my notes from the dinner which neatly fitted into the menu's envelope.

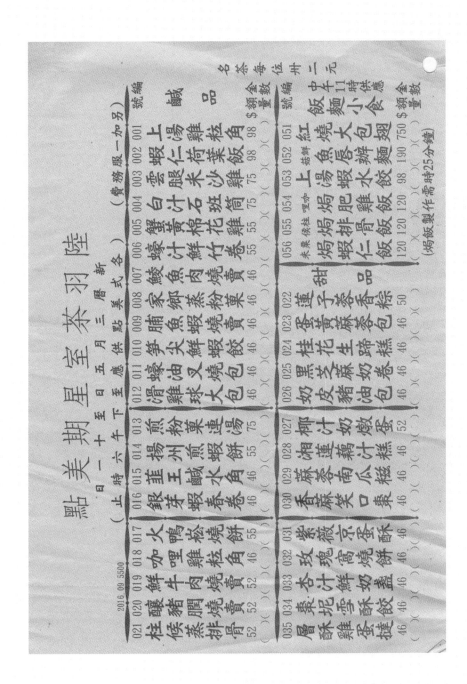

Luk Yu Tea House, Hong Kong

The classic dim sum menu from the famous Luk Yu Tea House, established in Hong Kong in 1933. Write down how many of each your table will want, hand the slip to the waiter and the food will arrive.

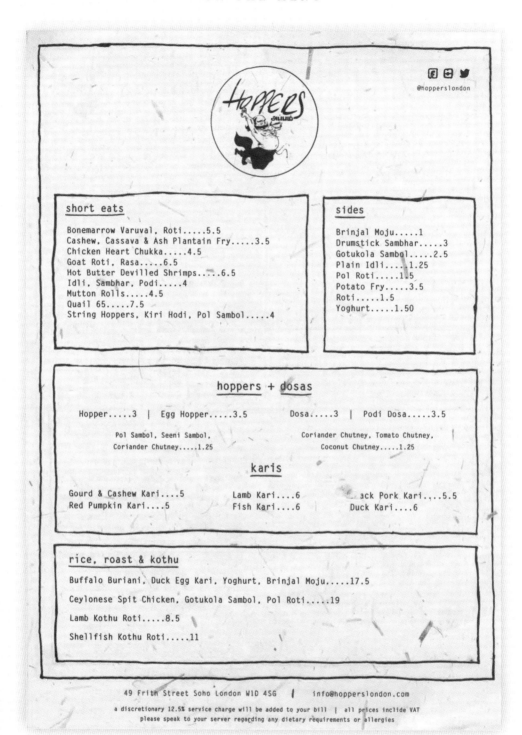

short eats

Bonemarrow Varuval, Roti.....5.5
Cashew, Cassava & Ash Plantain Fry.....3.5
Chicken Heart Chukka.....4.5
Goat Roti, Rasa.....6.5
Hot Butter Devilled Shrimps.....6.5
Idli, Sambhar, Podi.....4
Mutton Rolls.....4.5
Quail 65.....7.5
String Hoppers, Kiri Hodi, Pol Sambol.....4

sides

Brinjal Moju.....1
Drumstick Sambhar.....3
Gotukola Sambol.....2.5
Plain Idli.....1.25
Pol Roti.....1.5
Potato Fry.....3.5
Roti.....1.5
Yoghurt.....1.50

hoppers + dosas

Hopper.....3 | Egg Hopper.....3.5   Dosa.....3 | Podi Dosa.....3.5

Pol Sambol, Seeni Sambol,   Coriander Chutney, Tomato Chutney,
Coriander Chutney.....1.25   Coconut Chutney.....1.25

karis

Gourd & Cashew Kari....5   Lamb Kari....6   ack Pork Kari....5.5
Red Pumpkin Kari....5   Fish Kari....6   Duck Kari....6

rice, roast & kothu

Buffalo Buriani, Duck Egg Kari, Yoghurt, Brinjal Moju.....17.5

Ceylonese Spit Chicken, Gotukola Sambol, Pol Roti.....19

Lamb Kothu Roti.....8.5

Shellfish Kothu Roti.....11

49 Frith Street Soho London W1D 4SG   info@hopperslondon.com
a discretionary 12.5% service charge will be added to your bill | all prices include VAT
please speak to your server regarding any dietary requirements or allergies

@hopperslondon

Hoppers, London

Very authentic Sri Lankan food on offer in the heart of London's Soho.

hards

Tapper's Tipple.....8.5
Ceylon Arrack - Toasted Rice - Bittered Wine

Kung Fu Pandan.....8.5
Pandan Infused Ceylon Arrack - Vermouth - Coffee
Liqueur - Hazelnut

Pineapple & Black Pepper Punch.....8.5
Ceylon Arrack - Saffron & Vanilla Bitters -
Black Pepper Cream Soda - Pineapple Foam

Kandy Gunpowder.....8.5
Amrut Single Malt - Passion Fruit -
Green Peppercorns - Fino Sherry

Citizen Burgher.....8.5
Genever - Papaya - Coconut Water

Hoppers'G & T.....8.5
Lemongrass Infused Tanqueray Gin - Indian Lemon -
Lemongrass - Tonic

Colombo No.7 G & T.....8.5
Colombo No.7 Gin - Fresh Curry Leaves -
Cinnamon - Cardamom Tonic

beer

Lion Sri Lankan Lager.....4.5
Lion Sri Lankan Stout.....6.5

spirit

Ceylon Arrack.....6.5
Colombo No.7 Gin.....7.5
Zuidam Dry Gin.....7.5
Sipsmith Gin.....7.5
Bols Genever/Zeer Oude.....6.5/6.5
Fillier's Oude Graanjenever 5yr/12yr.....7.5/8.5
Sipsmith Vodka.....7.5
Amrut Single Malt/Peated Fusion.....9/10
More spirits available on request

wine

125ml.....5 | 375ml.....14

White - Gavi Le Marne
Michele Chiarlo 2014

Red - Barbera d'Asti Le Orme Superiore
Michele Chiarlo 2013

softs

Black Pepper Cream Soda.....3
Ginger Beer.....3
Coconut Water.....3
Seasonal Juice.....3
Curry Leaf Buttermilk.....3.5
Sweet Dilmah Metre Tea.....2.5
Sweet Frothy Kaapi.....2.5

glossary

Arrack - a Sri Lankan spirit distilled from the sap of the coconut flower and matured in vats made from teak or Halmilla trees
Brinjal Moju - aubergine pickle
Chukka - fragrant and spicy semi-dry masala from Tamil Nadu
Dosa - crisp fermented lentil and rice crepe
Genever - the precursor to English gins, as well as the origin of the phrase 'Dutch Courage'
Gotu Kola Sambol - pennywort relish with coconut, Maldive fish and onions
Hopper (or Appam) - bowl shaped fermented rice and coconut milk pancake
Idli - steamed rice cake
Kari - The Tamil term for Curry
Kiri Hodi - a mild coconut milk gravy from Sri Lanka, cooked with fenugreek and Maldive fish
Kothu - a Sri Lankan street dish made with a finely chopped roti cooked with vegetables, meat or seafood

Maldive Fish - sun dried bonito
Podi - coarse spicy powder mix of ground dry spices and seeds
Pol Roti - grilled coconut roti
Pol Sambol - Sri Lankan relish made with fresh ground coconut, Maldive fish, onion & red chilli
Rasa - gravy
Seeni Sambol - a Sri Lankan caramelised onion relish
String Hopper (or Idiyappam) - steamed handmade rice flour noodles pressed into string pancakes
Varuval - a classic Chettinad dish

49 Frith Street Soho London W1D 4SG | info@hoppersiondon.com

a discretionary 12.5% service charge will be added to your bill | all prices include VAT
please speak to your server regarding any dietary requirements or allergies

A la carte and 4-course dishes are served at the same size or portion
Our set menus are designed for 1 guest

ONE – COLD

Khao-Chae, shrimp & pork ball, radish, salted fish, jasmine ice cream   *300*

Raw Oyster, sweet acacia, chili gel, chili paste tuiles, spicy cilantro granite   *300*

Black Barracuda, chili, lemon, basil, red onion jam   *300*

TWO – FROM THE SEA AND FOREST

Local Mackerel, chu-chee sauce, pickled grilled leek   *600*

Duck & Prawn Wonton, pickled chayote, preserved lime gel, scallion,
duck broth   *400*

Wild Mushroom, mushroom broth, bottle gourd, Northern-style sausage   *400*

THREE – FROM THE RANCH

Local 30 Days Dry-Aged Beef Tenderloin, kale-salted fish puree, garlic jus,
 fried garlic, kale   *990*

Chicken, scallion, pickled ginger, soy-ginger jus   *490*

Free Range Pork, shitake mushroom, Chinese flower, warm-spiced jus   *950*

FOUR – SIN

Coffee Pudding, caramel ice cream, pandan cream   *190*

Pineapple, nuts, lemongrass, coconut ice cream   *190*

Pandan dough, toasted coconut ice cream   *190*

All prices are subject to 10% service charge
Please inform us if you have any dietary restrictions.

Le Du, Bangkok

Chef Thitid 'Ton' Tassanakajohn's clever menu which makes effective use of colour at his
Le Du restaurant in Bangkok.

4-COURSE*   *990*

Select 1 dish from each category

Supplements on

Local Mackerel	*– 200*	*add on*
Beef	*– 500*	*add on*
Pork	*– 450*	*add on*

Wine Pairing 4 glasses with food 1190   add on

LE DU 'S TASTING MENU   *2,300*

Amuse Bouche

Khao Chae

Barracuda

Mackerel

Duck & Prawn Wonton

Chicken or Beef or Pork

Pandan Dough

Wine Pairing 6 glasses with Foods 1690   add on

Iberico Ham & Chorizo 400, 800   Cheese platter 400, 800

BREAKFAST

Eggs

poached, fried,
scrambled *or* boiled

all served with buttery
fried bread

6

fresh fruit *or* fruit compote

with granola
yoghurt *or* ricotta

5·5

porridge

4·5

KIPPER

7·5

COOKED BREAKFAST

bacon, sausage, black pudding,
egg, roast tomato, fried bread 12

bacon roll

5

avocado, tomato & mayonnaise

on grilled bread

6.5

BAKERY

breads & buns
fresh from our ovens every day

*toasted and served with
butter, preserves, honey & marmalade*

4·5

fruit juices

orange & grapefruit

4

COFFEE

espresso 2.5

double espresso 3.5

americano 3.5

cappucino 3.5

latte 3.5

tea

english breakfast, darjeeling,
earl grey, autumn oolong
green, camomille, lemon
verbena, nettle, fennel seed,
rooibos, fresh mint tea

3·5

HOT CHOCOLATE

3·5

BREAKFAST IS SERVED MONDAY TO FRIDAY 8 - 11AM

PLEASE ASK A MEMBER OF STAFF FOR INFORMATION IF YOU HAVE A FOOD ALLERGY OR INTOLERANCE

A DISCRETIONARY 12.5% SERVICE CHARGE WILL BE ADDED TO YOUR BILL

Quo Vadis, London

Brought in by his friend, Quo Vadis chef Jeremy Lee, artist John Broadley's illustrations add a lively wit and humour and resulted in a significant upturn in sales.

thursday 15th september

quo vadis

'hot ticket' 24°c

BITES
AHOY!

smoked cod's roe,
lettuce & almonds
5.5

baked salsify
& parmesan
6

*smoked eel
sandwich*
9.5

QV
autumn salad
16.5

*BAKED
MUSHROOM PASTRY,
GREEN BEANS
& ONIONS*
19.5

warm grouse salad
21.5

today's tipple:
a glass of
langhe nebbiolo,
2013 cigliuti piedmont
10

crab & sea vegetable
salad
14.5

chilled celery & watercress soup 7.5

terrine, toast & pickles 9.5

fig, ricotta, cobnut & mint 9.5

grilled mackerel, fennel & coriander 9.5

leek, bacon, egg & bitter leaves 10.5

∞∞∞

rabbit, bacon, mustard & sage 19.5

salt cod, cockles & aïoli 21

hake & herb dressed sorrel 22.5

venison, artichokes & wild cress 24

onglet, girolles & green beans 23.5

QV APERTIVO
campari,
orange & prosecco
8.5

irish rock oysters
'carlingford'
2.5

The Theatre Set

pumpkin & spinach
& aubergine
-
chickpea pancake.
grilled vegetables &
coriander salad
-
'st. emilion
au chocolat'
19.5 for 2

*THE SANDWICH
CHIPS & SALAD*
17.5

green salad 5 ~ parsley potatoes 5 ~ chips 5
roast squash & herbs 6 ~ tomato, grapefruit & mint salad 6

PLEASE ASK A MEMBER OF STAFF FOR INFORMATION IF YOU HAVE A FOOD ALLERGY OR INTOLERANCE

26-29 DEAN STREET, SOHO, LONDON W1D 3LL
TELEPHONE 020 7437 9585

A DISCRETIONARY 12.5% SERVICE CHARGE WILL BE ADDED TO YOUR BILL

THE FRENCH HOUSE DINING ROOM

Wednesday 11 July 2001

Tomato & Bread Soup	5.20
Rabbit Rillette	5.50
Langoustine & Mayonnaise	8.50
Artichoke Vinaigrette	5.50
Pickled Pigeon & Watercress	6.00
Salt Cod, Tomato & Little Gem	6.50
Foie Gras	9.00
Buckwheat Pancake, Beetroot & Horseradish	10.50
Calves Liver, Turnips & Anchovy	12.50
Smoked Eel, Mash & Bacon	12.00
Pot Roast Old Spot Pork & Prunes	15.00
Roast Quails & Chard	13.00
Plaice & Tartare Sauce	13.00
Green Beans	3.00
New Potatoes	3.50
Green Salad	4.00
Welsh Rarebit	4.40
Caerphilly & Wigmore	5.20
Bowl of Cherries	6.00
Creme Caramel	5.20
Prune & Armagnac Ice Cream	5.20
Almond Tart & Raspberries	5.20
Chocolate Pot	5.20

The French House Dining Room, London

This menu, from 2001, predates Fergus Henderson's time at St John but reveals the underlying principles of his approach to writing a menu – why use two words when one will do?

SUPPORTERS

⸻

Unbound is a new kind of publishing house. Our books are funded directly by readers. This was a very popular idea during the late eighteenth and nineteenth centuries. Now we have revived it for the internet age. It allows authors to write the books they really want to write and readers to support the writing they would most like to see published.

The names listed below are of readers who have pledged their support and made this book happen. If you'd like to join them, visit: www.unbound.com.

Jesus Adorno

James and Nathalie
    Alexander

Jose Alvarez

Chris Ammermann

Paul Askew

Steve Ayres

Simon Baggs

Jason Ballinger

Sarah Barclay

Helen Barratt

Adam Baylis-West

The late Sally Beauman

Will Beckett

Rob Behrens

Bruno-Roland Bernard

Cat Black

David Blackburn

Scott Boden

Nick Bramham

Richard W H Bray

Tom & Gilly Brent

Stephen Browett

Claire Brown

Hennie Brown

MC Brown

Nate Brown

Johnny Burns

Marcus Butcher

Carmen Callil

Paul Campbell

Sarah Canet

Andrew Catlin

Miranda Cavanagh

Roger Cavanagh

Sarah Chamberlain

Philip Connor

Kevin Currey

Avalon de Paravicini

Thomas De Waen

Steve Dimmick

Kevin Donnellon

Suzannah Doyle

Edel Ebbs

Grahame Edwards

Danielle Ellis

Nick Emley

William Emmott

Tomas Eriksson

Anita Feiger

Sally Fincher

David Foster

David Giampaolo

John Gieve

Martin Gilbert

David Gleave

Judy Goldhill

John Gordon

Christopher Gorman-
Evans

David Graham

Voula Grand

Angela Greenfield

Marek Gumienny

James Hacon

Abel Hadden

Dorothy Halfhide

John Hamwee

Julia Harding

Gemma Harrison

Tim Hart

Richard Hemming

James Hockney

Ken Hom

Simon Hopkinson

Jenny Howard

Peter Howard-Dobson

Trevor Hudson

Spencer Hyman

Anne Hynes

Daniel Jackson

David Johnston

John Keith

John Kelly

Hilary Kemp

Dan Kieran

Caradoc King

Kenneth Lamb

Katie Lander

Rebecca and Ben Lander

Richard Lander

Johnny Leathers

Peng Hui Lee

Harriet and Bill
Lembeck, CWE,
CSE

Jonathan Levy and
Gabrielle Rifkind

Caroline Lien

Stuart Lipton

Tamasin Little

James Lo

Mike Lucy

Karl Ludvigsen

DeAndra Lupu

Sam MacAuslan

Sarah Maddox

Philippa Manasseh

Maya Matthews

Judith and Andrew
McKinna

Alasdair McWhirter

Patricia Michelson

Richard Milner

Robert Miskin

John Mitchinson

Allan Morgenthau

Guy Morris

Carlo Navato

Gary Nicol

Christopher North

Mike O'Brien

Douglas Oppenheim

Jennie Orchard

Howard and Kate
    Palmes

Gerard Pandian

Gemma Louise Pearson

Antony Peattie

Justin Pollard

Matthew Porter

Helen Reece

Nicky Richmond

Julian Roberts

Guillaume Rochette

Robyn Roscoe

Katharine Roseveare,
    Martin & Lucas
    Raymond

Harold Rubin

Nicholas Rudd-Jones

Joan Schopf

Tamsin Shelton

Linda Shoare

Tori Slater

Freya Smith

Snorag

Andre Sokol

Marcia Soldatos

David Somers

Andrew Stevenson

Kinan Suchaovanich

Geraldine A Sylver

Barrie Tankel

John Taylor

Maisie Taylor

Shamil Thakrar

George Theo

Susie Thompson

Ian Thompson-Corr

John and Lindsay Usher

Shaun Usher

Renaud van Strydonck

Marco Velardi

JC Viens

Nick Vincr

Richard Wassell

Wynn Wheldon

Andrew Wiggins

Cary Wilkins

Mark Williamson

Danny Wolfson

John Wood

Ashley Woolf

Phillip Wright

Ana Virseda Zamorano